OPENLY *Karl*

OPENLY *Karl*

A MEMOIR

BY KARL WELLS

BREAKWATER
P.O. Box 2188, St. John's, NL Canada A1C 6E6
WWW.BREAKWATERBOOKS.COM

ISBN 9781778530395 (softcover)
9781778530401 (ePUB)
a CIP catalogue record for this book is available from Library and Archives Canada

FRONT COVER PHOTO: Ed "Eddy" Ringman, Ringman Photography
BACK COVER PHOTO: Dave Howells
PAGE LAYOUT: Nadine Hodder

We acknowledge the support of the Canada Council for the Arts.

We acknowledge the financial support of the Government of Canada through the Department of Heritage and the Government of Newfoundland and Labrador through the Department of Tourism, Culture, Arts and Recreation for our publishing activities.

PRINTED AND BOUND IN CANADA.

Breakwater Books is committed to choosing papers and materials for our books that help to protect our environment. This book is printed on paper made of material from well-managed forest and other controlled sources that are certified by the Forest Stewardship Council®.

for Larry

CONTENTS

NOTE

Most of the names in this memoir are real. However, to maintain the privacy of several people and where an actual name was not essential to the story, I've used pseudonyms. These appear in quotation marks on first presentation.

PREFACE

This memoir focuses on my life from its earliest days to the end of my CBC career, with mention of events leading to and including marriage to my husband, Larry Kelly, who's been my supportive partner for forty-five years and counting.

I experienced my sexual awakening as a gay youth in an era when homosexuality was illegal in Canada. Growing up, I was aware of the rejection, ridicule, and worse that I might face, just as my gay friends did. In the following pages you'll read about how I navigated my personal life and my career as openly as I could as a full-time CBC on-air personality and employee, from the 1970s onward. It was a less tolerant time for 2SLGBTQI+ people, a time of ignorance, hatred, harassment, and sometimes physical violence.

Canada now protects the rights of 2SLGBTQI+ citizens, just as it protects the rights of all citizens. But make no mistake, homophobia and transphobia and the fear of anybody seen as different still exist. Kids are more likely to share feelings about their sexuality because they are less fearful of rejection by family and friends, but rejection still happens.

It's taken time, but there's growing acceptance of the 2SLGBTQI+ community in many countries. We have gay and transgender role models in media and in most areas of life. Many people today understand that there is nothing wrong with being who you are. We take pride in who we are, and all 2SLGBTQI+ young people should know they have a future ahead of them, one that is theirs to make.

My hope is that when you read this memoir, in addition to enjoying the overall story of my life and CBC career, you'll also appreciate the view from my perspective and that of my community during less tolerant times—particularly in the time of AIDS, well before gay marriage and the subsequent progress made by our community.

Writing a memoir never crossed my mind until friends and a former colleague suggested I should. They thought I had a story to tell. I'll leave it to you to decide if they were right.

1

COME QUICK! THE BABY'S CHOKING!

I was sitting on the green painted steps that led to the front door of our house on O'Neil Avenue. It was Easter 1958. I was four and a half. My mother had dressed me in grey short pants with suspenders, a white shirt, and bright red bow tie. The St. John's sky was blue, cloudless, and calm. Not a breath of wind. The sun was brilliant. I was by myself, eyes closed, head turned skyward, smiling and enjoying the warmth of the sun on my face. Quiet, blissful solitude. Thinking about nothing.

My reverie was shattered when my older sister, Betty, also in her Sunday best, came clambering down the stairs. She was holding her black Kodak Brownie camera with its big, round, prying lens. When she stood at the foot of the steps and pointed the thing at me, I bolted. "No!" I screamed. I have no idea why I was against having my picture taken, but I clearly remember that this was not something I wanted or was going to allow.

I ran, scraping the soles of my shoes on the gravel sidewalk. I barrelled down our street, kicking up a cloud of dust worthy of my TV favourites, Roy Rogers and Trigger, in hot pursuit of cattle rustlers. My sister chased me down the hill, yelling, "I jus wanna take yer pic-churr!" I reached the bottom of our street and turned left onto St. Clare Avenue. Going farther was impossible—I was too scared to venture beyond familiar landmarks. I stood, covering my face with my hands, beside the imposing house that stood on the corner. Betty clicked her Brownie. She got a picture, although not the one she wanted. A blurred black and white image of a little boy in short pants turned sideways, attempting to hide his face from the Kodak's mechanical eye.

This event is my first detailed memory. The irony is that when I grew up, I chose to spend much of my life in front of cameras—mostly CBC TV cameras that, day after day, would send my live image and voice across Newfoundland and Labrador, and for a few years across Canada.

We're told stories about ourselves by family or family friends that occurred before we were able to develop lasting memories. Sometimes, having no memory of such stories is a blessing. There's one such story about me. It happened in the place I was born, when I was still in diapers.

I was born on Friday, October 23, 1953, in the company mining town of Buchans, close to the centre of the island of Newfoundland. My father, Leonard, was a journeyman cook. He was hired by the Buchans Mining Company in the mid-1940s to manage the Buchans Hotel. The hotel offered temporary accommodation—plus meals prepared by my father—to visiting officials, mining executives, and salesmen. It also housed long-term boarders, mainly schoolteachers and seasonal workers. Many semi-professional hockey players, such as Scotty McPhail, Jimmy Hornell, Hugh Wadden, and others (imported by the company to boost the prospects of the Buchans Miners hockey team) took their meals in the hotel but lived in another company building.

The Buchans Hotel was a rectangular two-storey white building with brown trim that stood in the shadow of the company's ore mill. It and many other nondescript Buchans buildings would have blended in perfectly on a military base. My mother and father, Elizabeth and Leonard (Lizzie and Len to friends), along with my siblings, Betty and Len Jr., were housed in the hotel manager's apartment, which had access to the public areas of the hotel. I was an unplanned child, arriving nine years after the birth of my brother and eight years after the birth of my sister. I've been told that I was a very cute baby and quickly became a star attraction around the hotel.

One day in the waning summer of 1954 when I was ten months old, I crawled into the hotel's dining room, with its many tables smartly laid with white linen and cutlery. My audience that day consisted of a small group of hotel guests chatting and smoking

A family portrait taken at Buchans in 1954.

while they waited for supper. I must have impressed at least one of the male guests, because he decided to give me a treat. He bent down and carefully placed a LifeSaver candy in my open mouth. He did this with all the casualness of someone popping a coin into a jukebox. Was he hoping for a better or perhaps different performance from me?

Nobody was paying attention until things went horribly wrong. I swallowed the hard candy, but my throat wasn't large enough to accommodate it. When my progress across the dining room's rug ended abruptly and my baby gurgles changed to wheezing, the hotel guests froze in place. They stared as I crumpled. My body was deprived of oxygen. I began turning blue. Keep in mind that this was twenty years before the Heimlich manoeuvre was invented.

Panicking guests called out to my father, and while the colour was draining from his tortured face, mine was turning an even deeper shade of blue. He scooped me up and began probing my mouth with his forefinger. Paralyzed and not knowing what to do, he turned to the guests with a look of raw anguish. A tall, handsome salesman in a tweed jacket, Carl Woodworth, stepped forward and calmly told my father to take me by the legs, hold me upside down, and pat me on the back. My father, fearing I would be dead in a few minutes, did as instructed, and the candy flew out of my mouth like a dart from a NERF blaster.

Although this method of first aid is not recommended today, it did save my life, and I'm thankful to Carl Woodworth for supervising my rescue. Betty, who was playing outside at the time, remembers our father opening the front door, mad as hell, and pitching the candy as fast as he could. It went spinning through the air, far away from our door and far away from me.

We lived in Buchans only two more years. My father developed rheumatoid arthritis, and was in so much joint pain that he was forced

At front, the Buchans Hotel, with mine site in background.

to take sick leave. Mom took on the hotel cooking with instructions from Dad until a replacement was found. Sometimes Dad couldn't walk. Betty remembers seeing him shuffling from the bedroom to the bathroom on a kitchen chair. Eventually doctors told Dad that standing for hours in a kitchen (from 6 a.m. to 7 p.m.) had to stop until his symptoms could be brought under control or eliminated with medication. That's when it was decided that we'd leave Buchans and move back to St. John's, where my brother and sister had been born, into a house on O'Neil Avenue. In 1955 we said goodbye to our hotel home and my birthplace.

I was too young to remember anything about those Buchans years. My mother rarely mentioned the town, my father and Len Jr.

hardly ever. But Betty talked about Buchans often, so much so that I believe Buchans was one of the happiest chapters of her life. It's where she and my brother spent their formative years. By the time we moved back to St. John's, my formative years were just beginning. St. John's is where I would grow up, find my soulmate, and build a career in broadcasting.

By 1957 my father had established himself as a businessman in St. John's. First, he ran a shop in Rabbittown out of rented premises on Goodridge Street. He made fresh sausages, selling them mainly to small corner grocery stores around St. John's. There were few supermarkets at the time. He'd also travel to Bell Island and sell to stores there. Sometime during 1957, a property owner named Otto Small asked Dad if he was interested in renting a grocery store near the top of Golf Avenue. It was in what was then considered the city's west end. The rent was low, and Dad jumped at the opportunity. Wells Groceteria opened shortly afterward. Eventually Dad bought the building, and the grocery store became the family business.

In my preschool and early elementary school years I didn't see much of my father, apart from being taken to school by him. Dad worked long days and spent few of his waking hours at home. My life mainly involved Mom and sister Betty. My brother seemed, for all intents and purposes, to be absent from my early life. I've seen family photos of us together—there are a couple of cute snapshots of my brother holding me when I was a baby. Still, I have only one clear memory of him from my life before age ten.

When we lived on O'Neil, I was given a Rocket Radio. It was a small crystal radio set in the shape of a red-and-white rocket ship. I kept it on a bedside table. It came with a single tiny earplug. I loved to lie in bed and listen to the crackly sound of voices from near and far that came out of that little rocket ship. Those voices, travelling into my four-year-old head long ago, sparked my love of broadcasting.

At Buchans, eagerly anticipating a car ride. Perhaps to a new life in St. John's.

That little radio fed my imagination and enabled me to picture bigger, more exciting worlds. I wanted to play a part in whatever it was that brought them to me.

One day, my thirteen-year-old brother took my radio from me and proceeded to pull it apart piece by piece. I started to cry, and pleaded with him to stop. He replied, with a child's casual indifference, "I wanna see how it works." He said he would put it back together, but my precious radio was gone.

Before I was old enough to go to school, radio and television took up most of my time. Since I no longer had my Rocket Radio, I made the radio–record player console in our dining room my personal entertainment centre. I would sit in front of the console's speaker, with my ear inches from its gold mesh cover, and listen to radio programs like *Art Baker's Notebook.* Baker's fifteen-minute program came from Hollywood and aired on CJON Radio at 1:45 p.m., after Don Jamieson's editorial and the sports. Art Baker was a storyteller. His programs featured colourful tales about his family and everyday life, often with an uplifting message. The show's attraction for me wasn't the stories, it was the sound of the voice telling them: Baker's was warm, distinctive, and resonant. Over the years, my love of the human voice has never diminished. I marvel at its ability to produce such beautiful music and spoken words.

Many local broadcasters impressed me during my childhood, and there were some that stood out on TV. Unlike our radio, which had a dial that could tune to several stations, our first Westinghouse floor-model TV had a dial that never moved off the number 6, because we had only one channel: CJON TV. The picture was black and white. Colour TV didn't arrive in Newfoundland until 1966. Don Jamieson hosted the nightly suppertime news program called *News Cavalcade.* It began with the following energetic introduction:

> Presenting CJON's *News Cavalcade* with Don Jamieson: a television report of Newfoundland news of the day, a round-up of world events, with the weather story, the sports scores and special features, and Don Jamieson's guest of the day. *News Cavalcade* is presented each night at this time by Bowring Brothers Limited, everybody's store, and by Hickman Motors Limited, your Chevrolet-Oldsmobile-Cadillac dealer in St. John's. And now here's Don Jamieson.

Jamieson was most impressive, although he was perhaps a little too fond of the word "mighty." He did literally everything on *News Cavalcade*, including the live commercials. During commercials he was "mighty happy," and things were often "mighty big," "mighty fine," and "mighty handy." Jamieson was also the weatherman. An outline of Newfoundland was painted on a blackboard, and he used a large piece of white chalk to write the temperatures on the various coasts and capes. I remember thinking it looked like fun. In fact, I thought Don Jamieson had the best job in the world. I decided that when I grew up, I was going to be Don Jamieson. (Much later I decided I would become an actor instead. Eventually I fashioned a career that combined broadcasting and occasional acting.)

We had books in our home, and most important to me—as I couldn't yet read—were the ones with lots of pictures. I remember frequently turning to a hardbound illustrated version of the Bible. It had illustrations of David taking on the Philistine giant Goliath with his slingshot, spear-carrying Roman soldiers, Jesus walking on water and healing the sick. I would spend hours staring at those wonderful drawings, imagining myself living inside them.

But there was one book in our house that, over time, caused some grief. It was an illustrated tome that gave descriptions, symptoms, and treatments for hundreds of human ailments and diseases. It was called *The Universal Home Doctor*. My mother became obsessed with it. Every time she had a twitch, twinge, ache, or pain, she'd reach for the book and try to match her symptoms with a disease. She was regularly diagnosing herself (wrongly) with the most serious illnesses. When my father finished work for the day, she would report her conclusions to him. It might be, "Len, I've got leukemia," or "Len, I've got a growth on my liver." Dad would listen, knowing she'd been reading "that damn book." He'd say, "Lizzie, don't you be so foolish. There's nothing wrong with you." It made no difference. One day, without telling Mom, he tossed *The Universal Home Doctor* in the garbage. Dad's action didn't cure but it certainly quelled Mom's hypochondria.

Observing my mother at work in her kitchen was a favourite activity of mine. Certain days called for a specific meal. Thursday, for example, was pea soup with big, fluffy white dumplings, and Saturday we'd feast on dark baked beans with homemade bread. Sunday dinner was roast chicken or roast beef with boiled vegetables. Sunday supper featured cold chicken, cold beef, or tinned ham served with potato salad, Jell-O fruit salad, lettuce, and sliced tomato. I wasn't fond of Mondays because my mother fed us an awful fried hash of chopped vegetables from Sunday's hot dinner. It reeked of reheated cabbage and made my stomach do flips. I also recall eating a lot of pan-fried bologna smothered in ketchup, which I loved. Sometimes we'd have to eat food from dented tins that Dad brought home from our store. Anything that people wouldn't buy, we usually ended up eating. I got used to dining on tinned meatballs in gravy, tinned beef stew, and tinned spaghetti in tomato sauce. Despite being thought too thin in my early childhood, I enjoyed food very much. Efforts were constantly being made to fatten me up. I could eat whatever I liked, whenever I wanted. This policy would eventually backfire.

Occasionally we'd have special meals, including Dad's seal flipper pie. More often we'd have fish and brewis (boiled salt cod and steamed hard bread) with scruncheons (tiny cubes of pork fat, fried till crispy) and drawn butter. We were tea drinkers, mostly, but the only beverage ever served with our fish and brewis was sweetened instant Maxwell House coffee with a splash of Carnation milk. I soon acquired a taste for coffee and would ask Mom for a drink of "stars on top." (Maxwell House coffee came in a screw-top jar with white stars on its red lid, and 1950s TV commercials referred to it as being "in the jar with the stars on top.")

The most memorable food of my childhood wasn't prepared by my mother or father, though. It was from Archie's Snack Bar. On Friday evenings my mother would send my sister, my brother, and me for takeout fish and chips. We'd walk to the neighbourhood snack bar: down O'Neil Avenue, right on St. Clare Avenue, and right on Campbell Avenue to Archie's little building at the southeast corner of Campbell and Cashin. I would sit on the chrome barstool next to the kitchen pass-through window while we waited for our order.

My vantage point gave me a perfect view of the woman who hovered over the deep-fat fryer, cooking the chips. She was thin, with deep-set eyes and a narrow nose on a narrow, lined face; she wore a hairnet, a white uniform, and cat-eye glasses with a chain. I would watch as she lifted and shook, lifted and shook the fry basket again to release excess fat from the load of chips. (In the background, a low staticky radio would pump out songs by the Everly Brothers and Elvis Presley.)

Watching her was fascinating because she was a chain-smoker. I never saw her without a burning cigarette hanging precariously from her mouth. She smoked without ever touching it. Over time, the ash at the end of the cigarette would grow longer and longer. I stared at that cylinder of ash like a hawk as it grew, fractionally, with each passing second. I was certain the ash would break off and we'd end up having to eat fish and chips with salt, vinegar, and EXPORT "A" ash. Thankfully, the ash somehow stayed in place and we were able to take our grease-stained brown paper bag home and devour the battered cod and chips at our narrow, glossy white kitchen table.

My preschool life didn't include other children my age. Mom always kept me at home with her. There were children on the street, but I didn't play with neighbourhood kids until I was six or seven. The only children I saw near my age were on TV. Occasionally, I saw my peers on CJON's local version of *Romper Room*, and I never missed *The Howdy Doody Show* with Clarabell the Clown, Timber Tom the forest ranger, Howdy Doody, and the twenty or so children who sat in the Peanut Gallery. So, I started to get nervous in August of 1958 when my mother began dropping hints about my having to go to school in September with other children, though I kept my fears to myself. When the day arrived to leave the safe harbour of our O'Neil Avenue home, I panicked and hid inside a cupboard. I wanted nothing to do with other children. Hiding worked, and I continued to hide for the rest of that week. After each morning fuss that my refusal to go to school caused, things would calm down and I'd settle into my daily routine.

The idea of leaving my pleasant haven, of not having my mom nearby, of being with strange grown-ups and strange children terrified me. What would I say to them? Would they like me? Would they be mean to me? Would the teacher be nice? Whenever I thought about school, I'd get butterflies in my stomach and begin to feel physically ill. Perhaps if I'd met and played with children my age earlier, starting school would have been easier. My parents didn't try to allay my fears by speaking positively about school and reassuring me that everything would be fine. Instead, I was left to imagine that I was being forced into a scary place. But I was about to discover that scary things can happen at home, too.

2

I FELT ABANDONED AND BETRAYED

I remember the Monday when everything finally came to a head as if it just happened. A week had passed since I'd launched my first successful bid to stay home from school when I awoke with a feeling of foreboding. There was an atmosphere in our house. I decided to hide right away. Underneath my parents' bed seemed like a good spot, even with the dust bunnies. I thought that maybe I wouldn't be noticed if I curled up in the darkest, least accessible area, tight into the corner of the room. The chenille bedspread had a pink tassel fringe, which provided extra cover but still allowed me to see movement outside my hiding spot. Not long after I'd crawled underneath the bed, my mother began calling me. Her voice sounded different. Apart from being slightly louder, it was gradually taking on a hard edge of exasperation. I had, to paraphrase the proverb, sown the wind and was about to reap the whirlwind.

Suddenly, from my hiding place, I saw Mom's ankles and familiar white slip-on shoes. Next the pink fringe disappeared, revealing my mother's angry face. "Get outta there. Come on. You're goin' to school." She kept on ordering me out, eventually becoming angry, then angrier. When she left, I thought she'd gone to fetch my father, but no, she'd fetched a persuader—our flat, broomcorn broom. By the time Mom's face reappeared in the gap between the bed and floor, I hardly recognized her. She was boiling red, with narrowed eyes glistening, full of fire, voice at full throttle. "Get OUT!" she shouted. Then, in came the wooden-handled broom with its long, compacted straws that stung. She whacked me with it, making hit after hit as she grew even angrier. Then came the biggest outburst. "Get OUT you little BASTARD! Get OUT!" she shouted. I resisted, thinking my father would intervene any second and save me from this crazy person who used to be Mommy. Help never came. Afraid she'd seriously hurt me if I didn't surrender, I scampered out from under the bed like a terrified animal.

I was in shock and can't recall if I had breakfast or what transpired immediately after I surrendered. The next thing I remember is sitting in our Vauxhall Bedford delivery van with my father. There was stony silence. I could smell the pungent new leather from a bookbag that had been placed on my lap. On top of the bookbag lay a wafer-thin colouring book with a black cover featuring a giraffe, big bouncing letters, and colourful fruit. I stared at it, dazed and teary-eyed. My pyjamas had been replaced by a strange costume: a white shirt, long clip-on tie with red and blue stripes, a navy-blue blazer edged with red thread, grey flannel trousers, black shoes, and a navy-blue school cap. I don't remember a word being spoken from the time we left O'Neil Avenue until we reached Harrington School on LeMarchant Road. As we passed each familiar landmark, reminding me that we were getting closer and closer to our destination, I became more and more anxious. The butterflies in my stomach were flapping frantically and crashing into each other.

It was my first day of school: Monday, September 8, 1958. I was six weeks shy of my fifth birthday. I was late for my first class by just under a week and some 20 minutes. Dad walked me down an empty hallway that had an overpowering, almost nauseating smell of floor cleaner. The classroom's double doors stood at the very end of the corridor. We entered a big room with about thirty children seated at tables in a semicircle, all staring at us with a look of mild curiosity. Dad said something to the teacher, Mrs. Andrews, then he turned and left. I ran to the doors with tears streaming down my face. I pressed my nose against the glass, which was embedded with wire mesh to prevent it from shattering. The mesh reminded me of a

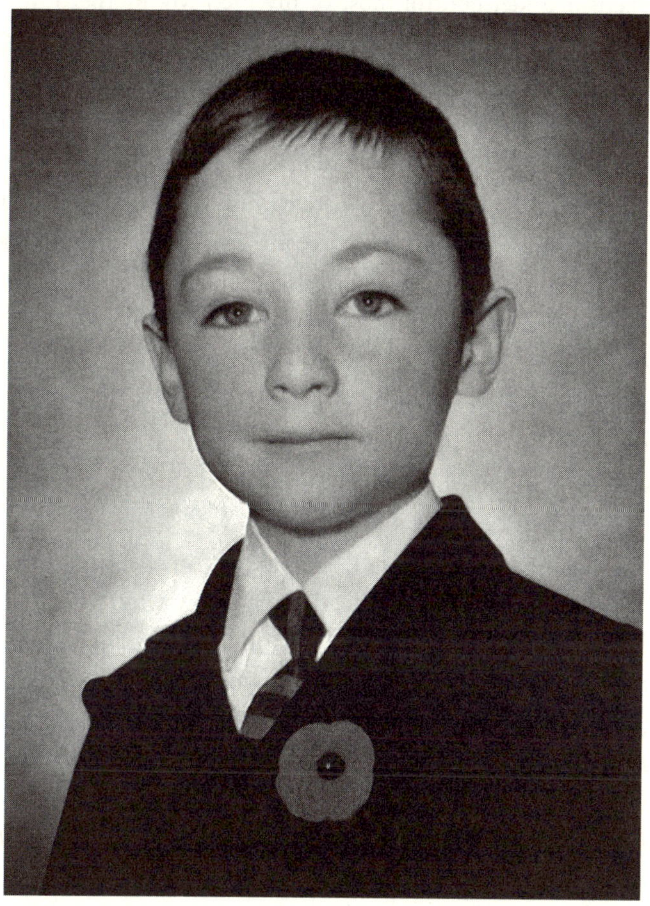

I overcame my aversion to having my photo taken by the time I reached school age.

cage. I watched my father walk away, back through the corridor, into a watery blur. I felt abandoned and betrayed. Dad never looked back.

My mother had a temper, but her outburst on my first day of school was unusual. I never witnessed anything like it again, and she never physically punished me again. Her temper was inherited from her father. (I inherited some of Mom's temper but, thankfully, have kept it under control most of my life.) My mother loved her children (and we loved her) but she had neither the temperament nor the patience for raising them. I came along at a time when she thought she would soon be freed from child rearing. Mom found the responsibility of keeping house and raising children overwhelming at times. Still, she did her best. My parents worked hard, but my mother would have preferred a more carefree life involving less responsibility.

I had no doubt my father loved us, too, but Dad's attitude toward children was Edwardian, like that of many men of his generation. He believed that raising kids was a wife's duty. When I was young, my mom and Betty shared the responsibility. My mother looked after me ninety percent of the time and my sister the rest. It's how my mother chose to cope with raising her new, unplanned child. Betty was barely a teenager when I entered kindergarten.

It was unfair on my sister. I even slept in the same bed with her for much of my young life (I don't know why). This became unpleasant for her and horribly humiliating and stressful for me when I became a bedwetter. To make matters worse, every time I'd wet the bed, both my mother and sister would be angry. I'd stand barefoot, in soaked pyjama pants, struggling to tune out their raised voices as they quickly stripped the sheets from the bed. Red-faced, freezing, my stomach in knots, I remember thinking I'm a freak.

We had a three-bedroom house on O'Neil Avenue and three beds. I slept in my sister's bed and sometimes with my parents, or on a small cot. Growing pains in my legs would often wake me. The pain was so

There's me, the sad-faced child at top left, in kindergarten.

bad that I'd cry and go to my parents' room for help. Dad would rub my legs with a milky-white patent medicine called Minard's Liniment until I settled. Then he'd let me get into bed between him and my mother. I'd snuggle my dad and go back to sleep.

One morning, when I was six, I woke and heard someone in the kitchen. I went downstairs and found Betty making breakfast. She was stirring a cup of Maxwell House instant coffee. I asked her to make me "some stars on top," but she ignored me. I asked again. Betty replied, rightly, "No. Children aren't supposed to have coffee." This was news to me, since our mom gave me coffee, and I'd always had my sweet milky coffee with fish and brewis. "Mommy lets me have it," I replied. She persisted, "You're not supposed to have it. You're too little!"

We went back and forth until I concluded that Betty wasn't interested in my argument that Mom's rules trumped anything she might decide. I thought Betty was being mean. I grew more and more exasperated, feeling wronged and not able to make my words convince her. Futility gave rise to overwhelming frustration. A hallway ran from our front porch straight into our kitchen. As I stood in the kitchen, I stared up the hall at the varnished French door leading to our porch. It was a beautiful door containing fifteen panes of clear glass.

I fixed my eyes on a middle pane. Before I knew it, I was racing up the hallway in a blind rage. I pulled back my right arm, forming a fist, and punched through the glass. Shards went flying. I moved my tiny arm back out of the window frame and, as if detached from reality, viewed with curious disbelief the bright red lines forming on the pale inside surface of my skin. The lines quickly became rivulets of red. Then everything went blank. I don't remember what happened next. Perhaps trauma erased the memory. The incident was never mentioned again, not by anybody, until May 2024, when Betty told me what she could remember of the aftermath.

"You began to cry, and Mom was close to hysterical. Your hand was bleeding and Dad wrapped it in a dish towel, I think. Then he took you to a drugstore up on Pennywell Road. He knew the owner who worked there. He bandaged it. I don't think there was a problem with the wound after that."

The drugstore was Fleming's Drugstore, a small family business, as most were in the 1950s. Mr. Fleming was a kind man. My father probably took me to him because my cuts weren't deep. He may also have thought that because I knew Mr. Fleming, I'd be more likely to settle down for him. There was no dedicated children's hospital in St. John's in those days. General hospitals were terrifying places for adults, let alone children.

For a child growing up in late 1950s and early 1960s Newfoundland, the world seemed built for adults. Apart from schools and churches and their affiliated activities, there was little available for kids unless you fancied wearing a sports jersey or scouting uniform. Services for youth, youth counsellors, and helplines did not exist. Supporting youth wasn't a priority, even though it was a time of rising anxiety because of the Cold War and anti-establishmentarianism.

My siblings often seemed angry at the world. As teenagers they weren't unique in this regard. My brother would act out by drinking alcohol before he was old enough. He did other dangerous things, too, like driving underage. One night while Mom and Dad were out, when I was nine, he took me and my sister on a joyride in Dad's delivery van. The van had only two seats—for the driver and a passenger. I was perched on a wooden box in the back, terrified that we'd end up in a crash or in jail, since my siblings kept talking about avoiding the police.

Betty often lashed out at our parents verbally. I remember a night when one of her outbursts made me wish I'd been born into another family. It was a school night and I'd gone to bed. My sister's raised voice woke me. She was in the kitchen launching a barrage at our father. She was defending our brother, whose behaviour at the time was causing family stress. Everyone was in the kitchen except me, but like it or not, I could hear every shouted word.

My sister's assessment of brother Len hinged on the fact that my father had never spoken the words "I love you" to him. She was attempting to make Dad say the words to my brother. Dad wouldn't or couldn't. She was relentless, but the most Dad would say was "Yes, I like him. Sure I do. I like him."

The whole episode was very painful to listen to. It hurt me so much that I began to shake, and tears streamed down my face. I began to sob into my pillow. Nobody heard me amidst all the shouting in our kitchen. I just lay there, miserable, for what seemed like hours, until I was too exhausted to stay awake. Sleep, when it finally came, was a relief.

I felt sorry for my father. There was and still is a strong bond between my sister and brother, likely because of their closeness in age and having been raised together. (That, and the gap between my age and theirs, made me feel very much like an outsider.) I doubt that my brother wanted my sister representing him in conflicts with our parents. Her confrontational approach probably rankled him. Although Len was able to speak for himself, he often chose not to communicate.

Neither my mother nor father told us they loved us when we were young, although in later years my mother did. Their generation wasn't brought up hearing or saying "I love you." My paternal grandmother, Eliza Wells (from the Methodist outport, Wesleyville), was averse to displays of affection. I remember her showing disapproval when she saw Mom hug my father. "Ahhhgt!" she'd snap. Dad would have learned in childhood to resist saying "I love you." But while Mom and Dad didn't voice the words, their love for us was obvious in their actions. I always felt protected and cared for by my parents. I knew I was loved and didn't need to hear the words spoken by either of them.

Not long after I started school, Dad's youngest brother moved into our basement apartment with his wife and little girl. Uncle Walt was unhappy living in New York and wanted to move back to Newfoundland. Dad wanted to help him get on his feet in St. John's. He offered him a job in our grocery business. That was Dad's story and he stuck to it. Uncle Walt maintained that Dad begged him to come home to go into business with him and save our store. They fell out with each other many times during the years they worked together. Sometimes Uncle Walt would quit and become a truck driver or a Bugden's cab driver. Once he quit and opened his own small store in Rabbittown.

Uncle Walt had met and married a fellow Newfoundlander in New York. Aunt Jean (née Strickland) was from King's Cove, near Bonavista. She'd given birth to my cousin Debbie a year or so before they moved back to Newfoundland. Debbie was a few years younger than me. I was thrilled to have relatives in our house, and I could visit them whenever I wanted. My Aunt Jean gave me lots of love and I came to regard her as a second mother. Debbie became like a sister.

We rode the brown and silver city buses frequently during my childhood. My first trips were to Bowring Park with Mom, Aunt Jean, and Debbie. I liked sitting in the higher sideways seat near the driver. In summer, special buses would take loads of people to the park, travelling west on Hamilton Avenue to Topsail Road, then south on Cowan Avenue to Bowring Park's main entrance. The trip seemed long, like going far into the country. It was an adventure.

We'd spend time watching the swans and ducks, and people rowing around the duck pond in small wooden boats. I'd wade and splash about in the Waterford River swimming pool, a dammed section of the river behind the tennis courts. We'd end every park visit relaxing on a blanket spread out under a tree on the Bungalow lawn. Mom and Aunt Jean would prepare a lunch of sandwiches and soft drinks for our day in the park. Our sandwiches would usually be made with Mammy's white bread, Good Luck margarine, tinned potted meat, sliced ham, or egg salad. We'd wash them down with Orange Crush for Debbie and me, and 7-UP for Mom and Aunt Jean.

My first visit to a movie theatre happened at age five, when my father took me to see the Disney film *The Shaggy Dog*, starring

My Aunt Jean and Uncle Walt. She was a second mother to me.

Tommy Kirk and Fred MacMurray. It was playing at the Paramount Theatre on Harvey Road. Years later, when I was ten, my mother took me to see a Bette Davis movie at the Paramount. My cousin Debbie came with us. Debbie was eight. I'm not sure why Mom chose the movie we saw. She may have been motivated by its popular theme song of the same name, "Hush . . . Hush, Sweet Charlotte."

I remember hearing the song on the radio. These days the movie has a PG rating and is described as a "psychological horror film." We sat and waited for the movie to start. I stuffed my face with warm popcorn from a yellow box with a clown on the cover. The lights dimmed and the curtain opened.

Early in the movie, before the title credits, the actor Bruce Dern's character, John Mayhew, sits in a darkened room. A close-up shows his hand resting on a piece of furniture. Suddenly we see the hand chopped off by a meat cleaver! Then we see a close-up of Dern screaming and holding up his grisly stump. Next, a shadow suggests his head has been chopped off too! I was terrified. Debbie hid under her jacket. I turned to my left to look at Mom, thinking she'd surely be just as horrified as us.

Amazingly, her face had not registered even the slightest sign of distress. Her expression was neutral, calm. We stayed through the entire showing. When we were back home, I asked Mom why she wasn't upset by the man having his hand and head chopped off. "Because I knew it wasn't real," she said calmly. My mother had, unintentionally, taught me an important lesson. Always question. Learn to tell the difference between what is real and what is fake.

After I started school and was allowed outside on my own, I began to make friends on our street. Sandra Barron, Patsy DuPree, and Gerry Power, a boy my age who lived next door, were frequent companions. Gerry and I would play in our backyard hunting for daddy-long-legs or other insects (anything more interesting than a housefly would do). We'd wrestle on the grass or pretend we were cowboys firing our toy guns at rustlers and bank robbers. My mother fed us slices of Mammy's white bread slathered with yellow mustard sprinkled with white sugar: tart, sweet, soft, and fragrant.

Sometimes an event brought all the neighbourhood children together, such as a visit by the Lawlors Meats delivery wagon—a wooden wagon pulled by a big horse, with a driver up front on a high bench. This throwback to a previous era was still around when I was a child. No doubt it was used for advertising purposes, which certainly worked for the kids of O'Neil Avenue.

More of an event was the late summer visit of Mr. Peanut. The monocled Planters mascot wore a black top hat and would travel up and down O'Neil and the other avenues, standing in the cargo bed of a pickup truck. He'd toss us little bags of peanuts. Nothing could have made us happier or more devoted to an eight-foot peanut with human arms and legs.

Gerry Power invited me to his house for dinner once. His mom, Clare, was a good cook. I enjoyed the food and was surprised by the large number of Powers around the table. It was the first time I'd seen them together in one place. Gerry had lots of brothers and sisters, and I couldn't help but notice several were close to his age. It must be fun having kids around your own age, I thought. At our house, my father solemnly said grace before we began a meal. At Gerry's house nobody said grace. Each just quickly made the sign of the cross on themselves. I remember thinking it was a much faster and more efficient way to invoke the Spirit of God at the family table. I made a mental note to strongly recommend it to Dad.

At our next family meal, immediately after my father said grace, I told him about the new high-speed invocation I'd learned at the Powers's dining table. Dad went icy silent. He glared at me as if I were the Antichrist in flesh. My father could scare the life out of me with a facial expression. It's what I would later name "the Wells look." I learned very quickly about organized religions and that my friend Gerry was of another tribe called Roman Catholics. We were Protestants. My father made it clear that if you were born into a religion, or joined one, you stuck with it and upheld its practices and traditions exclusively. We never discussed religious diversity again.

Underneath the stop sign at the top of O'Neil Avenue. I was seven.

For the earliest years of my life, three of my grandparents were living. Grandfather Wells had died in 1949, never to experience the change that came after Newfoundland joined Canada. Grandmother Wells, who would live many years beyond the others, was living in Gander with my Uncle Bert and Aunt Mabel. Grandmother and Grandfather Stockley were still living in Gambo.

Gramp Stockley wasn't well. He had palsy, likely Parkinson's disease. In the summer we'd drive to Gambo, or take the train if just Mom and I were going. I enjoyed the train but wasn't fond of driving because I got carsick. At the time there was no highway across Newfoundland, and what roads we had were gravel. Our Ford Customline four-door sedan would be oiled and gassed up, and we'd rattle and roll until we got to Bunyan's Cove. Once there, we and the Ford would sail across Clode Sound on a small ferry boat. Then we were back on the road for the bumpy drive to Gambo. If it was hot and the roads were dry, things got worse. If you wanted relief from the stifling heat, or a breath of fresh air, you rolled down the window and hoped the incoming cloud of dust contained a little oxygen.

In those days I found Gambo fascinating because of the contrast between it and St. John's. I lived in a city with paved streets, traffic lights, and department stores. Our house in the city had electricity, running water, central heating, a flush toilet, and television. Gambo had no modern conveniences. A visit to my grandparents' home was like stepping back in time. I likened it to one of those small places in the Wild West that I'd seen on *The Roy Rogers Show* and *Gunsmoke*. Those western homes had oil lamps, and so did my grandparents' house. Gambo even had what I thought was a herd of wild horses that would run down the unpaved main road, leaving clouds of dust behind. They were, in fact, work horses running to pasture, but you can imagine the thrill I felt watching a scene from a western movie come to life before my eyes.

A subdued atmosphere pervaded my grandparents' home in the summer of 1958. Since Gramp Stockley was in failing health, a bed had been moved downstairs into the parlour for him, where he lay, staring at the ceiling and covered in blankets up to his chin. He had a head of thick white and grey hair and a big, bushy white western moustache. I'd climb up on the bed and snuggle in next to his head. He couldn't speak. Every now and then he'd make a pitiful sound—plaintive, mournful mumbling. I'd sit quietly on the bed, wide-eyed, and watch as Gram Stockley gave him a shave.

Each careful step in the process fascinated me. She'd tuck a small terry towel under his chin and make a soapy lather in his shaving mug. Then she'd use the shaving brush to soap up Gramp's face. Finally, she'd use his safety razor to shave away, in gentle strokes, the stubble that had grown since the previous morning. Sometimes I'd stay on the bed and watch as she fed him tea with milk and sugar. He'd have a towel under his chin again. Gram would blow on the tea to make sure it wasn't too hot and carefully place the mug against his lower lip and gently tip it into his open mouth. Some of it would go into his mouth and some would escape out the sides. I was a tot, but I knew my grandfather was dying.

Despite my belief that Gambo was stuck in a time warp, a building directly across the road from the Stockley homestead stuck a tiny pin in my theory. It was a plain white wooden structure that looked like a small warehouse, but was actually a movie theatre with a generator powerful enough to run a 16 mm projector and a light bulb or two. Grandmother Stockley had figured out that on a warm summer's evening she could stand in her garden, leaning against the front fence for support, and look directly through the theatre's open door at the movie screen. She could see and hear, for free, whatever happened to be playing.

In summer it wasn't feasible to shut the outside door, because the usually full theatre was uncomfortably warm. I loved to stand beside my Gram, who'd still be wearing a long apron over her long dress, and peek through the fence and tall grass trying to see what she was looking at, often gazing upward to witness the various expressions crossing her face. One night I was at the movie fence with Gram and she was totally engrossed by the film (an Audie Murphy western, I think). Before I knew anything, she was shaking her fists and angrily shouting at someone across the road. A steady stream of vitriol poured from her mouth, including a few words I'd never heard before. What happened? Apparently, the projectionist decided his patrons had had enough fresh air, so he shut the door.

When the booming 1950s ended and 1960 was about to dawn, our family grocery business began to fail. Dad's takings were down. Profits weren't high enough to maintain the store, keep a house on O'Neil Avenue, and pay Uncle Walt's wages. Dad's only option was to sell our house on O'Neil and move to Golf Avenue, where we could live above the store.

An early version of our store, shortly after Dad set up shop in the late 1950s. That's cousin Mick Stockley climbing aboard our Bedford van.

3

I KNEW I WAS DIFFERENT

The apartment above our grocery store was spacious. It had nine rooms: a living room, dining room, den, kitchen, laundry, bathroom, and three bedrooms. I still had to share a bed with my sister, but within a few years I was given my own bed in my brother's room. Dad let me pick out the bed, a small single with a bookcase headboard. I loved having my own bed. I kept my *Hardy Boys* books and *Spiderman* comics in the headboard, which had sliding doors, and I put a lamp on top so I could read in bed.

I missed my O'Neil Avenue friends, who seemed far away even though they were just three streets over. Not having a front and back garden was strange. Our new home was bordered by concrete and asphalt. We were now in a livelier, more interesting neighbourhood. Our store stood at the corner of Golf Avenue and Mount Royal Avenue. We had lots of neighbours. The houses on Mount Royal, much like Golf, were a mixture of compact two-storey dwellings and a few small bungalows with dormer windows. All were close to the sidewalk, with tiny front gardens.

As a residential street, Mount Royal had an anomaly: a small mattress factory owned by a family named Keats. The low blue building, set back from the sidewalk, was full of dust, feathers, wool, and straw. It made mattresses, mainly for CNR rail construction workers. Not high-quality mattresses. The factory was poorly built, and our neighbours believed it was a firebomb waiting to go off. One hot, windy day, fire struck. They said it was caused by an electrical malfunction. I watched the factory being consumed by orange and yellow flames. Mattresses, mattress stuffing, roof, walls, all furiously devoured. Nothing but the building's foundation remained. Mount Royal's residents were relieved that no houses caught fire. The factory wasn't rebuilt.

Golf Avenue was longer and roomier than Mount Royal. Homes on Golf had larger front gardens with mature leafy trees: maple, dogberry, and chestnut. The folks who lived on both streets and in the general area were friendly people who came from all walks of life. Some were born and bred in the outports, others in St. John's. They were tradespeople, factory workers, businesspeople, civil servants, teachers, druggists, police officers, and doctors. A few neighbours worked in our store, and some helped occasionally. They were like family.

Ralph Spurrell lived nearby on Pennywell Road. He was eight years older than me. Ralph was kind, happy-go-lucky, smart, and full of energy. He filled orders, stocked shelves, worked the cash, and delivered groceries on a wobbly grocery bike that had a large box at the front. I visited his home and met his family, and we went places together. Ralph's older brother, Ron Spurrell, was a typesetter with the *Evening Telegram*. We went to the paper's big white building on Duckworth Street and saw the downstairs print shop. It was like something from *Citizen Kane*.

Farther down Golf Avenue, just below Raleigh Street, was an entrance to the Canadian military facility, Buckmaster's Field. Its inaccessibility made it mysterious to me. Commissionaires, in black uniforms with white covers on their caps, were posted at the gates. (There was a similar gate on Prince of Wales Street.) Just inside was a very high pole with a yellow air-raid siren on top, to warn of imminent nuclear attack. (We were well into the Cold War by then.) I heard the

Ralph Spurrell trying to get me to face the camera in 1963. Notice the grocery bike.

siren once when it was being tested. The sound was like the wail of a thousand tormented ghosts. Around 1965 the base was closed, and the personnel moved to Pleasantville, formerly an American base called Fort Pepperrell. I remember Pepperrell, which closed in 1960, being guarded by military police wearing MP armbands and white striped helmets. Dad and I drove along the Boulevard once, and there they were, Uncle Sam's finest, at the guardhouse and gates.

Plenty of neighbourhood shops surrounded ours. On Golf Avenue alone there was Fruitland, Two-Way Stores, and near Buckmaster's gates, Stanley's Meats, and Best's Store. Across the street from Wells Groceteria, on an opposite corner, was Hodder's Store, and from our main entrance you could look north to Pennywell Road and see Walsh's Store, where I got my *Spiderman* and *Batman* comics and Betty bought her Hollywood magazines, *Movieland* and *Photoplay.*

Our store was L-shaped. Customers entered the store at the corner of the L. To the left, just beyond the shopping trolleys, in the long part of the L, was a white wooden island of shelves stocked with tinned, bottled, and packaged goods. The top shelves were reserved for breakfast cereals and fresh Mammy's and Sunny Bee bread. In the 1950s and '60s, some of our stock was made in the UK or came through British supply lines. We sold British tinned Fray Bentos Steak and Kidney Pies, Rose's marmalade, Joseph Dobson & Sons Lemon Crystals, Ovaltine, Crawford's Garibaldi biscuits, and several other British products.

Beside one of the Golf Avenue windows stood a shorter island. Fresh fruit and vegetables were kept in the divided top bins, and below them, five- and ten-pound bags of potatoes. There were shelves dedicated to baking ingredients. To the right of the store's main entrance was our checkout counter. Behind the counter were shelves for Gerald S. Doyle's Newfoundland Cod Liver Oil, Dodd's Kidney Pills and other patent medicines, cigarettes, tobacco, cigarette paper, stationery, candy bars, Adams and Scotties chips, and Hawkins Cheezies. In later years we installed a custard cone (soft serve) machine behind the counter. Some of the candy bars came from England, including my favourite bar—Needler's Kreema Nut & Fruit Milk Chocolate, made in Hull. The wrapper had a drawing of the huge Hull chocolate factory on the back. I'd examine it and imagine what a wondrous place that chocolate factory must be.

Built above our cash register was a long shelf with well-worn invoice books stacked in alphabetical order; surnames were etched in ballpoint on the bottom edge of each book. These were essentially charge books. Dad allowed many of his customers to charge what they bought. They purchased weekly (or more often) and paid monthly. This was a common practice in small grocery stores of the era, but even as a young teenager I thought it a precarious way to make a living. It was the root cause of many of the arguments that arose between my mom and dad. Dad's creditors would call our home instead of the store phone when his payments were past due. My mother would answer and listen to payment demands from, for example, someone from the Gaden's soda company insisting upon immediate payment. I couldn't bear to hear the nervousness in her voice as she spoke with the anonymous debt collector.

When Dad came up to the apartment for his supper, things would kick off. My mother would weep and shout, "Why can't you pay the bills?" Dad would calmly answer, "Lizzie, they'll get their money when I get mine." It was like water off a duck's back to my father. Running a business isn't for the faint of heart. Meanwhile I'd worry about what might become of us. I was sensitive when I was little, but I've since grown a thicker skin. Those arguments turned me into a fiscal conservative: I vowed nobody would ever bother me for not paying on time.

At the back of the store, in the short part of the L, next to stacks of bottled soft drinks, laundry supplies, and a water-bath Coca-Cola drink cooler, was the heart of our store: the meat room. It had a staff entrance, and one whole wall was open from ceiling to floor to accommodate a long display cooler. You could stand against the open meat and dairy display case, and anyone who could tolerate the loud buzzing of the powerful meat bandsaw could watch my father in his long white apron deftly sawing up a hindquarter of beef.

Standing against the exterior wall were wooden barrels filled with large pieces of salt meat, pork riblets, and pork fatback. At the rear, next to a corner sink, was a heavy free-standing butcher's block. Just beyond were faded red-topped Arborite counters housing a commercial meat slicer, a scale, sheets of wax paper, a brown paper roller, and high above on a hook, a conical roll of store twine with a length of freed twine hovering over the paper rollers. Always at hand were ancient-looking, well-sharpened meat cleavers and butcher knives.

If you wanted a quarter-pound of boiled ham, Dad would ask, "How thick do you want it?" Using our big electric slicer, he'd slice your ham onto a piece of wax paper laid on his left palm. Then he'd tear off a piece of brown paper, put the ham and wax paper on it, place another piece of wax paper on top and wrap the whole package up neatly. Next, he'd spool off whatever string he needed, snap it in two with a quick jerk of his wrist, and tie up the package of ham. Finally, he'd write the price on the outside in black wax pencil. I was never able to snap the string like Dad, even though I kept trying, sometimes until my hands were blistered and raw. My skin wasn't thick enough and my wrists weren't strong enough.

On a typical day, Wells Groceteria buzzed, not only with the sound of the meat saw, but with human activity. In the morning, just after the door was unlocked, the Coke or Pepsi truck arrived, and driver and helper would start lugging in thick, heavy wooden crates filled with bottles of Coke and other soft drinks. I'd watch them from a bedroom window overlooking Golf Avenue as they carried those full crates with the ease of someone carrying a block of foam rubber. I thought the Mammy's Bread man—who arrived in the afternoon in his distinctive white box truck with *Mammy's* writ large on its sides—had a much easier job. Mammy's bread was like fluff, feather light compared to crates filled with Coca-Cola.

One day, my mother was chatting with a Mammy's delivery man named Forward Wicks. His full name was sewn in luminous yellow thread on the front of his sharp blue uniform.

"Forward? That's a funny name," I said. He chuckled.

My mother, who was leaning against the meat cooler, which I was barely tall enough to see over, replied, "Forward by name, forward by nature." They laughed heartily.

"Lizzie by name, Lizzie by nature!" I shouted reflexively, even though it made no sense.

Mom didn't laugh and neither did Forward Wicks. In fact, they blushed. Lizzie was short for Elizabeth, and it's what my dad always called Mom. I knew, almost immediately, what I'd said didn't make sense and wasn't worth a laugh, but I wondered why it made them blush and look so uncomfortable. Later I asked Mom why my comment made her turn red. She told me that Lizzie or, more accurately, "lezzie," meant that a woman was a homo, and homosexuals were bad people. (Homosexuality was illegal at the time. Men had been jailed for being intimate with one another.) Mom awkwardly tried to explain homosexuality to me. I mulled it over. It scared me. I didn't want to be a homosexual. Yet, intuitively, I knew I was different and that I might be a homosexual. I was eight at the time.

Some remarkable characters shopped at our store. Florence "Flo" Kavanagh wore metal-framed glasses, the thick lenses of which made her penetrating eyes look slightly bigger, more intimidating. Her manner was gruff, her voice low pitched, but she had a kind heart. Bruce Tizzard, a teenage neighbour who often helped in the store, told me about one visit made by Florence Kavanagh to Wells Groceteria. It was typical.

"It was a Monday morning. Your father was putting the meat saw back together after cleaning it. Mrs. Kavanagh walked in and leaned over the meat cooler and mumbled something about 'the price of a bit of meat these days.' Your father turned toward her, but by this time she'd come round the corner and was standing over a barrel of salt meat. 'I want a nice piece,' she said, 'I'm makin' a Jiggs' Dinner.' Mr. Wells said, 'Okay, my dear, I'll pick out a few pieces for you.' As he started to do so, Mrs. Kavanagh said, 'Not too much fat . . . no, too many bones.' She took a few of the pieces between her index finger and thumb and turned them over, inspecting with her keen eye. By now the barrel was almost empty. As your father began putting the pieces back in the barrel, she complained about the price, saying it was hard to get good salt beef anymore. She ended up taking the first piece he'd picked out. Your father had the patience of Job, bless him."

Moving to Golf Avenue and above our store had an unexpected physical effect on me. Before the move from O'Neil Avenue, I rarely ate junk food. It wasn't available. My parents didn't give me junk food or have it in the house—apart from candy and Moirs chocolates at Christmas. Living above a store, or more significantly, above a trove of every kind of junk food, put me in a special situation. I wasn't just "a kid in a candy store," I was a kid living in one, able to take and eat what he wanted. In the beginning I doubt my father cared or noticed. He felt I was too thin anyway. In retrospect, the result of my unrestricted access to junk food was predictable. Gradually I began to gain weight. I became overweight and was made fun of at school. Some boys called me Fatso. I was already perceived as being strange because I was shy and indifferent to pursuits such as sports, outdoor recreation, and girlfriends. Now my size became something else to pin a label on.

My father's solution to my weight problem was to put me to work in the store. I swept the floors, swept and then spread fresh sawdust on the meat room floor. I scrubbed and stacked shelves, bagged groceries, filled one-pound plastic bags with dried beans and peas. I'd also help Dad package wedges of cheese, which he'd carefully cut from a huge, heavy wheel of cheddar. He usually cut off a small piece for me as a treat. I was banned from working the till or cash because I proved utterly useless at making change. I'd often give people more than they were owed. It was before the days of smart tills that tell you how much change to make. Dad's weight reduction scheme didn't work. I got hungrier and ate more.

What I enjoyed most was helping Dad deliver groceries in our Bedford van and joining him on his rounds to wholesalers and

Wells Groceteria in early 1960s, from an oil painting by Jason Jenkins.

suppliers. Sometimes we'd collect Dad's freshly laundered white aprons from a nearby laundry. Hai Wong operated Hai Lee Laundry at 85 Casey Street. Dad's aprons got bloodied and soiled from sawing and chopping meat and required professional cleaning. I remember the laundry well, because it was so different from anything you'd expect.

All anybody got to see was a quiet, unadorned, dimly lit front area where you either delivered or collected your laundry. Unless someone was leaving laundry, you didn't see any. That's because, once laundered, dried, and pressed in a back room, your items were wrapped in heavy brown paper, tied with string, and kept at the front of the store for pickup. Behind the Hai Lee Laundry counter, a wall of shelving was divided into large pigeonholes. Each pigeonhole contained one or two brown packages. Dad would send me in, I'd give the man—or sometimes a woman—my father's name, and they'd hand me one of the brown paper packages.

Whether it was stopping for aprons, picking up supplies for our store, or darting down to the harbour with a case of Carnation milk for a fishing boat, there was a period of my early adolescence when I spent much of my free time touring around St. John's as my father's helper.

I had no interest in learning how to run a grocery business; I just wanted to be with Dad, to chat with him and learn about the places and people we'd encounter. I was a curious kid and although shy in school, I never hesitated to ask questions of my easy-to-engage father.

"Dad, why does Joey [Smallwood] hate Prime Minister Diefenbaker?" I was nine when I asked that one. We were driving along Pennywell Road. It was the winter of 1963. Dad was wearing his flat winter cap, gripping the wheel in gloved hands as we watched the road through a windshield unevenly framed by snow and ice. A federal election was happening that spring. I'd heard Premier Smallwood on CJON Radio fuming about some terrible thing that Prime Minister John Diefenbaker had done to Newfoundland. Dad was a news junkie (like his late father), so he eagerly told me "that bad man Diefenbaker won't give Newfoundland the money we're owed for joining Canada." It was much more complicated and involved a simmering dispute of some years about the terms of union signed by Newfoundland and Canada in 1949. Dad gave me an answer I could understand, albeit a partisan one. He was a staunch Joey supporter.

We are all products of our parents. Some of what we inherit is good and some not so good, but it's who we are. When I look in the mirror, I see bits of my mother and my father. I inherited from Dad the common default facial expression that some wag labelled "resting bitch face." When people ask me, "Why aren't you smiling?" I like to give them the late actor Geoffrey Palmer's answer: "I am smiling. It's just that my face isn't co-operating." My father wasn't a dancer, nor am I. My mother could sing and dance. I can sing. Mom had the performance gene, which was passed to me. She was a mimic and loved to take off people. I was her audience.

Whenever Mom felt like it, she'd have me in stitches doing Jackie Gleason, one of the ladies from our church (Wesley United), an aunt, or an uncle. When I was eight, I started doing impressions, too.

President John F. Kennedy was elected in 1960 and rapidly became a celebrity around the globe. He was young, with a young family and a beautiful, elegant wife. He was on radio and television quite often. I began doing my impression of President Kennedy as soon as I became aware of him. His Boston accent made it easy. Sometimes, when we had company, I'd stand on one of the living room ottomans and do my impression of JFK, followed by my impression of Elvis Presley singing "You ain't nothin' but a hound dog." Later I created a small space in the huge basement of our Golf Avenue building where I'd put on shows for, and with, my friends.

After first grade, I went to Holloway School on Long's Hill. I never enjoyed school, and my awful first day didn't help matters. I spent five years at Holloway before moving to junior high. I was content rather than happy at Holloway and did earn good grades. My Holloway teachers—except my grade three teacher, Miss Templeman, who would crack us across the knuckles with a long wooden pointer for the slightest infraction—were kind and professional. I developed a lifelong appreciation for visual art at Holloway, and later in high school, from art teachers Gwen Seary, Robin Cook, Frank LaPointe, and Reginald Shepherd. Art class was a refuge, a place where I felt nourished. I loved learning about art and making art.

My favourite teacher, and I suspect of many fellow students at Holloway, was Lima Davis. Miss Davis taught grade five. She was lean and tall and possessed a perfect complexion. Her refined features were framed in short, dark hair with a wave at the front. Miss Davis wore harlequin glasses. Of all the weekly activities at Holloway, there were two I really enjoyed. One was the regular CBC Newfoundland School Broadcast. A radio would be set up in the classroom and we'd listen to a dramatization of an event from Newfoundland and Labrador history, or a profile of a hero or heroine from the past, or perhaps something adapted from classic literature. (Little did I know that I would give my first professional acting performance on a CBC Newfoundland School Broadcast.) The other activity was Miss Davis's regular reading. It was her custom to read a novel to students during the school year. Every Friday she'd read as many of the novel's pages as she could. During my year with Miss Davis, she read aloud *David Copperfield* by Charles Dickens.

Seared in my memory is the afternoon of Friday, November 22, 1963. Miss Davis had just started a fresh chapter of *David Copperfield.* You could hear a pin drop as her calm, clear voice described David's London reunion with his friend James Steerforth. Suddenly we were snapped out of Victorian London by someone knocking at the classroom door. Miss Davis, as surprised as we were, closed her book and went to the door. She partially opened it and began whispering with whoever was outside. Then she opened the door to allow the person to enter the classroom. It was Holloway's headmistress, Miss Sophie Edgecombe. Her normally pale complexion was even paler than usual. She entered gravely with hands folded in front of her. Miss Davis spoke: "Boys and girls, Miss Edgecombe has something to tell you." Miss Edgecombe stepped forward.

"We've just heard that President Kennedy, the president of the United States, has been shot. So we're going to dismiss school for the day. Your parents have been called and they're coming to pick you up."

By the time I was walking across the school playground, my father was parking our new Mercury Comet station wagon on Long's Hill, bright red signal light flashing in the grey fog that had crept in from the nearby harbour. Once home I ran up the stairs to our apartment. Straight ahead of me, on our living room TV, was the face of Walter Cronkite, removing his black-framed glasses as he told viewers, "President Kennedy died at 1 p.m. Central Standard Time." Nobody ever did an impression of JFK again.

4

MY SEXUAL ORIENTATION WAS MOST LIKELY HOMO, NOT HETERO

As with President Kennedy's death, the tumult of the '60s played out on our TV screen. We watched coverage of the assassinations of Martin Luther King Jr. and Robert Kennedy, FLQ bombings in Quebec, race riots, the Vietnam War, and the counterculture's embrace of recreational drugs and sexual liberation. Our lives weren't directly affected by it.

The Vietnam War resonated with me when I was a young teen because so many of its soldiers were just a few years older than me, and indeed, before the war ended on April 30, 1975, many of my age would serve and die in that senseless conflict. In the fall of 1969, during a free period, I spent time in the school library. I like magazines, and as I scanned the meagre offerings on the magazine shelf, I was drawn to the cover of a dog-eared *Life* magazine from June 27. It featured a close-up black and white photo of a young man with haunted eyes staring directly at me. Printed over his left temple were the words "The Faces of The American Dead in Vietnam ONE WEEK'S TOLL." The boy with the haunted eyes was one of the dead.

I sat and laid the magazine on the large table in front of me. I opened it and slowly turned the pages. Every page was covered with photos of kids, arranged like a school yearbook. It was a book of the dead. Many were eighteen, nineteen, twenty years of age. Looking at those young faces, hundreds of them, I was filled with sadness. I thought of the lives cut short, the grief of families, potential that would never be realized. I continued to stare in a kind of daze, oblivious to anything else. But for geography and nationality, I thought my photo could easily have been among those of the fallen youngsters. Nothing before or since made me more aware of the human cost of war.

As I sit now, distanced from that long past autumn day, I'm still aware of how fortunate I and my schoolmates were to be citizens of Canada. Today I have an American friend, Dale Green, who served in Vietnam. Luckily, he wasn't injured. It seems absurd that while Dale was trying to stay alive in Vietnam, here in St. John's I was living a comfortable, safe teenage life, my head filled with mundane thoughts. Like, for instance, figuring how long I'd have to sleep on the spare cot to make room for visiting relatives.

St. John's families with strong outport roots, like ours, always made room for visiting relatives, and we had our fair share of house guests. Stirling "Mick" Stockley was exceptional in that he became like a brother to me and like a son to my father. Mick was Mom's nephew, son of her favourite brother, Winston Stockley. Mick arrived from Gambo full of youthful enthusiasm, ready to break into broadcasting. His goal was to be a successful radio disk jockey. While he was applying for jobs at VOCM and CJON, he worked for my father in our store and became one of Dad's steadiest and most dependable employees. Mick was gregarious, well-spoken, and funny. Customers liked him. Our mutual interest in broadcasting bonded us. Mick had completed a home-study course in radio announcing from the Career Academy School of Famous Broadcasters, which provided a study guide, instructional vinyl records, and a tape recorder. He could, as they say, talk the legs off an iron pot, and was self-confident. He was a natural for radio or television.

Mick brought his tape recorder and microphone to St. John's and set them up on a small table in his bedroom. He'd regularly compile news clippings from the *Daily News* or the *Evening Telegram* and read them into the tape recorder as if doing a newscast. Then he'd rewind and play the recording to analyze his performance. He let me use the recorder and I started recording my own newscasts. I didn't like my squeaky boy voice but was determined to make the most of what I had by speaking as smoothly and clearly as I could. A jubilant cousin Mick came home one day and told us he'd gotten a job as an announcer with CJON Radio. It was the overnight shift but big news for Mick and our household. As excited as I was for my cousin, it was a struggle to stay awake long enough to hear him, but I did. Hearing his familiar voice over the radio made us proud.

When Mick got settled at CJON, he took me there for a visit. In the 1960s, CJON Radio and TV was in the former Canadian Forces' barracks on the edge of Buckmaster's Field. I got to see the impressive TV control room, which had recently started broadcasting shows in colour. During our visit they were running a new variety show called *The Pig and Whistle*. Regrettably, our visit was cut short.

Out of curiosity, I opened a door and startled an announcer recording a commercial. His name was Dan Sheridan. There was a red light on next to the studio door, meaning do not enter, because somebody inside was on-air. I didn't know about on-air lights. Announcer Dan really told me off. Mick hustled me out, saying, "Don't mind him, he's an arsehole." Mick eventually left CJON to work for VOCM in Grand Falls and then in Marystown. He continued his broadcasting career in the Maritimes at Amherst, Nova Scotia, and Moncton, New Brunswick.

While I kept busy trying to teach myself to be a broadcaster, writing scripts to record and critique, my formal education continued. Holloway School may have looked it, but United Junior High was closer to Dickensian in my experience. Several of the teachers appeared uninterested and bitter, and the school's principal, Clarence Button, was a real-life Mr. Squeers from *Nicholas Nickleby*. One day he walked into our grade seven classroom and asked a boy named Reg to stand up. Reg, who was thirteen at the time, had been overheard saying that a girl in our class was "a fine-lookin' piece o' stuff," or something along those lines. The girl told her mother, who formally complained to Principal Button. When Reg had admitted his guilt in front of the class, Mr. Button ordered him to put out his hands. Then, out of nowhere a short, thick leather strap appeared in the principal's right hand, coming down again and again like lightning on Reg's palms.

The principal was leaning into the strapping so hard that his grey forelock came loose and began swinging back and forth in time with each punishing stroke. It was frightening. Reg's hands got redder and redder, his eyes wetter and wetter. A tear spilled and quickly ran down his cheek. When the strapping was over, Clarence Button casually smoothed his hair back in place, folded his strap and left with a self-satisfied expression on his sharp face. We speculated after school that he must have had the strap hidden underneath his suit jacket near the collar, just behind his neck, for it to have magically appeared. Principal Button had planned and achieved a startling effect. Having come from a school where the headmistress disciplined with a harsh look, I found corporal punishment at this level sobering.

Not long afterward, I too would be humiliated by Clarence Button. My punishment involved a barrage of verbal abuse, not the strap. My grade eight teacher was a humourless woman, Mrs. Woods, who wore the same Britannic ensemble daily: pleated wool skirt, white blouse with collar brooch, and grey cardigan. She kept a tissue under the cuff of her sweater and would occasionally blow her nose in it and stuff the tissue back in her sleeve. A pair of reading glasses hung around her neck on a chain. She specialized in Latin.

Her approach to teaching us Latin (back turned, endlessly chalking declensions on the blackboard) did little to grow my interest. Unlike French, Latin seemed pointless to me. (I came to appreciate its linguistic usefulness later.) I couldn't muster any enthusiasm for it. By mid-year I was failing Latin badly. Principal Button paid a surprise visit to class when report cards were ready for our parents. He asked the teacher for them and, as he went through them one by one, he called on the poor performers, individually, to come to the front of the room.

As each student went to the front of the class, Mr. Button would pass comment on their performance. When my turn came, he stiffened and glared at me. "What do you call this?" he said, pointing to the Latin mark, adding, "Only 31 percent in Latin! You should be ashamed of yourself. This tells me you've done no work on this subject since the fall! Are you lazy? Is that it? Why do you think you're here? Do you want to fail grade eight? Is that what you want? Because that's where you're headed, man!" He continued with more of the same as I turned crimson from embarrassment. I passed grade eight, but never conquered Latin. Clarence Button's verbal pounding accomplished nothing.

Because I was shy and passive at an age when boys tend to want to show off and be macho, I was an easy target for bullies. A fellow student and bully named "Jeff" zeroed in on me. He'd grab me and haul me in among the coat racks in the corridor. Then, with a vice-like grip, he'd pull me by my shirt and tie toward him. He would breathe heavily in my face and stomp on my foot, grinding his heel into my toes. It was painful and terrifying. Jeff derived satisfaction from his sadistic behaviour. My foot still bears a reminder of the damage he inflicted. Some months after these assaults Dad took me to the Grace Hospital, where I had surgery on the injury, which had become infected. I never told my parents about the bullying.

Forty years after Jeff physically assaulted and terrified me, fate brought us together. My husband, Larry, had hired a contractor to do some renovations on our house. The contractor had subcontracted the electrical work to an electrician friend of his. That electrician was Jeff. As I was leaving the house for work, the contractor arrived with Jeff. Smiling broadly, he introduced me to Jeff: "I believe you guys went to school together." There was no need for an introduction.

As soon as I looked into his eyes, I recognized him. I was seized by the same panic I'd felt decades before when confronted by him. I couldn't speak. I was literally unable to form words. My old tormentor's expression changed. He knew exactly what was happening. He approached me, but instead of saying that he was sorry, he said, "Yeah, let's forget about all that now." The contractor looked puzzled and uncomfortable. Jeff completed the electrical work and I never saw him again.

In the summer of 1966, we were invited to attend the New York wedding of Dad's grandniece, Linda (granddaughter of Dad's eldest brother, Art). Linda's father, Walt, oldest son of my Uncle Art and Aunt Evelyn, had been killed in a car accident the year before. Uncle Art lived in Smithtown, New York. I knew as soon as the invitation arrived that, somehow, we were going to get to that wedding on Long Island's North Shore. Dad was devoted to his brother and wanted to be with him, as well as his family, during a time that would be happy but also difficult for them.

Dad decided that he, Mom, and I would drive to New York. He insisted we drive to save money, but also because my father was terrified of planes and flying. This would be our first vacation outside Newfoundland, an opportunity to visit other family members who had visited us. Dad had a plethora of relatives in New York, including his sisters Sadie and Annie. I became map reader and navigator. Just outside New York City we stopped for a rest and something to eat at a Howard Johnson's Motor Lodge. It was a blistering hot summer, heat that we three Newfoundlanders had never experienced. The hotel had the chain's familiar orange chalet roof and mid-century lobby. As we walked out of the heat and into the cool, spacious foyer, I saw something unexpected and shocking.

A gaunt Black man wearing a long-sleeved shirt, work pants, and dusty boots was lying quietly on his side on the floor beside a red leather sofa, lit by soft afternoon sunlight. As we walked near him, I saw that he was chained, literally chained, to the sofa. My parents saw too, but like everyone else in the lobby chose to ignore what was confronting them. This was the first time I'd seen a Black person in the flesh. (Few, if any, Black people lived in St. John's in 1966.)

I'd seen coverage of race-related demonstrations on TV and knew immediately what the man was doing. Witnessing this one-man protest against racial injustice when I was thirteen made racism real to me; it was no longer a brief news story on TV. I felt empathy. Even though it had been almost two years since President Lyndon Johnson had signed the American Civil Rights Act into law, little had been done to enforce the new legislation. Black people still faced discrimination in housing and job opportunities, and many schools were still segregated. There was plenty for them to protest—individually and collectively.

Our visit to New York was beyond exciting for a thirteen-year-old. I'd never attended a wedding before. It seemed lavish (at least to my inexperienced eyes). Events took place at a graceful venue suffused with tradition, dressed in plenty of rich, dark wood. Bride and groom revealed the perfection only seen on a wedding day. No doubt everyone wished that Linda's dad had been there to see it.

In New York we also experienced things I'd only read about or seen on TV. We visited Jones Beach and Montauk Point State Parks and picked strawberries almost as big as my fist at a new venture called a U-Pick farm; we saw the United Nations Building, tasted real pizza for the first time, dined in a fancy Manhattan eatery, and then went to a show at Radio City Music Hall, where we enjoyed a performance by the famous high-kicking Rockettes.

Having experienced New York, including Long Island and Manhattan, and having guided my parents safely there and home, I was proud of myself. I began another year at United Junior High more confident. Adulthood didn't seem far away. A sign of this was something that began later that fall—my sexual awakening. I was seeing other boys in my class differently, the way they were seeing girls differently. A powerful physical attraction drew me toward "Alex," a classmate. Alex had vivid blue eyes and bronzed skin. He was lean and strong. It was a struggle to avoid staring at him. At some point he must have become aware of my interest but took no notice. It didn't matter, because I was content just being in the same room with Alex. Despite knowing that most boys are attracted to girls, I wasn't surprised by what I was feeling. Physical and mental stirrings had already led me to realize that my sexual orientation was most likely homo, not hetero.

After my fourteenth birthday I became close to "Lee," a neighbourhood boy I'd known since kindergarten. We often played outdoor games with a few other neighbourhood kids. Sports weren't for me, but I had lots of fun when we role-played TV secret agents from *The Man from U.N.C.L.E.* It brought out the actor in me. I loved portraying Napoleon Solo or Illya Kuryakin. Occasionally, when the weather was miserable, Lee and I would explore our vast basement with walk-in freezer, abandoned store equipment, old pieces of furniture, and musty books from as far back as the 1930s.

One cold afternoon while we were exploring the basement, Lee did something unexpected. He seduced me. It began with a loving embrace, which Lee initiated without the slightest hesitation or

Grade 8, me in the middle, the round-faced kid who lived in a candy store.

embarrassment. I didn't resist but welcomed the intimacy. We found a hiding place and lay down, eventually becoming naked and aroused. Lee was attractive, fair, blond haired, and athletic—an excellent hockey, basketball, and soccer player with a toned body. His manner was comfortably masculine, confident. Lee wasn't the slightest bit self-conscious about showing me his fully aroused body and letting me touch him. Our intimacy didn't go beyond embracing, caressing, and stroking, but it was thrilling and wonderful. We enjoyed our secret time and wanted more.

Lee and I continued our trysts for weeks, but a thought wouldn't leave me. If we continued to have such encounters, we might get caught. The prospect frightened me. Even though I knew instinctively that being gay wasn't a choice and knew that I and every other gay person was normal and not deviant, I was aware that homosexuality was against the law. Also, I had no idea how my parents might react if my secret was discovered. I was aware of the hurtful language and epithets used to describe homosexuals—queers, fairies, pansies, sissies, and fruits—though they had never been directed toward me up to that point. So, after some weeks I ended our intimate relationship.

I didn't hear the epithet *fag*, or *faggot*, until it began showing up in the dialogue of many '70s movies, such as *The Love Machine*, *Rituals*, and *The Private Files of J. Edgar Hoover*, and then in Mel Brooks's *History of the World, Part 1* (1981). The term *fag* didn't have the visceral impact on gays of my generation that the word *queer* had. Many of us born before 1965 still wince when we hear *queer*. When I was growing up in St. John's, fags were cigarettes. "Ya gotta fag? Give us a fag b'y," was a common after-school request.

A black comedy called *Something for Everyone*, starring Michael York, which I saw as a teenager at the Capitol Theatre on Henry Street in 1970, featured a scene that affected me far more than a word. It was a kiss. Seated in the familiar darkness of an almost full theatre among the Saturday matinee crowd, I couldn't have been more surprised when I saw Michael York give Anthony Higgins a sensual, on-the-lips kiss. As I watched this amazing scene on the huge screen, I became aware of jarring, discordant sounds around me. People in the audience were booing and mimicking vomiting sounds to register their disapproval. I must have been the only person in the audience who enjoyed the onscreen kiss. The audience's reaction made me feel helpless, and worthless as the stale gum stuck to the floor.

What I felt wasn't just about moviegoers booing a gay kiss. When I saw those two guys kissing, I thought, wow, finally something for my tribe. It was an affirmation. I briefly allowed myself to think that things might be changing for the better. Then came the booing: instant, and searing. It was as if the people surrounding me had heard what I was thinking and were booing me as well. Was this what lay ahead for me, I wondered. Hatred, ridicule? It was crushing. Newfoundland and Labrador, like most of the world, wasn't friendly to gays in 1970. It would be many long, difficult decades before any significant change happened.

Lee and I remained friends. I suspect he viewed our hidden relationship simply as a rite of passage. For me, it was emotional and romantic. Lee eventually married a woman and, from what I know, lived an enjoyable life. I was forced to think about what ignoring who I was might mean in the long run. My future seemed uncertain. I was scared. I decided that, for the time being, I would bury thoughts about my sexual orientation. (It would be six years before I got together with a man. I had a brief relationship with a woman, and while the sex was mutually enjoyable, I soon realized that I was only capable of developing a strong, loving bond with a man.)

Remembering the day my mother gave me her explanation of homosexuality, albeit a negative one, I at least knew I wasn't the only homosexual around. If Canada didn't have homosexuals, I reasoned, there wouldn't be a law against us. (At the time I had no idea that some gay men were sitting in jail for no other reason than being themselves.) Keeping my sexual orientation quiet, at that time, seemed important. Apart from how my parents might take the news, I had no idea how my siblings, friends, and relatives might react. I assumed that many, like the people I saw react to the gay kiss at the Capitol Theatre, would be disgusted. My fears were somewhat lessened when I heard about Tom.

When my family lived in Buchans, my parents became friends with a married couple named Margaret and Tom. The couple divorced and Margaret moved to St. John's. When we came to St. John's, Margaret would occasionally visit my mother for a cup of tea and a chat. I asked my mother once about the man named Tom who was sometimes mentioned in their conversations. She told me, without equivocation: "Tom was Margaret's husband, but they got divorced because he's a homo." It was the last thing I expected her to say.

A few years later, when I was helping my dad deliver groceries, we made a delivery to an apartment building outside our neighbourhood. There weren't many apartment buildings in St. John's at the time. Many of our customers called in their weekly grocery list, and I assumed it was a phone-in order. We each carried a bag of groceries into the apartment of a man in his mid- to late forties. He was thin, just under six feet tall, wore wire-framed glasses, and had short grey hair. Over his plain shirt he wore a cardigan. He also wore soft leather slippers.

His apartment was small and decorated with what appeared to my young eyes to be antique furniture. Everything was spotless and nicely arranged. I was surprised that my father and this man appeared to know each other. Even though little was said, their body language and faces told me they had known each other for a long time. I kept thinking it odd that I'd never seen or heard about this man before. I thought I'd met all my father's friends. Was he a secret friend? The man looked sad. It was as if he wasn't sure what to say. My ability to spot another homosexual, my "gaydar," was starting to develop. It told me that this reticent, timid gentleman was gay. When we were leaving, my father said, "Bye, Tom." After we'd climbed back into the van, I asked my father about him. Dad told me that he was the "Tom" of Margaret and Tom. At that moment I knew my father would never reject me for being homosexual.

I finished junior high school in June 1968. That summer, prior to entering high school at Prince of Wales Collegiate, I went on a crash diet. I was tired of being body shamed, being seen as different, and being bullied. I knew I couldn't change my sexuality; I was who I was. But I could change my body by losing weight and I could continue to put my sexuality out of mind for as long as possible. In September I started grade ten weighing 155 lbs. I had lost 30 lbs. My former classmates didn't recognize me.

My high school years were marked by some high points and one low point. When I was in grade ten, my homeroom was the biology lab. It had rows of long black benches, stools, sinks, and Bunsen burners. More benches and shelving bordered the room's interior, accommodating big, clear glass bottles filled with formaldehyde and small, lifeless animals. My homeroom always smelled of solvents and chemicals.

One Friday I spent most of the midday break sitting by myself at my assigned bench in the empty lab daydreaming, sketching my teachers, and reading. About twenty minutes before classes resumed, four or five girls came into the room and sat about twelve feet away. They began whispering, giggling and staring at me. I felt uneasy and sensed trouble. Their whispering was conspiratorial.

"What are you lookin' at?" shouted one of the girls. (I wasn't looking at her or any of the girls.) I ignored her.

"Are you lookin' at us?"

"Have we got somethin' you want?" asked another.

Then it started. All of them surrounded me and were joined by others who poured in from the corridor. I froze. They ran their hands through my hair, tried to rip off my jacket, loosened my necktie. One put her hands down my chest and pretended to kiss my face as the hands of others moved all over my body. There was more laughter, distant male and female laughter that gradually grew louder.

It became cacophonous as the room and the outside corridor filled with spectators. Half the student population showed up. Hands went down my back and inside my pants. I couldn't move. The room was spinning. A combined smell of perfume and sweat made me feel sick. I was in shock, but I remember thinking, "Why is this happening? What did I do? What did I do?"

Mercifully, my homeroom teacher, Robert Crane, showed up and took in what was going on. He smirked. Everyone who wasn't supposed to be in the room left, including my tormentors. People took their places as if nothing had happened. I was left to pull myself together, red-faced, hurt, confused, humiliated. The teacher never asked me about the incident. At a subsequent parent-teacher meeting he did ask my mother if I had a girlfriend and suggested maybe I should get one. That's about the level of enlightenment most schoolteachers possessed in the 1960s. Other than telling me about it, Mom appeared to place little importance on Crane's comment. She never mentioned it again and, thankfully, she didn't pressure me to get a girlfriend.

I still wonder why those girls chose to swarm me. They'd probably concluded I was gay. I didn't flirt with girls, and almost everyone then was homophobic, even many homosexuals. I've never tried to act gay or straight. Still, there must have been something about my behaviour that the girls picked up on.

I began my last year of high school in September 1969. That year, Joey Smallwood, who had been premier of Newfoundland since 1949, decided to step down. The provincial Liberals organized a leadership convention to be held at Memorial Stadium on Saturday, November 1. Prior to the convention, Premier Smallwood reconsidered his decision to step down and decided to run for leader after all. He came to this decision when it looked as if he might be replaced by his nemesis, John C. Crosbie. The idea of Crosbie assuming the leadership was completely unpalatable to Smallwood.

Here I am in Grade 10, having shed 30 pounds. Svelte and shy.

The convention promised to be one of the most exciting political events ever held in Newfoundland and Labrador. Smallwood had been premier since before I was born. Gavel-to-gavel coverage of the convention had been scheduled by local television channels, and there would be lots of attention paid by major Canadian media outlets. I looked forward to a full weekend of TV convention viewing. Little did I know that my convention experience would ultimately be on-site.

In high school I hung out with a group of artsy types and geeks. Our domain was the yearbook office at Prince of Wales Collegiate. Few of us fit in with the guys who were focused on sports and girls. Our interests were different and included school, provincial, and federal politics. One of our number was Tim Kemp (today a highly successful management trainer in the UK). Tim had come to us from Alberta. He was bright, a born leader, planner, and organizer. Our gang all pitched in to help him with his campaign for student council president. Tim's campaign slogan was "Your Opinion Is My Concern." Unfortunately, it turned out to be a popularity contest, and one of the school's star jocks won.

Tim's dad, in his bold, black eyeglasses, looked a lot like Clark Kent. He was a handsome, well-dressed, well-spoken, affable man in the provincial government. I suspect he, like most who served under Smallwood, viewed working for the government as working for the Liberal Party of Newfoundland and Labrador.

Tim showed up at school in late October with fantastic news for the gang. He said that thanks to his dad he could get all of us into the Liberal Leadership Convention on the day of the big vote. We were thrilled. The catch was that we'd be working as volunteers for something called Committee Services. Each of us would be assigned to a group of delegates. Our job was to be their servants—get them tea, coffee, soft drinks, and snacks, show them where the restrooms were, that kind of thing. But we were rarely called upon, which left us to take in the atmosphere of the convention and view the day's unfolding drama.

The stadium was jam-packed. It was clear that most of the delegates on the floor were for Smallwood. There wouldn't be a second ballot. But up in the rows of seats, high above the main floor, sat hundreds of Crosbie supporters. They couldn't vote, but they were vocal, which no doubt gave TV viewers the impression that Crosbie had a shot at winning.

I found myself standing directly in front of the John Crosbie camp when Herman Batten, the convention chairman, announced the result of the vote. Three key people sat on John Crosbie's platform: John Crosbie, Jane Crosbie, and Clyde Wells. A calm descended on the stadium as Batten announced the results in his booming baritone: Peter Cook, 3; John Crosbie, 440; T.A. Hickman, 187; Randy Joyce, 13; J.R. Smallwood, 1,070. As soon as Smallwood's count was read, there was an explosion of sound that reverberated throughout the stadium. I was momentarily stunned by the reaction.

As I stared ahead, I saw John Crosbie looking stoic, Jane Crosbie looking concerned, and Clyde Wells (who helped manage Crosbie's campaign, along with Andrew Crosbie and others) looking livid. Then I noticed candidate Randy Joyce and his camp, who were situated nearby. They rose and, led by Joyce, began giving Nazi salutes, like Rudolf Hess saluting Hitler. Things escalated after that; the anger in the room was palpable. I'm sure many delegates were concerned for their safety. I was. The Crosbie observers and delegates in the room began swearing and referred to Smallwood as a dictator. Many were throwing placards to the ground, stomping on them, and shouting that they were finished with the Liberal Party. Some employed less polite words.

Very soon after the announcement we heard Joey Smallwood's familiar voice. Clyde Wells, his face red as a peeled beet, looked disgusted. Smallwood declared from the convention podium that he had been congratulated by Mr. Hickman, and said, "Now I wonder about Mr. Crosbie. Will Mr. Crosbie come up and make it unanimous?" It was clear to me, from my close vantage point, that Crosbie wasn't sure what do to. Should he rebuff Smallwood, as his supporters no doubt wanted, or should he be magnanimous and go up and congratulate him? When he finally made the move to rise from his seat, I saw Clyde Wells tug on his sleeve and heard his voice cutting through the humid air: "No, John! No! Don't give the old bastard the satisfaction!" Crosbie ignored him. Both men then went to the podium, where Crosbie made a brief concession speech and called for party unity.

I'd witnessed, first-hand, history in the making. Not many sixteen-year-olds could claim that they were inside Memorial Stadium on that remarkable day. It was an inflection point in Newfoundland and Labrador history, and in my life. High school would soon be ending, and important decisions would have to be made. Not long before I began high school, my father had suggested I start thinking about a career. If I chose to further my education at university, I could remain at home and he'd support me. If not, I'd have to find a job and get out on my own.

5

THERE IS A BALM IN GILEAD

I'd been inside Wesley Church many times for services and Sunday school, but Wesley's attached radio station was unfamiliar. VOWR, Newfoundland's first radio station, has been a part of the church's physical structure since its founding as 100-watt station 8WMC by Reverend Joseph G. Joyce on July 20, 1924. VOWR is entirely run by volunteers. By the winter of 1970, the station was broadcasting at 5,000 watts, and I was sitting in VOWR's large recording studio for the first time. In front of me was an intimidating RCA 77 microphone, shaped like a giant Contac cold capsule.

My interest in performing had developed to the point where I was certain my career would be in acting or broadcasting or both. I was sixteen and about to finish high school. Since no drama schools would admit me until I was eighteen, studying English at Memorial University for a few years seemed like a good option. (This was decades before MUN established a theatre school in Corner Brook.) I also reasoned that experience in broadcasting wouldn't go astray, so I sought an audition for the position of volunteer announcer at VOWR.

Through the control room window, framed by studio walls that looked like pegboard, I could see station manager Everett Hudson. He stared at me with curiosity, waiting to hear this kid—the youngest person he'd ever auditioned—speak the first words of the VOWR audition script. I had no doubt that Hudson was the author of the script. Hand trembling, I turned the cover page and saw the first few lines I was to read. I smiled to myself. My confidence returned.

I'd checked out VOWR's shows. At the time, the station featured primarily religious and serious classical music programs. Boning up on the pronunciation of classical music terms and names seemed wise. My preparation paid dividends because there, at the top of the page, were three of the names I'd practised: Chopin, Rimsky-Korsakov, and Beethoven. I passed the audition mainly, as Hudson later confirmed, because I knew how to pronounce the classical music names, titles, and terms.

Everett Hudson was VOWR's grand arbiter and his was the final word on every programming decision taken at the station. Nobody questioned his authority, and he had ways of making sure his instructions were followed. If Hudson didn't want a certain piece of music played, he would physically remove the record from the library or do something to the vinyl that I considered hideous.

VOWR (Voice of Wesleyan Radio) is a semi-religious, conservative station—in those days even more so—and our station manager was obsessed with song lyrics that might contain a hint of sexual innuendo. A Tom Jones record containing the song *Love Me Tonight*, for example, would have that track deliberately damaged by Hudson. He would take his car key and, with the precision of an engraver, scratch across the song cut multiple times so that it couldn't be played. I watched in disbelief as he methodically destroyed a track in front of me one day.

My first shift at VOWR was on a Thursday night, hymn night. I was responsible for announcing duties, from sign-on to sign-off. Technical operations were handled by another volunteer, Hubert Garland, a grey-haired gentleman approaching sixty. Hubert sat in the control room surrounded by a horseshoe of dials, switches, turntables, large rack-mounted reel-to-reel tape machines, and the transmitter. We could see each other through a window. I sat in a small, attached announcer's booth behind a battered, box-shaped mic that had most likely been in service at VOWR since the 1940s. The only technical operation I could perform was to turn off the microphone if I coughed, using a switch attached to a metal box next to the microphone.

My inaugural broadcast on live radio was a success. I was soon lined up for more VOWR shifts. Several hymn nights, as it turned out, because few of VOWR's volunteer announcers wanted to work the hymn shift. By the end of my first broadcast, I was beginning to feel the same way. VOWR's Thursday broadcast was a five-hour endurance test. I appreciate some of those hymns now, but back then, introducing musty old hymns from scratchy records was no fun.

"And now let's listen again to George Beverly Shea singing that old, old favourite, 'There Is a Balm in Gilead' . . . 'a balm to make the wounded whole.'"

It was enough to make a teenage announcer lose the will to live, balm or no balm. I soon created a plan to end my Thursday night purgatory, a plan I hoped station manager Hudson would endorse.

Friday evening was a dead zone on the VOWR schedule. When the station signed off on Thursday evening, everything fell silent until Saturday. No Tennessee Ernie Ford, no Mahalia Jackson, not so much as a middle C from George Beverly Shea. I asked Everett Hudson why we weren't on-air Friday night and in a fretful voice he answered, "Because I can't get anybody to work on Friday. It's the weekend and they want to be out on the town, I suppose." This information kick-started my plan, which, to have a reasonable chance of success, required me to become an announcer-operator. Soon enough, with the help of a few fellow volunteers who were willing to teach me, that's exactly what I became.

A very proud teenage announcer-operator at VOWR. I was hosting my first big Friday night broadcast.

When I was proficient at both announcing and operating the control boards and related equipment, it was time to present my plan to the boss. The motivator I used to convince Hudson would be powerful, I thought. If he agreed to my proposal, I would guarantee that I would work every Friday night for at least a year, and because I was able to do the announcing and the operating, no other volunteer would be needed. He looked at me with a half-smile and said, "What's the catch?"

Standing beside me in the VOWR control room, he waited. I opened a file folder containing copies of a Friday night program schedule that I'd mocked up. I said I wanted to create the program schedule for Friday and select all the music for Friday's various programs. I explained that the shows listed were meant to provide an alternative to the rest of VOWR's weeknight fare. Within seconds he was pointing to a line on my schedule with a look of shock. "What's this?" he asked, as if he couldn't believe what he was seeing.

Scheduled after a classical music show I'd created called *Evening Serenade*, and just before a light, instrumental show, *Music for Relaxation*, was a half-hour country music show I named *Thirty for Country*. Country music was about as welcome at Everett Hudson's VOWR as a fart in church. I knew this, but I also knew that VOWR then had a minuscule audience. It was a broadcasting backwater compared to other radio stations, with, perhaps, the exception of another religious station, VOAR (Voice of Adventist Radio).

Having spent many summers in rural Newfoundland, I was aware that country music was extremely popular outside St. John's. Unlike rural radio stations at that time, the St. John's stations (commercial and non-commercial) avoided country music altogether. Given the numbers of rural Newfoundlanders living in St. John's, I felt there was an audience for country music in the capital city. I was more than confident that if VOWR offered a show on Friday night playing thirty minutes of country music exclusively, it would increase VOWR's audience share.

"No, no, no. We can't have Tammy Wynette an' all that stuff on VOWR," said Hudson. "Classical music, yes, and instrumental music. But no country music."

I had some convincing to do. I presented my argument for the Friday night schedule, focusing on my firm conviction that the best way to grow support for VOWR, a not-for-profit radio station, and one totally dependent on public financial support, was to grow our listenership. The new schedule with all its elements, most especially *Thirty for Country*, would help do the job. Hudson's head kept shaking from side to side as the speaker above us purred out another movement of Rimsky-Korsakov's *Scheherazade*. We agreed to talk it over later, despite his offer to let me go ahead right away without the country music show. I was reluctant to give up on my idea to introduce country music to VOWR. A few weeks of reflection on Everett Hudson's part, I thought, might yield a better result.

I was somewhat surprised that Hudson made no mention of taking my proposal to the VOWR board of directors. Notwithstanding the substantial latitude of his personal power, I still thought a plan to create an additional evening of programming was worthy of consideration by the board. Then I learned from a fellow volunteer, Hubert Garland, that the board's main function (in those days) was to assist in fundraising, not to get involved in programming decisions. It made some sense, given that VOWR was a community volunteer station totally dependent on donations and fundraising projects, of which the annual VOWR Radio Auction and sale of turkey teas was most important. (Turkey teas were cold, boxed meals containing salads and slices of turkey.) Hubert explained that that was why all board members (it was a male board) had to be married: "Their wives have to cook turkeys for the VOWR turkey teas," he said. I started to laugh, thinking it was a joke, but Hubert's sad face said otherwise. That, and the fact that Hubert was a bachelor and a long-time VOWR volunteer, gave me pause.

Meanwhile I carried on doing my regular shifts at VOWR, and in fairness to Everett Hudson, he was very supportive of other projects I developed. If I had an idea for a show, or a Christmas special—once he'd listened to a sample and liked it—he didn't hesitate to give me the go-ahead. It was on one of those Christmas specials that I first performed *A Christmas Carol*, by Charles Dickens, doing all the characters' voices. Years later I would give an annual public performance of the piece with Chad Stride's chamber choir, Cantus Vocum.

In time, Everett Hudson broached the subject of Friday night broadcasting with me again. I sensed that the possibility of going live on Fridays, more or less permanently, was becoming a great temptation to him. So great a temptation (I hoped) that he would finally see things my way. He made another attempt to convince me to drop my country music show, but I held firm. We came to a compromise. I'd go ahead on Friday of the following week with my full schedule of programming, including *Thirty for Country*, but if the station received a significant number of complaints about the country music, the show would be axed.

News of the arrangement I'd struck with Hudson spread to all members of the VOWR staff, and from them to their families and friends. Word of mouth, along with a few on-air mentions of the upcoming Friday broadcasts, ensured that I'd have a small but interested audience for the inaugural Friday shows. Saying I had butterflies before going on the air that first Friday doesn't adequately describe how I felt. More accurate would be a Newfoundland expression: "Me nerves were rubbed raw!"

Making a success of the night, especially *Thirty for Country*, was very important to me. My gut was telling me that everything I'd argued in favour of the new programming was right, but it was now up to the listeners. I'd purchased country records with my own money and donated them to VOWR and borrowed some records from home. Established stars like Charley Pride, Johnny Cash, Loretta Lynn, and, of course, Tammy Wynette were among the first country artists to make their debut on VOWR that night. I'm happy to say they all returned frequently in the weeks that followed. *Thirty for Country* was a hit. The audience loved it.

My VOWR years, from 1969 to 1973, were well spent. I learned the production and technical sides of radio and gained confidence and experience behind the microphone. My main contribution was in developing a much bigger audience for the station (and consequently more financial support) through the introduction of country music. During subsequent years I took pleasure in seeing how the tiny seed I'd planted grew. *Thirty for Country* evolved into *Sixty for Country*, then *Ninety for Country*, then *800 Country*—a full afternoon of country music on Saturdays.

In the early 1990s, I was having a beer at Schroeder's Piano Bar on Bates Hill in St. John's where the gentleman sitting next to me at the bar appeared to be drowning his sorrows. Looking up from his drink, he recognized me from TV and introduced himself. His name was Hilary Montbourquette. He told me he was the General Manager of KIXX Radio, a new country music station in St. John's. When I told him I was the person responsible for introducing country music to VOWR, he was gobsmacked. After a pause of several seconds he muttered, "So you're the S.O.B."

"Excuse me?"

"VOWR: you're responsible! If they weren't playing so much country, KIXX's numbers would be higher!"

Apparently, an analysis had discovered as much. I smiled and said, "Sorry about that, Hilary."

I was a lousy university student. I loved anything that took me away from my studies, mainly working part-time at Memorial's Educational Television Centre, volunteering at MUN Radio, and acting—sometimes onstage but mostly as a paid performer on CBC Radio. Paid work at ETV and the CBC did help fund my education, but I took on too much of it.

The Educational Television Centre became a second home during most of my university years. ETV, which in 1972 was a fully equipped professional television studio, was established to produce credit courses in various subjects on videotape. These videotaped lectures were shipped around the province and played in the evening (using playback equipment provided by MUN, in a community's borrowed high school classroom) for part-time university students. This allowed students to complete a university education without physically being on campus.

ETV employed full-time professional technicians and producers. It also employed MUN students whom the centre trained to be floor directors, production assistants, and operators of camera, audio, and videotape machines. Most of the equipment then was supersized. The silicon chip hadn't yet begun to shrink computers and TV equipment. Over four years I received first-rate training in literally anything I was interested in. I was paid two dollars an hour.

I sometimes operated the leviathan floor-model quadruplex videotape machines, which stood about five feet tall. The two-inch-wide quad tapes were used for master recordings, from which all copies of lower grade but smaller tapes were made. Mostly I worked in the studio or control room—in studio as a floor director (the person who relayed information between host and control room) and in the control room as the audio operator.

As soon as a few ETV producers found out I was also interested in doing work in front of a camera or behind a microphone, I was asked to contribute to their productions as a performer. Once, for a MUN course ETV was producing for teachers in performance and communication skills, I was asked to do a memorized on-camera rendition of Edgar Allan Poe's story *The Tell-Tale Heart.*

Some of my voice work was done for a history course hosted by Professor Gerald Panting (later to become leader of the Newfoundland and Labrador New Democratic Party). Andy Wells (who went on to become mayor of the City of St. John's) was the producer. In addition to voicing bits of scripts, I was the main audio operator for the course, which consisted of many on-camera lectures by Professor Panting. This meant that over many hours, for several weeks, I operated the audio console while Andy operated the video console. We were control room companions. It's often the case that what you hear in a TV control room is much more entertaining than what's on the actual program. Being in a control room with Andy Wells was easily twice as entertaining.

Andy was bright, well-read, opinionated and, to many, an unyielding pain in the ass. In the 1970s, Andy was an active member of the NDP and was preoccupied with organizing a union for ETV's full-time employees. To say he became a thorn in the side of ETV management would be an understatement, especially for the director of educational television, Duane Starcher. Andy was successful in his unionizing efforts, eventually becoming a leader in Newfoundland and Labrador's trade union movement. (Ironically, in his later years, Andy turned against unions, declaring them corrupt.)

I remember that when we were making the Gerry Panting history lectures, Andy, in the relative privacy of the control room, would occasionally take issue with something being said on-camera by the professor. "Lies. All lies," he'd say, or, "Go way, Gerry b'y." But Andy took greater offence with Panting's bushy eyebrows. They were so thick and full that they shaded his eyes like window canopies, making them quite difficult to light properly. Andy often threatened to show up with a pair of scissors "to trim those jeezly eyebrows!" Of course, he never did. Some years later, when Panting became leader of the provincial NDP, it looked as if his eyebrows had finally been pruned. Media scrutiny had perhaps succeeded in getting the job done.

Speaking of politics, while I was in university, Andy ran as a candidate for the NDP in St. John's East in the provincial election. He'd been active in the NDP for years. I volunteered to help campaign door to door and made phone calls on election day to help get Andy's vote out. The NDP was a hard sell in Newfoundland in those days, especially for a candidate with no public profile. Many doors were shut in my face. One day, after Andy's defeat, he and I were discussing politics and his interest in running in another provincial election. I suggested he try for city council instead. It would, I argued, build his public profile before another provincial run. He didn't react much, but I could tell he was mulling it over. The suggestion took hold because Andy later ran for City Hall. He won a council seat, becoming deputy mayor, and finally, mayor of St. John's. (He never did occupy a seat in the provincial House of Assembly.) He was a controversial councillor and mayor, often receiving unflattering national media exposure. Andy was willing to lose friends and votes to get things done. He strongly agreed with the adage attributed to President Harry Truman, which I'll paraphrase: If you want a friend in the game of politics, get a dog. Andy had many dogs. At least five. All at the same time.

6

HE WAS MOTIVATED BY THE SHOW

Like all teenagers, I had crushes. Mostly I fantasized about being embraced and fervidly kissed by any of several TV stars I found attractive. While my male friends had crushes on The *Mod Squad's* Peggy Lipton, and Linda Evans of *The Big Valley,* I was secretly crazy about the dedicated and dashing *Dr. Kildare,* Richard Chamberlain; the towheaded academic *Mr. Novak,* James Franciscus; and Canada's dark-haired man-of-the-people, *Quentin Durgens, M.P.*, Gordon Pinsent. I had no idea my Quentin, or rather, Gordon Pinsent, was a Newfoundlander; nor did most Canadians at the time. He was simply a handsome man with a brand of onscreen sensitivity that I, as a young gay boy, found irresistible. I watched Quentin religiously every week as he fought the system and advocated for the little guy. With each battle won or lost, my feelings for Quentin grew.

In August 1974 I saw a small text advertisement in the *Evening Telegram* inviting actors, singers, and dancers to audition for *The Music Man*, a St. John's Arts and Culture Centre production directed by Ian Mennie, with musical direction by Frances Dawson. I'd seen the Hollywood version of the musical, starring Robert Preston, and loved it. The most significant information in the ad (after the name of the musical) was conveyed in seven words beneath the title: "starring

Gordon Pinsent as Professor Harold Hill." The chance to perform onstage with my teenage crush was too tempting.

On Tuesday, August 27, I auditioned in the centre's Rehearsal Room B for Frances Dawson and Ian Mennie. The room was hot and crowded. I felt completely unnerved by Frances Dawson, a strikingly handsome woman who evoked the strict teachers I'd had in school. She sat perfectly upright at a slightly battered rehearsal piano with note taker and assistants beside her. She asked me what I wanted to sing. I obediently said, " 'Edelweiss,' from *The Sound of Music*." She looked up at me with piercing dark eyes, raised her jet-black eyebrows—which matched her jet-black hair—and said, "Hmm . . . okay." She played the intro; I slowly inhaled, then sang, "Edelweiss, edelweiss, every morning you greet . . . " At the end of the song, she half-smiled and nodded. I walked out very relieved, feeling optimistic that I'd soon be rubbing shoulders with Quentin Durgens, M.P.

The Music Man was about a travelling salesman, Professor Harold Hill, who would convince the citizens of a targeted town that the solution to juvenile delinquency was to form a youth marching band. He would guarantee to teach real or potential juvenile delinquents how to play various instruments, and (or so he told the townspeople) he would also lead the band. All the townspeople had to do was pay him up front for the instruments and lessons. Of course, it was a con. Harold Hill was no professor. He knew nothing about music, and as soon as the second-rate band instruments arrived, he flew the coop.

Ian Mennie and Frances Dawson put me in the chorus and cast me as one of eight travelling salesmen who open the musical with the patter song "Rock Island," performed aboard a rocking railway coach heading to River City, Iowa. Gordon Pinsent was in the scene with us, but didn't speak until the end of the opening number. Meeting a TV celebrity in person can be risky: they can be friendly and kind, or a shit. They can look just as you remember them from the screen, or totally different. Gordon Pinsent was very pleasant and kind but didn't look like the character he'd played on TV. He was heavier, his handsome face looked older, and his hair was longer, bushier.

My only interaction with Pinsent happened onstage and in the wings before entrances. Once he asked me, "How am I doing?" "Great, Gordon, just great," I said. Because he was, in so many ways. Later in life I had the privilege of interviewing Gordon Pinsent many times. I was honoured to be one of the dais speakers at his seventieth birthday roast in Grand Falls, where I met his family and close friends. *The Music Man* is a wonderful memory. I am happy to be able to say I worked with Gordon, a consummate professional and gentleman.

In the early 2000s, *CountryWide*, a national CBC morning television show on which I was a regular, aired a short tribute to me on my last day with the program. Ian Mennie, *The Music Man* director, was asked what he remembered about me from that 1974 musical. Ian was interviewed from Fredericton, New Brunswick, where he had moved since retiring from his day job as a MUN physics professor.

"I think Karl was about seventeen, incredibly shy, if you can believe that. He was motivated by the show in the sense that at rehearsals, in the good old Arts and Culture Centre, he would sit there against the wall, just sitting there very quietly, and then as director—Gordon Pinsent was in the show and so on—as director I would say, 'Now I want someone to run right across the stage, run twice and back.' And Karl would say, 'I'll do it.' And he'd get up and go berserk, leaping in the air and doing all kinds of schtick, and then go right back and sit down and become quiet again. In any crowd scene where I wanted someone to go wild, he would be the guy who went wild. And then he switched it off the moment it was over."

It was Ian Mennie who suggested something after *The Music Man* closed that led to the next and most significant phase of my

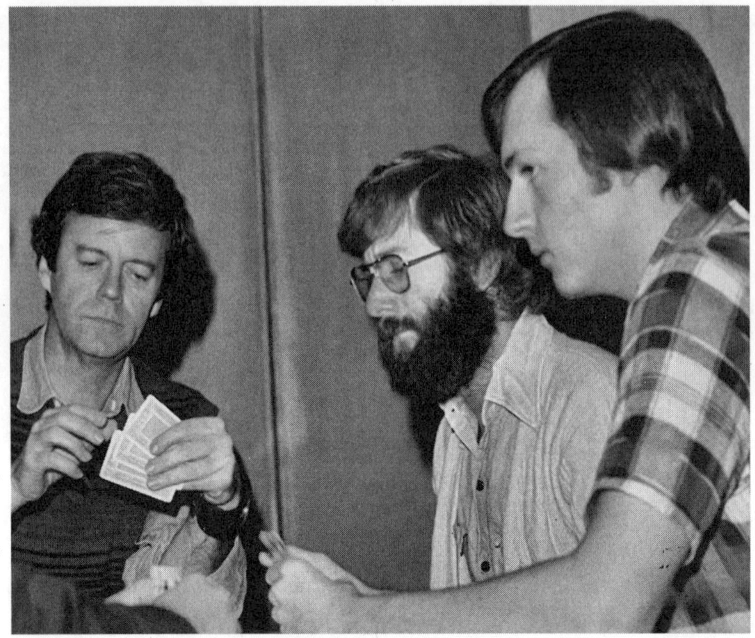

Rehearsing the train scene in The Music Man *with Gordon Pinsent and Tols Barrington.*

acting career. He told me that I should contact CBC Radio and try to get some work as a radio actor. At the time, the corporation was attempting to beef up its stable of radio actors with young talent.

Having become a regular radio listener in my childhood, I was familiar with some radio drama. Before kindergarten, I remember listening to a radio serial on CJON Radio, and at about age twelve I discovered Max Ferguson and his one-man program of topical satirical skits on CBC. *The Max Ferguson Show* utilized the medium perfectly. Each weekday morning, Ferguson would take a handful of articles from the day's newspapers and create humorous skits based on those stories. Ferguson was a terrific mimic who was particularly effective in creating vocal caricatures of politicians, such as Pierre Trudeau. His sound effects technician contributed finishing touches that made for visually rich "theatre of the mind."

Max Ferguson's performances allowed listeners to imagine faces, action, and settings—often fantastical settings. His work influenced the one-man radio sketches I would later be contracted to perform on CBC Radio (most written for me between 1978 and 1995 by Fred Armstrong and Ray Guy). Ferguson's show taught me about comedic timing, vocal inflection, tone, colour, and how to control the voice. It wouldn't be a stretch to say that Max Ferguson gave me a comprehensive education in solo radio acting.

Getting hired as a radio actor at the CBC couldn't possibly be as straightforward as calling up and saying, "I'd like to be a CBC Radio actor, please." Making an audition tape seemed the thing to do. I was an ETV audio technician, so it would be easy for me to record myself once I'd decided what to put on my newly purchased Sony reel-to-reel tape.

CBC was highbrow compared to other stations. A little Shakespeare might be appropriate, I thought. My first choice was Hamlet's "To be, or not to be" soliloquy. The other piece I recorded was a portion of Edgar Allan Poe's *The Tell-Tale Heart*. My ETV on-camera performance of it had been well received by a MUN professor, so I didn't hesitate to include it.

Once I was satisfied with what I was hearing on my tape, I researched exactly where and to whom I should send it. I began paying attention to the credits at the end of locally produced CBC Radio dramas. The producer whose name was mentioned most often was John Holmes. I recognized the name because John was an actor. I'd seen him at the Arts and Culture Centre as Polonius in *Hamlet*, and as Sir Joseph Porter in *H.M.S. Pinafore*. I composed a short letter of application and placed it in the box with my tape, wrapped the box in brown paper, stuck on an address label which I'd typed up on our clunky old Remington typewriter, and off it went to John Holmes, CBC Radio, St. John's.

The more I thought about being in front of a CBC Radio microphone, acting in professionally produced plays, the more I wanted it to happen, to be challenged to bring to life a character from a playwright's script. Happily, it was only a few weeks later that a large white envelope arrived in the mail bearing the CBC logo. Inside it was a CBC Radio script. A script! John Holmes had hired me to play the Unicorn in *The Lion and the Unicorn,* an episode of a series based on *Through the Looking-Glass* by Lewis Carroll. Alice's adventures were being produced for the Newfoundland School Broadcasts—the very ones I'd listened to as a boy at Holloway School.

Before long, on a grey Saturday morning, I was sitting outside CBC Radio's Studio A on the third floor of the art deco CBC Radio building on Duckworth Street, holding a Bic pen and signing my first CBC contract as a principal actor in *The Lion and the Unicorn.* A woman with a kind face, a production assistant with the CBC Arts Department, gave me my copy and informed me I'd need to join a union called ACTRA if I intended to do much more radio acting. "You're allowed to do a small number of engagements before you become a union member," she said. Not a problem: I couldn't wait to join the union. As far as I was concerned, my future was going to be filled with all kinds of exciting radio drama. (And it was.)

John Holmes invited me into the studio, where most of the cast had already assembled. John was trim and middle-aged; he wore a tie and worsted wool jacket. He had a pleasant face dominated by thick, black-framed glasses, and his hair was dark grey and slightly wavy. He spoke with an English accent in a well-modulated baritone.

He said as soon as the entire cast was assembled, we'd have a read-through of the play. Michael Cook, our narrator, was running late. (I was to learn that Michael had a penchant for the grand entrance.

He was a star in the theatre community and received lots of adulation wherever he turned up. "Michael! How the hell are you?" "Michael! Read your piece in the paper! Spot on, me son! Fabulous stuff!" Arriving late guaranteed an audience and made his entrance an event.)

Studio A was then the largest CBC Radio studio in Newfoundland. It was rectangular, brightly lit, carpeted—not for comfort but for sound—and smelled of stale cigarette smoke. Soundproofing tiles covered the walls, much like VOWR's. A worn piece of curtain hung on the back wall, and a well-used grand piano stood in front of the curtain. Nearby was a round table covered in felt that held microphone stands. John Holmes sat there with his script and pencil in hand. Against the side walls were stacking chairs where we actors sat with our legal-sized scripts.

One wall of the studio housed a large window where we could see the control room. John and the production assistant would eventually sit on a high rostrum and, just below, with his head above the parapet of the control board, its mass of wires pressing against the glass, was sound technician Bern Penney, a large, curmudgeonly man in suit and tie, puffing on a pipe. Next to Bern towered a stack of sound effects cartridges. One might be the sound of a door opening, another the sound of wind whistling through trees. He'd pop the sturdy tape cartridges in and out of a player at John's direction. Above the window was a large clock and on-air light: red for on-air on top, green on bottom.

Standing at each end and mid-room were tall chrome microphone stands. Screwed atop each pole was an omnidirectional microphone, looking more modern than the ones I'd used at VOWR. After our read-through, Michael Cook took the mic at the front end of the studio, Eugene Young (Lion) and I (Unicorn) took the mic at the opposite end, and at the middle microphone were Louise Nugent (Alice) and John Moyes (King).

John Holmes's casting was impressive. Outwardly, Gene Young appeared very leonine—not that it mattered for radio, but it certainly helped me imagine I was addressing a contrary old lion. Gene had a face that looked like it had been slept on. (He would have made a good Winston Churchill on film.) His reddish hair, receding at the temples, was (helpfully) a touch wild. He spoke with a gruff, affected English accent. Not just for the part—that's how he spoke. Whenever he asked John Holmes a question he'd bellow, "Jaaawn!" (In those days, quite a few St. John's professional men and women affected what was called a mid-Atlantic accent, a blend of drawing room English and Upper Canadian. Christopher Plummer spoke much the same way.)

Louise Nugent made the perfect Alice, sounding every bit like a young, inquisitive girl. John Moyes possessed the plummiest upper-class English accent and could not have sounded kinglier. Finally, Michael Cook, also English, spoke in resonant, measured tones with a husky timbre, the result of excessive smoking. I couldn't help noticing the index and middle fingers of his right hand were stained deep orange from decades of cigarettes.

"Stand by!" called John from the control room. On went the red light and Michael Cook began our story. I'd created a high-pitched, self-satisfied voice for my unicorn. It seemed to contrast well with Eugene Young's rumbling, ill-tempered lion. Our dialogue went smoothly as we stood performing before our shared microphone. John was happy. The recording was done in a flash. It felt good to be part of this creative team. There was a magical quality about what we'd done: making pictures from sound.

Many years ago, novelist Brock Brower wrote an essay about this aspect of radio theatre. Specifically, he made the case for radio plays and their unique power in a 1960 piece for *Esquire* titled, "A Lament for Old-Time Radio": "Nothing like them will ever be done on television because they demanded the very thing TV has scotched: imagination.

The listener produced half the show right in his own head, taking his lead from a range of voices, a musical bridge, and a few sound effects."

For the next five years after my CBC Radio drama debut in a school broadcast, I was cast in many plays for weekly, stand-alone CBC Radio theatre programs. I will always be grateful to John Holmes and his CBC Arts Department colleague John Puddester for casting me in those shows. I appeared in plays produced for Newfoundland and Labrador's Terra Nova Theatre and for national drama programs such as the highly respected CBC *Stage*, CBC *Tuesday Night*, and *The Bush and the Salon.*

I found great satisfaction and fun in learning the technique of radio acting by doing the job—simple but important lessons such as moving your script away from the mic when turning the page (so rustling paper couldn't be heard), moving away from the mic to sound like you're walking away or in another room, getting close to it to sound like you're whispering in someone's ear. Creating individual performances was all down to the actors themselves. I was viewed and treated as a professional from the day I walked into the CBC. We were on the clock with no time to waste, and producers left it to us actors to deliver our best work.

From time to time, I was cast in a play where an accent was required. This was challenging but fun. In Michael Cook's play about the Beothuk, *On the Rim of the Curve*, recorded in 1976 for broadcast on CBC *Tuesday Night*, I played Lieutenant David Buchan. I gave Buchan an upper-class British accent. Michael himself played John Peyton, who murdered the Beothuk Nonosabasut and his wife, Demasduit.

We had a wonderful scene together where he and I went at each other, me giving him a dressing down with dire warnings. Michael was a brilliant actor as well as remarkable playwright. He brought gravitas, intensity, and nuance to each of his performances. (Michael Cook's voice, for me, was as easy to recognize as that of Newfoundland poet Al Pittman, with whom I'd performed in Dylan Thomas's *Under Milk Wood* for a basement theatre production in 1974.)

I played yet another military man in a CBC *Stage* production based on the story *The Helicopter That Couldn't Be*, by J. C. Charleson. It was called *Red Alert*, and, like the Cook play, had a large cast. Again, I performed with an accent. My character, Colonel Urquhart, was American. I spoke deferentially in a dialect that straddled America's north and south. My favourite scene was a telephone conversation my character had with General Mancino, played by Dick Buehler. Dick was a gracious, deep-voiced, soft-spoken American.

To paraphrase the late American theatre director and critic Harold Clurman, most plays are bad, but occasionally a good one comes along to make it all worthwhile. I was fortunate to appear in several excellent plays, *On the Rim of the Curve* being one of them. Some, however, were weak efforts quickly churned out and, I suspect, purchased by the CBC only because it was desperate for original local scripts.

Willy Wins Again, by Evening Telegram editor and columnist Wick Collins, is a prime example. It was supposedly a comedy about two Newfoundland servicemen, Willy and Sam, going AWOL in England during World War II. Remember the *Carry On* movies made in the UK between the 1950s and 1990s? *Willy Wins Again* was a tamer radio version of the genre. Today, and rightly so, *Carry On* films come with a warning. They're sexist, homophobic, racist, and filled with sexual innuendo. I played Gunner Willy Duggan, the Willy of *Willy Wins Again*.

I recall only one engagement during those radio drama years when I felt thoroughly unprepared, unnerved, and intimidated. It was February 1976. There were two reasons for my discomfort. One was the actor Mary Walsh. I'd seen CODCO's *Cod on a Stick* and had placed Mary on a pedestal. The notion of working with her in any capacity intimidated me. I feared not being able to measure up. The other reason, I was convinced, could scuttle my radio acting career. It was major, existential. Our characters, Mary's and mine, were required to engage in a short scene with amorous kissing. Female-on-male kissing—a monumental challenge for me. I had to act something of which I had no practical life experience.

The play Teddy by Tony Cochrane, originally written for the stage, had been adapted for CBC Radio's *Terra Nova Theatre*. It was about a neglected boy, played by Chris Warrick, who lives alone with his widowed mother, a functioning alcoholic. The young teen has retreated into a fantasy world with his best friend, a teddy bear. Mary played the mom, and I played her sketchy drinking companion and casual boyfriend.

On Friday night, the eve of taping day, I was feeling the pressure someone must feel when they're about to be exposed as a fake. I couldn't decide which was worse: looking like someone with no acting ability or someone who'd obviously never been intimate with a woman. Panic was setting in. It was too late to back down. I had to rehearse. Mine and Mary's dialogue was on the spare side, but our direction (in the script) called for "kissing sounds et cetera."

Then, as I turned the page of the script, I saw the back of my left hand. Suddenly a conversation I'd had with another radio actor came to mind. It was about simulating kissing (and other sounds) for radio drama. He told me that kissing scenes were done by kissing "the back of your hand." (You didn't get physically intimate for radio acting, only for TV, film and stage.) So, I rehearsed all evening, making sure to include frequent hand kissing, sometimes pecks, sometimes prolonged kissing. I kissed that hand until my lips hurt.

The day arrived and as I walked, wobbly-legged, along Henry Street toward the staff entrance of CBC Radio, on the rear, east side of

I received star billing for this CBC *radio play,* Willy Wins Again *by Wick Collins.*

the building, I felt queasy. I was so preoccupied that all I remember is sitting, waiting for Mary to arrive, and searching for a way to make my romancing believable. Then, my addled brain provided an answer like a gift, just in the nick of time, because within seconds Mary walked into the studio. She was twenty-four, had long, rich hair, and wore a brown raglan, tied at the waist. I'd never met her. Mary appeared indifferent, as if she would rather be anywhere but in Studio A that morning. I was twenty-two and temporarily tongue-tied. Right away we were called to the mic. Everything was strictly business. No rehearsal. Straight to tape.

I'm happy to report that I got through the scene unscathed and lived to act another day. Now you're probably wondering how I finally managed to give an acceptable performance. Simple. I imagined I was kissing Richard Chamberlain.

7

MY PATH WOULD BE DIFFERENT

When I reached my twenties and no longer had even a scintilla of doubt about my sexual orientation, I decided it was coming-out time. In the mid-'70s I knew there might be future employers from whom I'd need to keep this information, and others who could jeopardize my well-being or my ability to earn a living. But they were far less important than family and friends. They needed to know, regardless of how they might react. It would not have been possible for me to live a healthy life with such a secret.

Nobody has ever had a contented life hiding who they are or, worse, being in denial about who they are. I'd seen what happens when you live a lie. Dad's friend Tom married a woman, knowing he wasn't who she thought he was, knowing that he could not give her, emotionally at least, everything she deserved and that she could not give him what he deserved. It resulted in misery and heartache for both, and, years later, divorce. My path would be different—alone or, hopefully, with a man I loved.

There is truth to the cliché "mothers are always the first to know." Mom was sitting at the kitchen table when I told her. As she looked into my eyes, her expression changed. She knew I was about to broach a topic much more serious than the latest storyline of her favourite TV soap opera, *Another World*. I didn't beat around the bush. "Mom there's something I need to tell you," I said. "I'm gay."

I'd barely spoken the word "gay" before she flushed and burst into tears. Her reaction wasn't unexpected. My mother cried a lot. Any number of tragic stories, events, or slights would set her off. She was a champion weeper. Nonetheless, seeing her cry always made me sad for her. There are few things more gut-wrenching than a mother weeping, her usual neutral expression turning to hurt and anguish.

Once she'd regained her composure and wiped away the tears with the back of her hand, she said matter-of-factly, "I knew anyway. I always knew. You never showed any interest in girls." She then went on to express—as I suspected she would—concern about what people might say. I told her that I didn't care what people might say or think, and that it was none of their business.

My father wasn't home at the time; before I was able to tell him, my mother had taken care of it for me. He was subdued, only offering that it made no difference to him, that I was still his son, and it was important for me to live my life as I saw fit. Although it was what I thought he'd say, I remember being proud of Dad. His response was atypical for a man of his generation. I was fortunate. Several of my friends didn't fare so well, with one or both of their parents reacting with bitterness and anger that sometimes took years to resolve, if it ever did.

My brother Len was more reticent. His only comment was that I "was in for a hard life." Sister Betty, a nurse in Montreal, advised that I see a psychiatrist. I didn't. Neither of my parents endorsed Betty's advice. I thought my mother might, in a desperate attempt to ward off the inevitable. But in their hearts, my parents always knew that the sensitive child they'd raised, who loved to play make-believe and lived largely in his own world, was not like most boys. I was who I was, and they would continue to embrace and love me.

It's often said that when most gay kids realize they're gay, they think they're the only gay on the planet. My experience was different. I'd learned early on from Mom about "homos." My question was how and where to connect with other gays. An answer came from a university friend with whom I'd shared my sexual orientation. It turned out that he thought he might be bisexual, and to my surprise he'd been downtown on a reconnaissance mission, to discover where gays might gather or where gays and straights might mix. He'd even discovered the less busy areas of Water Street where gays cruised, hoping that someone might come along with an offer of intimacy or quick, anonymous gratification. Sex workers cruised the same areas.

My friend took me with him one night so I could see it all for myself. The experience felt scary, exciting, and depressing. You may find the idea of people getting involved in such activities seedy, unhealthy, dangerous, immoral, or all of the above. But consider this: in early 1970s Newfoundland, apart from certain downtown areas of St. John's or Bannerman Park, if you were a local gay man or perhaps a visiting gay man, there were few options if you wanted to connect with another homosexual. This was decades before smartphones and apps. There was no Grindr, no internet, not even an exclusively gay bar.

Homosexuality had just been legalized, and Canada was still heavily infected with the poison of bigotry and homophobia. Gay bashing was commonplace in the '70s and '80s. It still happens today, just not as often. And yet we 2SLGBTQI+ folks come from all levels of society, all walks of life. We are judges, doctors, lawyers, actors, politicians, journalists, plumbers, TV hosts, social workers, civil servants, retail workers, and everything else. Most citizens of Canada know or are related to an 2SLGBTQI+ person.

A majority of 2SLGBTQI+ folk believed they had no choice but to keep their sexual orientation secret. An acquaintance of mine was badly beaten in downtown St. John's for being gay. Did he go to the police? Of course not. The police force was no more enlightened than most of society. There weren't out and proud police officers. Back then, local police were more interested in pursuing and arresting consenting adult gays in the darkest, most secluded areas for what was called gross public indecency. Never mind that an arresting officer would have to be very fast and very close and have a very powerful flashlight to confirm such activity. Authorities weren't interested in heterosexual couples engaged in a gross public indecency unless a street worker was involved. Heterosexuals making out was somehow less gross and more decent.

I soon discovered a couple of safe bars where I could meet other gays. They weren't gay bars as such, but it was possible to find some gays nursing a beer in the Admiral's Keg at the Newfoundland Hotel, or a place in Baird's Cove called Fogo-a-Gogo. Eventually a small number of gay-friendly downtown bars became my entry point to a close-knit community of mostly gay men who cared for, counselled, and looked out for one another. Lesbians tended to be more discreet and stayed away from bars, with some exceptions. I remember one butch woman named Jude who, despite her threatening countenance, had a heart of gold. If you ever found yourself being harassed by a homophobe, Jude would soon warn them off.

There was lots of casual sex in St. John's in the early 1970s, but not a lot of drugs. Poppers (pure amyl nitrite then) were popular on gay dance floors. The drug, an inhalant, came in a bottle branded Rush. It gave some a quick high after a sniff. All I could manage was a headache. It smelled like solvent to me. Some would try almost anything that came their way. When I was introduced to marijuana it made me extremely anxious and paranoid. I decided to stick with beer.

My friend "Gerard" offered me acid (LSD) once at a party. He was ten years older. He said, "Acid is a much better trip than weed. You'll like it." So, for the only time in my life, I took LSD.

I still shake my head in disbelief. No excuses, but my young life was rapidly opening to new people, new ideas, and new experiences. It was exciting. I naively thought I shouldn't miss a thing.

Gerard gave me an acid tab, a minuscule square of blotting paper absorbed with a tiny drop of LSD. I placed it on my tongue. Slowly, every part of my body became infused with a feeling of confidence, energy, and strength. I felt as if I could climb Mount Everest, or scale the CN Tower in an instant. I felt invincible, beyond euphoric. At one point I was fearlessly leaping off furniture and jumping up and down on a bed as if it were a trampoline. Distorted, blurry, kaleidoscopic images of my friends grinning and waving in slow motion came and went. The trip lasted through the night, or so I was told.

Tripping on LSD was fun, far better than my awful marijuana experience. Thankfully, the after-effects of my LSD trip were so bad that I swore off acid and all recreational drugs for the rest of my life. I woke the next morning and every bone, every joint, every muscle of my body ached. I could barely stand and walk. The fatigue was profound. I was spent. My physical condition so alarmed and frightened me that the decision to avoid drugs forever was easy.

In 1975, roughly eighteen months before I graduated from MUN, I got a summer replacement job at the CBC as a television announcer. It was assigned shift work, meaning I wasn't attached to a particular show. One day I might do the sign-on and midday TV news at CBC Television on Prince Philip Drive, and in the afternoon record intros or promos for radio programs at the radio building on Duckworth Street. Another day I might read the six o'clock radio news, later the radio marine weather forecast, and end my shift doing the late-night TV news and weather. It was all very low-tech in those days. Neither CBC Radio nor CBC Television owned or operated a single computer. CBC Television was still gathering in-the-field news images using 16mm film cameras. Sound was recorded on tape—reel-to-reel or cassette tapes. Film, and sometimes reel-to-reel audio tape, was physically edited by cutting it with a blade and joining pieces together with tape.

I was required to audition on-camera for the CBC announcing job. I was slightly intimidated, sitting in the busy modern lobby of CBC TV, waiting to be ushered into Studio One. My nerves were edgy, but I was in control of them. Despite my long-held dream of attending drama school, I knew that if I didn't screw this up, I'd at least have my foot in the door at the CBC. And if the opportunity for full-time employment came, I'd have the option of going for a career in broadcasting.

Jim Byrd began his career at CBNT TV in St. John's and rose to the top at CBC TV as vice-president of the Canadian Broadcasting Corporation's English Television Networks. It was young, ginger-haired production assistant Jim Byrd who met me in the lobby and directed my audition. Jim is a kind and decent man who did his best to put me at ease. On a riser was a very brightly lit area with a chair and desk in front of a green, textured fabric backdrop. On the desk was the audition script. Jim put on his big headphones and stood next to the giant Marconi studio camera. When the control room was ready and rolling, Jim would cue me by quickly swiping his right index finger under the camera lens to begin.

I was pretty sure the CBC wanted announcers to dress well, so I had deliberately selected a dark suit, white shirt, and matching necktie. A fresh shave and haircut completed the look. I wanted to counter anything lacking in my speech with an impressive visual appearance.

Here's a taste of what I had to read for this video audition:

> "We're going to begin today with a recording by a brilliant young Dutch soprano whose voice may be familiar to you, Elly Ameling. Hers is not, perhaps, the biggest voice you've heard, although she has sung some opera, but it is a voice that is rich and clear and true.

> "Here's Elly Ameling, then, with Jörg Demus at the piano to sing 'Die Forelle,' The Trout, by Schubert."

Although I was sure I'd bombed, Jim was kind enough to say that I'd done very well. He also commented that I sounded like I'd worked in the "business" before. I guess my experience at VOWR and ETV and my radio acting had paid off, because later I received word that I'd been hired for the summer of '75. It was such a thrill to think that I was going to be a CBC announcer. My parents were very pleased and perhaps a little relieved. I know that my father was very proud because he couldn't stop telling his friends. It was heartening to know. We had grown close, and I respected him for his work ethic, his sound advice, generosity, and devotion to family and friends.

My desire to make it in big-time broadcasting (I'd placed the CBC on a pinnacle) was top of mind the first time I toured the TV station in St. John's. My tour guide was Geoff Seymour, a fellow announcer, fine actor, and generous human being. Geoff had been assigned the task of giving me a quick orientation and tour of the CBC buildings where I'd be working. There was one head-scratching moment. When Geoff brought me into the newsroom, he introduced me to Bren Walsh, a respected CJON and CBC veteran newsman. Bren asked me what part of town I grew up in. Back then, if you lived west of Prince of Wales Street, you were a west-ender. I told him Golf Avenue, a west-end guy.

Bren made a joke about me being a token Protestant. I didn't understand until I realized that most Catholic families did indeed come from the east end and south side of St. John's. (During my career, a few technicians sometimes referred to me, jokingly, as the "black Protestant.") When I started at the CBC, most staff and managers were Roman Catholic. In fact, I was later told by Harold Morris, a former CBC announcer, that there was a time when the Roman Catholic

Archbishop of St. John's made an annual visit to CBC Radio on Duckworth Street. CBC staff formed a welcoming line on the top floor, led by station management, and as the archbishop made his way down the line, each employee would kneel and kiss his ring.

As I walked the corridors of the ground floor of the television building, all I could think was: this is Tinseltown. Ninety-five University Avenue was sarcastically called "the palace" by CBC Radio employees. (Some radio staff disliked the television service, thinking it received too much funding, was wasteful, less serious, and had far too much power. I didn't agree.) The building's narrow passageways were filled with colourfully costumed performers, office workers, news reporters, producers, and technicians, all scurrying here and there. As they say today, "the place was on wheels." It was exciting. "My God," I thought, "this is what Hollywood must be like."

When it came time for me to start on-air work, I spent a week shadowing other announcers. The idea was for them to show me how things were done and then allow me to do some live announcing while they observed and assessed my performance. I still remember the first words I spoke live on CBC Radio. I was in a tiny studio off the central control room, then on the third floor of the CBC Radio building. As the dean of Newfoundland and Labrador announcers sat beside me, I waited for the on-air light to glow red and then announced to all of Newfoundland:

"From Ottawa, the National Research Council official time signal. The beginning of the long dash, followed by 10 seconds of silence, will indicate exactly 2:30 p.m. Newfoundland daylight saving time [pause for ten beeps, followed by a sustained beep]. It's 2:30 p.m., Newfoundland daylight saving time."

I waited for the dean to say something, positive or negative, but he said nothing. In the daily stream of thousands of words spoken live on CBC Radio, my utterance of approximately three lines was insignificant. However, for me the experience felt monumental. I wanted to hear "Well done," or "Good job," or "Better luck next time." But my elder colleague appeared bored and indifferent.

Looking back, we must have seemed an interesting pair. Me barely in my twenties, wearing a suit and tie, and him in his sixties, wearing a trilby hat, a colourful shirt, and tweed jacket. His strong-browed face was long and drawn, with deep lines around his mouth. He was Aubrey MacDonald, the longest-serving announcer with the CBC in Newfoundland and Labrador. He was also known in his career with VONF and the Broadcasting Corporation of Newfoundland (BCN) as Ted Mack, and then Aubrey Mac at CBC Radio.

Aubrey was a famous sportscaster and after-dinner speaker in Newfoundland and on the mainland. In June of 1963, for example, he spoke at events in Perth and Toronto, Ontario, and Rochester, New York. He had modelled himself on NBC sportscaster Bill Stern, a theatrical announcer famous for his *Colgate Sports Newsreel* on NBC Radio. Stern presented short biographical stories about athletes, often embellished (to the dismay of fellow broadcasters) with pure fiction. Aubrey covered mostly local and provincial sports in his day but, like all sports fans, followed the big leagues with interest.

He also read newscasts, sometimes the famous *Gerald S. Doyle News Bulletin*. In earlier years, before telephone connections were easily made, the *Bulletin* would contain messages from people in outports to their relatives in St. John's on business or at hospital for treatment. The messages could be unintentionally hilarious. Once a message was a note to a husband in St. John's in which his wife wanted him to know his mother had had an attack of kidney stones, causing vomiting. The announcer, possibly Aubrey, read the note: "Mother up all night over the sink with her kidneys."

By this time Aubrey had already had a long and fulfilling radio career. In the twilight of his time at the CBC, I found him a sad figure.

I was the future, fresh and filled with enthusiasm. He probably saw himself as the past, the end of his career looming. And for a man like Aubrey who thrived in the limelight, it must have been terrifying. He had been given two shows, *Mac's Music*, and *Mac's Scrapbook*, to see him to his retirement and pension. Both were much the same; one aired around 9:30 a.m. and the other (pre-recorded) near midnight. Between a song by Sinatra and a film theme by Mantovani, Aubrey would read a poem or tell a story that tied into the subject of each musical selection. Sometimes the link would be tenuous; for example, after recounting a nauseating ferry trip in stormy waters off Port aux Basques, Aubrey might segue into the romantic love song "Beyond the Sea," by Bobby Darin. Control room operators would roll their eyes, shake their heads, and smile.

Stories about Aubrey are numerous. My favourite is quite short. During his years with VONF, Aubrey had a drinking problem. Because it had interfered with his work, he had—more than once—been threatened with firing. One morning when Aubrey was scheduled to be on the air, he was nowhere to be found. VONF was situated on a floor of the Newfoundland Hotel. Some of the rooms on the VONF floor hadn't been altered much to accommodate the radio station's studios and offices. One or two bathrooms, for example, still had bathtubs.

Eventually the errant broadcaster was found. Out on the town the previous night, Aubrey had managed to make his way up to the station, where he had fallen asleep in one of the bathtubs. Dishevelled, tie askew, and in need of a shave, he was marched into the office of VONF general manager William F. Galgay.

Standing like a condemned man before the desk of the legendary executive, Aubrey shrugged and fidgeted as Galgay lectured him on the importance of professionalism, et cetera. Finally, leaning back in his leather swivel chair, Galgay asked, "Now MacDonald, what have you got to say for yourself?" Noticing that Galgay had a plate

A young man on track for a long career in the perfect workplace (or so I thought), the CBC.

of buttered toast and a cup of tea on his desk, Aubrey sheepishly responded, "Well, Mr. Galgay, I was wondering if you're going to finish that toast, because I'm starved."

In his day, Bill Galgay was quite well-known. As an announcer, he was famous for an expression he used during coverage of the rowing at the St. John's Regatta. His anchor position was at the end of Quidi Vidi Lake, where the rowing shells rounded the buoys. When the announcer mid-lake tossed to Galgay for his live description of the turning of the buoys, he would invariably begin with, "This is Bill Galgay at the bottom of the pond!"

I was much less confident about securing a permanent job at the CBC after I worked with radio producer Leo Thistle. I was assigned to host his weekly radio program called *Hymns of Praise*. Leo Thistle was an amiable man, with whom I'd later have many wonderful conversations about everything from broadcasting to his theories about who killed JFK. I had only known Leo from watching television, because when CBNT TV went on the air in the mid-'60s, Leo (once a CBC announcer) hosted a serious music program showcasing many well-known Newfoundland musicians: pianists, violinists, cellists, and singers.

It was a black and white show featuring a typical early TV set: white pillars surrounding the performance area, set against a limbo (black) backdrop. Leo Thistle, as host, appeared between the pillars on a high riser above the performers, seated on a blocky armchair made to look like white marble. The whole arrangement was like Zeus's throne.

When I sat before the studio microphone and saw Leo Thistle on the other side of the window separating the control room from studio, I shivered at the sight of Zeus holding a copy of the script he had written. The very script I was charged with voicing—with conviction and feeling. I'd practised all the hymn introductions several times beforehand. One was especially melodramatic. By way of introducing the hymn "Rock of Ages," I was to recount (as per Leo's script) a marine disaster where dozens of passengers of a sunken ship (which apparently had no lifeboats and an inadequate supply of life preservers) spent ages (pardon the pun) bobbing up and down in a cold sea joyfully singing "Rock of Ages." This activity, supposedly, saved them all from certain death. I was a trained lifeguard (having learned to swim at MUN and through Red Cross swimming courses), and had been shown, quite graphically, how most people react when faced with drowning. They don't sing "Rock of Ages," or anything else.

In those days I was immature and too cynical for my own good. I was undone when I heard myself reading the intro aloud. Specifically, the portion about the adrift souls singing while they were (I assumed) panic-stricken and struggling to keep their heads above the ocean surface and the briny water out of their mouths. I visualized people who couldn't swim, weighed down by water-logged clothing, spitting out buckets of water, going under and resurfacing in full voice with "Rock of Ages" lyrics like "While I draw this fleeting breath"!

My voice control began to fail as I felt my stomach begin to shake. At first it was a slight quaver in my voice. Then every part of me tightened as I tried to suppress a giggle that was determined to be heard. Suddenly, out it burst, followed by a flood of giggles. I turned crimson, began to sweat, and wanted to crawl under the studio table. I contemplated fleeing the studio, never to return to the CBC. My humiliation was complete. Leo folded his arms and looked downward. Now, I'd like to think he was suppressing laughter too, but at the time I felt he was signalling regret at having witnessed the end of a promising youngster's career before it had even begun. Thankfully, after a few tries, I redeemed myself by doing a reading that was acceptable to the author.

Forty-one-year-old announcer Wilf Dyke oversaw my first live CBC Television newscast, in (believe it or not) black and white. It was the weekday sign-on news, seen immediately after the airing of the "Ode to Newfoundland" and "O Canada." In 1975, CBNT still retained one black and white television camera; the other five were colour. It was the same set used for my audition. This time, to my surprise, there would be nobody in Studio One to cue me.

The sign-on news didn't rate a crew, just a technician who pre-set everything and then returned to the control room. Wilf showed me a naked lightbulb dangling from the back of the studio. "When this lightbulb goes on, look at the camera and start to read," he said. Below the camera lens was a large black-on-white analog clock with a hand that moved precisely as each second passed. When the hand reached the top of the clock, a slide popped up on the screen to the side of the camera. The slide showed the unpopular new CBC logo, which had recently replaced the multicoloured butterfly. It was called the Gem. CBC staffers had taken to calling it the "exploding pizza" or, less politely, the "exploding arsehole."

There was no teleprompter in those days, so I had to develop the technique of looking up at the camera lens every few seconds while reading. That, and keeping an eye on the distant lightbulb, the clock, and the monitor, was a little pressurizing. If that wasn't enough, Wilf decided to pull up a chair and sit, legs crossed, hands folded, right beside me. He was off-camera, of course, but I found this disconcerting. Did he want to be nearby in case I suddenly bolted, or passed out? Perhaps he'd push my limp body aside and complete the job for me. Well, I got the job done, but I was sure viewers could tell I was nervous. I found going live on TV much scarier than radio. After many TV broadcasts, I learned to control my nerves and began to build the confidence that eventually would get me noticed by viewers.

The CBC technician working that day was Pat Ryan, a mild-mannered guy from Torbay, Newfoundland. Pat had two careers. He was a part-time vegetable farmer and a full-time CBC TV technician.

He eventually quit CBC and moved to PEI to farm parsnips. Pat and I chatted while Wilf took a break. He told me that Wilf was the only on-air person who didn't have to look directly into the camera lens when he presented the news. "How's that?" I asked.

Pat explained that Wilf had a turn in his right eye, which I had noticed. Apparently when he looked directly at the camera, he appeared not to be looking at the camera, which was disconcerting for viewers. However, Wilf and Pat discovered that when Wilf looked directly at the dangling lightbulb, he did appear to be looking at the camera. Henceforth, Wilf Dyke delivered the CBC TV News to a dangling lightbulb.

As time passed during that first summer with the CBC, I slowly realized that my face was starting to be known by the public. A few who recognized me were members of the gay community, people I'd already encountered. Word soon spread amongst St. John's gays that the new young fellow doing the fringe newscasts (early morning and late night) on CBC TV was one of their own. This development led to my receiving a phone call at my parents' house late one evening. It was slightly unsettling. This total stranger told me he knew I was gay and that if I wanted to meet with him, he'd be happy to help me safely navigate the often rocky shoals of gay life in St. John's. I didn't recognize his voice and he wouldn't tell me his name.

My gut told me to hang up the phone. I didn't. I've often wondered how my life would have turned out if I'd hung up on the stranger. No doubt it would have been different. There are lessons I might not have learned, people and friends I might never have known—many experiences I would have missed.

8

LIFE WOULD NEVER BE THE SAME

The stranger ended the phone call when I agreed to meet him for coffee. During our conversation, I was convinced he was sincere. We met a few days later at his small, tidy apartment on St. Laurent Street in St. John's. His name was Jack Clarke, an inside worker for Canada Post. Originally from Victoria, Carbonear, he loved to say, "I'm from Victoria, B.C.—behind Carbonear." He wore clothing popular with gays of the era: faded blue jeans, wide belt, plaid shirt. Jack was about five foot eight, trim, fit, nose slightly upturned, balding at front and back. His expressive eyes made him a poor liar. An easy sense of humour, combined with free and joyous laughter, made Jack approachable. We talked for a few hours.

Jack was completely immersed in the gay life of mid-'70s St. John's, a walking reference guide to everything anyone might like to know about anything gay: people, places, local and national gay organizations, gay newspapers, gay rights, gay books, et cetera. As time passed, we met several more times. Jack began to have get-togethers to introduce me to his friends. I liked most of them. Before long I realized I felt safe and protected with Jack.

He was a few years older than me, and street-smart. Eventually he suggested we become a couple. I agreed. My one stipulation was that our relationship be monogamous. In the '70s, most gay relationships were open. Many are today. Sharing my partner with someone else was unthinkable. He agreed, and I moved from Mom and Dad's to St. Laurent Street. They put up no resistance. I think my parents, both in their fifties, were secretly delighted to see the last of their brood leave the nest.

After graduating from MUN with degrees in English and Education, I was offered full-time employment at the CBC by Des Brown, executive producer of radio current affairs. Des explained that announcer Charlie Veitch was to become a producer and they wanted me to replace Charlie on the announcing staff. It was a case of being in the right place at the right time. I would be paid a starting salary of $12,000 annually. The CBC became my second home for the next thirty-one years.

Full-time permanent employment at the CBC was a baptism of fire. CBC Radio decided to revamp its weekend morning show, which mainly offered light music, news, and weather. It was to become an information show focused on the arts: theatre, music, visual art, writing, and artists working in those fields. I was assigned to host on both days for the foreseeable future. Once the new program was well established and running smoothly, I could return to my previous routine of alternating TV and radio assignments. I was relieved to have an escape hatch because I very much wanted to do more TV work.

The name of our new program would be *Weekend A.M.* (the A.M. had a dual meaning: the obvious one, and "Arts Magazine"). My producer was fellow announcer John O'Mara. I liked John. He was a no-nonsense leader and had years of experience hosting shows such as *On the Go* and *Radio Noon*. We worked well together. We shared interest in the arts, and we had a similar sense of humour—always a good thing when a deadline's approaching. He pushed me to take on tasks that were slightly out of my comfort

Graduating from Memorial University, May 29, 1976.

zone. This was exactly the right approach to take with a young, less experienced broadcaster.

I'll give you an example. In 1977, the great actor Sir Michael Redgrave was touring Canada in an anthology production called *Shakespeare's People*. Having performed on the mainland, the UK company was preparing to open at the St. John's Arts and Culture Centre. A press conference was scheduled for the Battery Hotel a few days before the St. John's opening. John wanted me to attend, but he made it sound (to my twenty-three-year-old self) tricky, if not daunting.

I was in a dreary office not much bigger than a broom cupboard. I'd just taken a staff memo out of my mail slot and was about to read it when John approached, looking like he was about to lean in to share something top secret.

"Sir Michael Redgrave's in town," he said in a slightly conspiratorial tone. "He's touring with an English company doing readings from Shakespeare. Are you thinking what I'm thinking?"

"An interview? God yes, that's a fabulous way to kick off the new show."

"Absolutely. But here's the thing, I'm not sure we can get him."

"Why, John?"

"Well . . . I was told Peter Gzowski interviewed him at some point, or tried to interview him, and apparently it didn't go well."

"What happened?"

"Not sure. All I was told was that Redgrave is difficult, and Gzowski said he was pompous and awful, and that he never wanted to interview him again."

"Oh . . . "

If Peter Gzowski couldn't deliver a successful interview with Sir Michael Redgrave, then how in hell could I?

"But," continued John, "we need to try. Get yourself up to the Battery Hotel this afternoon and see if you can do a one-on-one interview with him."

"Aa . . . heh . . . how long an interview, John?" I ventured nervously.

"Five or ten minutes."

I was starting to think I was about to face a real ogre. Someone who would take me for a fool and dismiss me from his presence for fear of fouling the air with my witlessness. Just the thought of occupying the same room with the acclaimed actor, star of *The Browning Version*, father of brilliant Vanessa Redgrave (star of *Mary, Queen of Scots*) would ordinarily have been enough to intimidate me. Now, thanks to John O'Mara and Peter Gzowski, he'd been transformed into Sir Michael the Horrible.

Summoning the small amount of courage that I still possessed, I walked into the Battery Hotel salon. I scanned the bright, wood-panelled room, nodding to Shirley Newhook, the Arts and Culture Centre's public relations person. Shirley looked concerned as she spoke with a young, smartly dressed man in a Savile Row suit. He looked concerned, too. I assumed he was with the UK contingent.

When the press conference was about to begin, the actors arrived with the man in the suit and took their places at a long table before our small media group. For some reason, Sir Michael Redgrave sat at the back of the room in one of the salon's upholstered armchairs. It was a short press conference. Most of the media looked as bored as the actors. One of them was a sports reporter, no doubt sent because he was available.

As the actors were filing out of the room, I approached the man in the Savile Row suit. I asked him if it might be possible to be granted a one-on-one interview with Sir Michael for the CBC. He glared at me with a face that said, "Really? Why not ask me to cut off my arm instead?" After a long pause, he turned and slowly approached Sir Michael in his armchair. He bent over and whispered something; Sir Michael turned and sized me up. He gave a faint smile, followed by an almost imperceptible nod. Cripes, the dragon had invited me into his lair.

The Savile Row man came back with a stern, disappointed face and said, "Sir Michael will speak with you, but only for a few minutes." I thanked him and managed to get to Sir Michael before my trembling legs gave out. He was sitting, backlit, in a window with the stunning backdrop of St. John's harbour. It took a few seconds for my eyes to adjust and properly see his face, which was at first a shadowy blur. Gradually, he came into focus, now smiling a little more broadly and looking very comfortable in a wool cardigan, corduroy trousers, and suede shoes. He looked every bit the grey-haired, cherub-faced lord of the manor.

I thanked Sir Michael for allowing the interview, pulled up a chair, and with my Sony cassette recorder on my lap, I began. During the interview, I noticed Savile Row pacing, looking nervous as a cat. He was putting me off, so I decided to keep my eyes on Sir Michael, who appeared fixed, if not fixated, on me.

We spoke mostly about Shakespeare: blank verse, how it was being spoken then by new actors, and acting in general. Sir Michael could not have been sweeter. I was beginning to relax. He seemed genuinely interested and was clearly enjoying our chat. It was thrilling to hear him refer to Lord Laurence Olivier as "Larry." I had the impression he would have allowed me to remain with him for hours. What on earth was Peter Gzowski talking about? Sir Michael Redgrave was an absolute gem.

Then I began to notice something. In addition to his smile, which had gotten progressively warmer, Sir Michael now had a twinkle in his eye. A twinkle that shone brighter and brighter every second. Then it hit me. Yes, I recognized that come-hither look. It was unmistakable. God! Sir Michael Redgrave has the hots for me! I'd never suspected that Sir Michael was gay or bisexual, but it was obvious.

I've since discovered that Sir Michael was indeed bisexual and that he was known, throughout his life, to have enjoyed casual sexual encounters with men. I guess that's why Savile Row appeared so uneasy with my request, and with Sir Michael's agreeing to it so readily. Part of his job may have been to prevent such encounters. Having chatted well beyond my allotted time, I decided to leave. I thanked Sir Michael and wished him well with the remainder of the tour. He was polite to the end, and I was very happy to have met him.

John O'Mara was delighted but clearly shocked to learn I'd bagged an interview with Sir Michael Redgrave. When I saw his jaw drop, I realized he'd fully expected me to return empty-handed. Asked how I managed it, I demurred. A shrug of the shoulders was all I could offer. Candour about homosexual attraction would not have been welcome at the CBC in 1977.

One of the early interviews we pre-recorded for *Weekend A.M.* was with the great Joan Morrissey. Joan was known as Newfoundland's "First Lady of Song," unquestionably our most famous singer, an iconic star beloved for her records, TV and radio appearances, club and stage work—not the least being her starring role as Annie Oakley in *Annie Get Your Gun*, produced by the St. John's Arts and Culture Centre. She made an impression visually as well, with her long dark hair and eyebrows, dark eyes accented by eyeliner and mascara, and a smile and laugh that automatically lifted your spirits. Her slightly husky voice was instantly recognizable. I'd already met Joan from having temporarily stepped in as her co-host on a few instalments of CBC Radio's *Country Jamboree*. Joan liked to refer to me as "the posh one," which I think had to do with my clothing and appearance.

Apart from being kind and generous, Joan was a consummate professional. During our *Weekend A.M.* interview, billed as a chat about the province's developing music industry, she said performers needed to work harder on their stage presence, especially on how they spoke and interacted with their audiences between the songs. Joan believed you had to be "in the moment," laser focused on everything you sang, said, and did onstage, from stepping on to stepping off. Telling a quick story or the background of a composition to the audience was as important to Joan as striking the right notes.

Joan Morrissey left us on Tuesday, January 10, 1978, at the age of 42—decades too soon. I was at work in CBC Radio's arts department office on the Wednesday we received word that Joan had taken her own life. The entire office went silent, all of us stunned, saddened beyond measure as we struggled to process the news. We loved Joan. All of Newfoundland and Labrador mourned her passing.

My home life in early 1978 was good, although Jack insisted on drawing lines. I paid half the rent; furniture purchases, restaurant and bar bills were 50/50; grocery bills also had to be split down the middle. When I saw him approach with a handful of bills and a ballpoint pen, I'd feel like I was about to be audited by Revenue Canada. He also insisted I do things his way in keeping house, be it washing and folding laundry, dusting furniture or handwashing dishes. To this day I think of Jack every time I iron a shirt, still doing it his way: sleeves

Jack Clarke, my first boyfriend and partner.

inside-out, back first, then front (button side first), collar back and front, pull out one sleeve, iron, then the other. Done.

We had an active social life. Jack was known for throwing parties; we continued the tradition and attended many. If we didn't meet with friends in their homes or apartments, we'd see them at the few gay bars that opened in the late '70s, such as Friends, Katz, and the Brahma Room (it had a mechanical bull). I recall one costume party where I dressed as Buck Rogers, complete with white boots, rainbow armband, belt, and holstered sonic ray gun, which I fired too frequently as we danced and partied to the music of Gloria Gaynor, Blondie, Donna Summer, Alicia Bridges and, of course, the original Village People. I wasn't the best dancer, but God I had fun.

Except for the obvious differences, gay house parties weren't much different from straight house parties for twenty-somethings in the 1970s and very early '80s. Apartment walls were usually vibrating from stereo speakers on bust, pumping out that disco beat. Those dancing wannabe *Saturday Night Fever* Tony Maneros also caused the floor to undulate. The air was usually thick with cigarette smoke, hints of marijuana or Brut aftershave (possibly Polo shave balm if you fancied yourself sophisticated). Attendees who weren't dancing were drinking beer, cheap wine (Blue Nun or Ruffino Chianti), or rum and Coke.

They were colourful parties, and we tended to wear shirts in bold colours. Most people wore snug blue jeans, sometimes flared at the ankle. Neck chains and bracelets were popular. In the waning hours, the lights dimmed and the music softened. You might see a couple embracing on a couch.

Jack had a few gay friends from St. John's living in Montreal. We sometimes made trips there in late spring and summer. A few times I went alone. One friend, Jerry Bartlett, became a good pal of mine. We first met at a party on Waterford Bridge Road in St. John's. He stood out in white jeans, crisp white shirt and loafers. He was good-looking, thin and tanned, had dark hair and a moustache.

Jerry's first name was Vince, but he preferred Jerry, which I assumed was a middle name. He was about two years my senior. At the time he was teaching at one of Montreal's private English high schools. He'd gone to Brother Rice High School in the '60s and graduated from MUN a few years after I started. Jerry was eager to teach me everything he knew about Montreal: the nightlife, Quebec politics, theatre, art, literature, music, and film. When he saw I was interested, I became his pupil.

We'd go on long walks all over Montreal. Jerry was a tireless, enthusiastic guide. Once, we stood at the foot of the steep concrete staircase leading up the hill to Saint Joseph's Oratory of Mount Royal. Originally built from a modest shrine to St. Joseph established by Brother André Bessette, it became a magnet for pilgrims after André supposedly performed miracles for visitors. Jerry was skeptical, but he had regard for the deep devotion shown by believers. Pointing toward the stairs he said in a voice filled with awe and respect, "When my aunt visited, she climbed those stairs on her knees, all the way to the top."

Sometimes we'd tour interesting neighbourhoods near McGill University and have lunch at one of many side-street bistros. In the evening Jerry took me to gay bars and clubs. Le Jardin was a popular spot with lots of disco dancing. Then we'd hit Lentzos, a small, late-night delicatessen frequented by gays (especially the Le Jardin crowd) for a smoked meat sandwich and fries. Montreal nights and vacations were lots of fun. It was easy for gay men to love the city. Back then, Montreal was one of Canada's most progressive cities. Gay citizens felt welcome there, free from the oppressive homophobia of less-enlightened places. It was the first big city I got to know well, and I always wanted our holidays there to last longer.

Jack didn't enjoy Montreal as much as I did. Large cities and different cultures were out of his comfort zone. Jack's idea of enjoyable travel was our weekly visit to Victoria, Carbonear, to have Sunday dinner with his surrogate parents, Uncle Walter and Aunt Ethel—whom Jack, since childhood, had called Net. Jack's lineage was murky to me, and perhaps to him. All he offered was that he was born out of wedlock to a young single mother related to Walter and Ethel Clarke. His biological father was never mentioned. His young mother was unable to raise him. Walter and Ethel, who operated a small grocery and general store in Victoria, adopted Jack and raised him as their own.

Walter and Ethel were Pentecostal, though Ethel took religion more seriously than Walt. Jack's sexual orientation was known to them but never mentioned. They continued to treat him as they had from infancy, with much love. He was their son, not biologically, but in every other way. They offered him an education, spiritual instruction, piano lessons, and invaluable guidance.

Jack was actively involved in the Pentecostal Church until he accepted his sexual orientation. Like most churches at the time, Pentecostals believed homosexuality was sinful. (They still do.) Regardless, Jack had absorbed enough Pentecostalism to sustain him. He just ignored the homophobic parts. He could readily quote verses from the Bible or sit at Ethel's living-room pump organ and play any hymn you could think of, singing every verse from memory at the top of his lungs.

I was accepted by Walter and Ethel unconditionally, without a hint of animosity, only kindness and warmth. Every visit to their store-attached home included the offer of a pre-dinner drink from a large wine bottle bearing a ragged, faded label. Being a small business owner like my father, Walter Clarke kept some wine and liquor on hand for business associates, salesmen, and special guests. I always accepted a glass of Walt's so-called wine to be polite. Of course, he never joined me. Walt would just sit back and smile proudly as I pretended to enjoy the strange liquid, which seemed to change colour every few weeks.

Walt had a practical rather than cultivated way of looking at the serving and consumption of alcoholic beverages. If he had a few bottles that were half-full, he saw absolutely nothing wrong with taking the contents of one and pouring it into the other to make one full bottle. This would have been acceptable if each bottle contained the same thing and the contents weren't spoiled. However, Walt would mix Riesling with Burgundy, Crown Royal with Baby Duck, and so on. I made the mistake of asking him why he did this.

He looked at me as if I'd asked the most ridiculous question. Throwing up his hands he said, "But it's ALL alcohol, isn't it? I'm just adding more flavour to it. Besides, your body can't tell the difference." My stomach certainly could. Yet I continued to be polite and make Walt happy by accepting his hospitality. I'd pour myself the tiniest amount of the concoction and, smiling, sip it very slowly. Out of deference to his Pentecostal parents, Jack never asked for a drink (not that he'd want one), nor was he offered one. He was aware of Walter's chemistry projects and would laugh about my regular predicament all the way back to St. John's.

Monday, May 8, 1978, began routinely. It was to be one of the most consequential days of my life. My workday started at CBC TV presenting the sign-on news. I finished the morning doing the midday news on *Broph's Half Hour* (later called *Brophy's Corner*), a talk show hosted by veteran broadcaster Doug Brophy, known for his acerbic wit. My on-air interactions with Doug always kept me on my toes. He was known for giving fellow announcers a hard time. It stemmed from having had responsibility for reading the news on his show taken away from him because he wouldn't stop expressing opinions

Living away from home in Jack's apartment on St. Laurent Street in St. John's. Uncertain of what lay ahead.

about the stories he was reading. Other announcers, such as yours truly, were scheduled to read instead. One day Doug introduced me, with his guest sitting beside us.

"Karl, our guest here is from Buchans," said Doug. "Do you know where Buchans is?"

I responded, "Yes, Doug, I do. It's a mining town. I was born there."

"Which shaft?" replied Doug.

Eventually I got my own back. Peter Kent had recently quit his job as anchor of *The National*. A search for his replacement had been underway, and Knowlton Nash was picked to take over. Doug asked me, again while introducing me on-air, "A lady viewer told me the other day she thought you looked like Peter Kent. Who is Peter Kent if you're writing home to mother?"

Without missing a beat, I answered, "Oh Doug, you know who Peter Kent is. He's the guy whose job you applied for but didn't get." Broph was dumbstruck. Finally.

After lunch, I headed downtown to the radio building to finish my shift, which usually ended around 4 p.m. I was assigned to work with a producer to record public service announcements, intros, and promos. Before my shift ended, I went downstairs to chat with Howard Moore, the scheduling officer for the announcing staff, about future assignments.

Unbeknownst to me, the CBC switchboard operator in the TV building had been trying to track me down for a call from the United States. I'd lingered a little after my conversation with Howard to talk with some of the staff who worked in a pool outside his office. One of the administrative staff was Shane LeMessurier. Shane was a high school classmate. I remember we talked about his aging Oldsmobile, parked in front of the building, and why it ran so well. He told me the secret was frequent oil changes.

I wasn't home very long before the phone in our apartment started ringing. It was Jack. "Karl," he said, followed by a pause. His voice was different. Low, flat, nervous. I knew immediately that something was wrong. I had no idea where Jack was or why he sounded so anxious.

My parents had been vacationing in Florida since March. They'd begun travelling there for regular winter breaks. Not by plane, by car, due to Dad's fear of flying. I'd recently spoken to them on the phone. They sounded in good spirits, which made me happy. They loved the sunshine, the warmth, and the blue ocean. My aunt and uncle—Dad's sister Mabel and her husband, Absalom Kelloway—had joined the trip to Florida at Nova Scotia, where they lived.

"Jack where are you?"

"I'm at your brother's. You need to come out here."

"Why? What happened?"

"Just come out to Len's."

"Jack, what is it?"

"It's about your mom and dad. They were in an accident."

My heart raced; I couldn't catch my breath. I felt a chill. I knew someone was dead.

"Are they both dead?" I asked.

After a long pause, Jack said, "Your father didn't make it."

Just those words. Five words that meant my life would never be the same. I went numb. The following thirty minutes are largely blank. Jack and I were living in an apartment on Terra Nova Road in St. John's, and Len was living with his wife, Marg, and their two girls in Mom and Dad's basement apartment near Bowring Park. In retrospect, Jack should have come to pick me up or sent a cab, but none of us was thinking straight. It was all so incomprehensible.

My parents had spent their winter break with my aunt and uncle in a rented house in Fort Myers, Florida, not far from the white sandy beaches of the Gulf of Mexico. On the morning of May 8, they awoke to yet another day of sunshine. It was the day they were to drive home to Newfoundland, stopping for a few days at West New Annan, Nova Scotia, with Mabel and Ab. It was an early rise. On travel days, Dad favoured a quick getaway to beat work-bound traffic. His cream-coloured Chrysler Newport, which he'd purchased a few years earlier, was already packed, gassed up, and ready to go. It would be a tiring trip, but they were happy to be heading home, tanned and refreshed.

Just before they left, Dad complained of having a headache, not unusual for him, as he suffered from headaches more than most people. He took a couple of Aspirin. A bottle of the pain reliever was always nearby, since he took it for his arthritis. Shortly afterward they climbed into the Chrysler and pulled out of the driveway, heading for the highway.

Mom and Aunt Mabel were seated in the back, Dad was driving, and Uncle Ab was up front with a road map. Mom and Aunt Mabel, perhaps mesmerized by the fast-moving scenery and tired from the restless night spent anticipating an early morning trip, fell fast asleep, safely buckled into their seatbelts, as were Dad and Uncle Ab.

Around 8 a.m., still within the Fort Myers region, Dad approached a highway intersection and stopped at a red light. Uncle Ab was studying his map; my mother and aunt were still sound asleep. The interior of the car was silent except for the idling engine and the regular whoosh of vehicles passing in front of the Chrysler. Uncle Ab remembered sensing the car slipping forward into the intersection. He raised his head to look at the traffic light. It was still glowing red. Turning to his left he saw Dad, unconscious, grey-faced and slumped over the wheel. Ab could also see a large truck approaching. It was about to directly hit the driver's side of their car. He attempted to reach for the steering wheel and brake, but was prevented by his seatbelt and shoulder harness.

The approaching tractor trailer was carrying a full load of Florida oranges to market. The young driver saw the vehicle suddenly obstructing his path and applied the brakes, but it was too late. The truck struck the front half of the Chrysler on the driver's side. It dragged the rapidly crumbling car for hundreds of feet in sparks and smoke.

My mother, sitting directly behind Dad, was roused from unconsciousness by an emergency medical technician. She remembered opening her eyes and seeing the back of Dad's head. "I knew he was

Leonard Wells Sr., July 4, 1917-May 8, 1978.

gone." My father was killed instantly. He had borne the full impact of the crash, suffering multiple injuries, each of which could have been fatal. The accident was probably caused by Dad having a stroke while stopped at the intersection. His father had died from a stroke twenty-nine years earlier at the age of seventy-two. Dad would have been sixty-one on July 4th.

I walked into Len's apartment feeling like I was in an alternate universe. Passing through the small, empty kitchen, I stood at the living room entrance and took in the scene. I stared, saying nothing. Jack sat silent, bereft, across from my brother, who sat on the sofa. Len was bent over, hands on his knees, weeping. His wife, Marg, must have taken the kids out so they wouldn't be exposed to the thick pall of grief in the apartment.

Len and I flew to Boston and met Betty, who had flown there from Montreal. Together we flew to Page Field Airport in Fort Myers. We went straight to the hospital to see Mom. She was badly bruised, with broken ribs. Otherwise, she was physically okay. Mentally she was bewildered but comforted by our presence. My Aunt Mabel was in similar condition. Unfortunately, Uncle Ab had suffered a brain injury—from which he eventually recovered.

We flew back to St. John's with Mom and Dad. It was the first and last time my father would fly in a plane. The accident and Dad's death came as a huge shock to hundreds of people outside our family. Leonard Wells Sr. knew or was known by many people through his business and the various organizations with which he was associated. Hundreds attended his funeral service at Wesley United Church; the main floor and balcony were full.

My family was profoundly affected by my father's death. As I joined the congregation in singing "Eternal Father, Strong to Save" at the top of my lungs, I thought about Dad's boyhood years spent on the wild North Atlantic aboard his father's schooner and the treacherous voyages he made to the ice floes to harvest seals in support of his family. I wept at, "O hear us when we cry to Thee / for those in peril on the sea." Finally, I thought about the giant void Dad's passing had left in our lives and wondered how we could possibly move forward without our beloved captain.

9

HE SLAPPED ME HARD ACROSS MY FACE

My mother was fifty-eight when Dad died. Apart from family and social gatherings, and shopping on Water Street for clothes, she rarely left home. Her role was circumscribed and domestic: to wear an apron, keep house, and raise Len Jr., Betty, and me. Dad took care of everything else. Mom had never shopped for groceries, had never been to a bank, had never written a cheque, had never paid a light bill, had never driven a car. Now she was alone. I knew, from the moment I accepted that Dad was gone forever, how ill-equipped my mother was for life on her own. Thankfully, Len and his family planned to remain in her basement apartment for a few more years.

In the aftermath of Dad's passing, when things settled, I decided to abandon the dream I was nurturing to one day pursue my career in Toronto. My brother couldn't spend the time required to support and instruct our mother in how to survive on her own. Betty lived in Montreal. It would be my responsibility. As her son, I needed to do this.

She'd done her best for us when we were growing up. I recalled times eighteen or nineteen years past, when I was a little boy and Mom would have me hold on to the hem of her flowery nylon dress so I wouldn't get lost. On hot summer days we'd walk downtown from O'Neil Avenue and travel from one Water Street store to the next, shopping for clothes. Then we'd walk back home, Mom carrying a few Ayre's or Bowring's shopping bags and me still tightly grasping her dress in my moist hand. We'd begin by slowly making the steep, tiring climb up Casey Street, and then head home.

I'd never seen my mother look as vulnerable as she did on a cold June day in 1978. I'd taken her to the Bank of Nova Scotia on Hamilton Avenue. It was the bank my father used, and she was there to open her own, her first, bank account. My mom was like a child about to venture into a new, scary world. My emotions were mixed. While my heart was breaking for my mother, I felt angry at Dad for not preparing her for this day, for not allowing her to be more independent during their marriage.

We approached the teller. Mom answered several questions in a small, hesitant voice. If there was something she didn't know, I stepped in. She was handling a lot of stress but coping. I watched as she signed *Elizabeth Wells* in her elegant script. Mom's handwriting was the best of all of ours, certainly better than mine and Dad's. Finally she was handed her first bank book and some cheques. Opening her purse, she dropped them in and closed it. Then she looked in my eyes. I saw the pain of grief on her face. "Let's go home now, Mom," I said gently. That was the day I was proudest of my mother.

As weeks and months passed, Mom gradually grew stronger emotionally. There were times I'd walk into her kitchen (always the kitchen) and find her sitting by herself, crying. She avoided most of the house—the living and dining rooms where she and Dad had hosted so many parties, the TV room where they'd sat with King Cole tea and biscuits and watched *Another World*. Sometimes I'd hear them debating what "that Iris Carrington" might get up to next. Those rooms reminded her of loss. The loss of my father, her husband of thirty-five years, of a life she'd never see again. Many of Mom's married friends abandoned her, but she slowly made new friends: single women and other widows. I grieved with her. We got

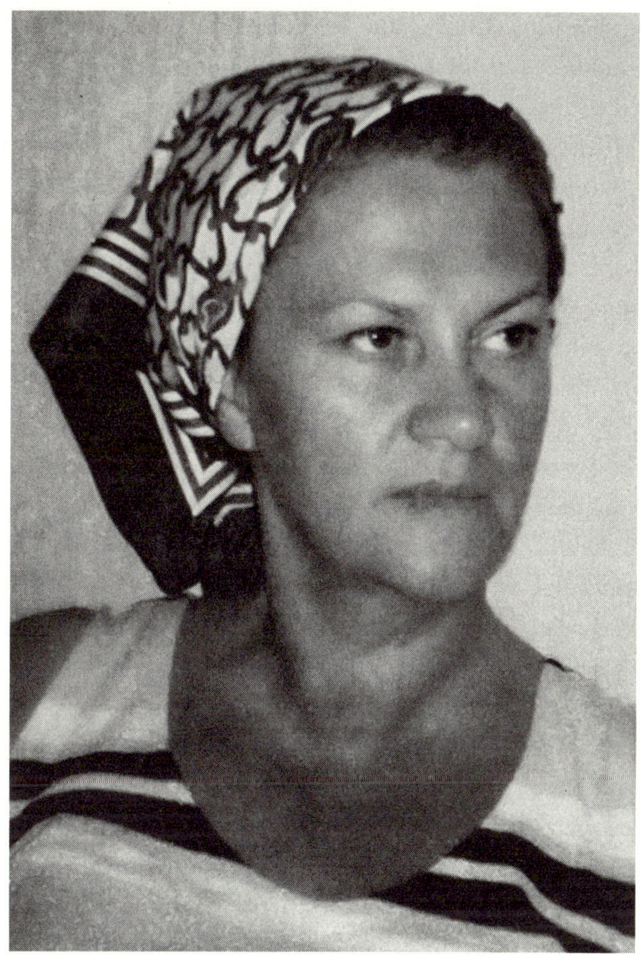

A photo of Mom, taken a few years after Dad's death.

through the darkest days together, and along the way, we occasionally managed to cheer each other up.

In the wake of my father's death, I had descended into a dark depression, numbing and claustrophobic. Jack found it difficult to cope with my unfamiliar mood and my inability to talk about my feelings. I started checking and rechecking things. I'd check a dozen times to make sure the stove was turned off before I left the house. I did the same for the iron, making sure it was unplugged, even though I knew it was unplugged and that I hadn't plugged it in again. I'd go back and recheck because I felt compelled to do so. This would continue multiple times before I'd be able to rush out the door and drive to work. Once at work, I'd settle down as I donned my actor's mask and played the role of a professional CBC broadcaster.

Making my mental anguish worse was phobia, specifically the fear of dying. Even though I'd had aunts and uncles, distant relatives and even a few former high school classmates pass away, my father's death was the first in our immediate family. It was as if I'd never given the inevitability of death a thought before. But now we were four in the family, not five. The fact that I would never see, hear, or talk to my father again was a profound loss.

I began having panic attacks. Explaining a panic attack is hard because the symptoms are both physical and mental. My heart would race, I'd lose my breath, I'd want to run away, escape into an open space and fresh air. You think catastrophe is imminent, but you have no idea what will happen. Something bad. Your mind races. An explosion? Ceiling collapse? Gunshots? Death? My first panic attack happened at a movie theatre in the middle of a matinee. I remember abruptly rising from my seat and racing up the aisle, through the lobby and eventually out into sunlight and fresh air. Running, then walking fast. I only began to slow down after the panic subsided.

One evening, in our Terra Nova Road apartment, Jack was in the living room watching TV. I was trying to rest in the bedroom but began having thoughts about life and the finality of death. Playwright Tennessee Williams once said in an interview that life is such an intense experience it's hard to imagine it ending. Rational acceptance of death as a part of life is one thing, but out-of-control fear of death is something else. In a flash I went into another full-blown panic attack. Rushing out of the bedroom, weeping and frantic, I ran into the hall and in and out of one room after another. "I don't want to die!" I said over and over. As I moved down the hallway, Jack came toward me, staring, saying nothing. Suddenly, he grabbed my right shoulder, and with his other hand, at lightning speed, he slapped me hard across my face.

With my cheek stinging and flushing with heat, I pushed Jack away and stepped back, staring at him in disbelief. He looked at me and said in a matter-of-fact, almost casual way, "Karl, I had to snap you out of it." My first thought was that he'd probably seen a slap in the face used in a movie to shock a frantic person back to normal. But physical assault is not the way to calm distraught people. It hurt and disappointed me that instead of using a compassionate, loving approach, Jack had employed the palm of his hand. He never apologized, but I forgave him. His next mistake was not so easy to forgive.

Jack and I began to drift apart. We tried to make things better, but I was slowly realizing that he was deceitful. The slap affected me more than I thought it would. I began to see it as a betrayal. Then came the day I was blindsided by news from an acquaintance of ours. He contacted me to say that Jack was having casual hookups for sex with strangers. I asked Jack if it was true. Knowing I could easily see through his lies, he said yes. That was the end of our relationship. He wanted us to continue sharing the apartment as roommates. I was reluctant, but eventually said yes, with the understanding that it was temporary.

It was an uneasy arrangement, mainly because Jack never showed remorse. Despite our firm agreement to be monogamous, I don't think he thought casual hookups qualified as betrayal. If he had strayed once, I would have forgiven him. But his infidelity went too far. Lines were drawn. We slept separately, travelled separately. I no longer yielded to his direction, as I had so often to get along. He tried to convince me that I wouldn't survive without him. I told him not to be so foolish. But he did sway a few friends. They thought I'd be lost. Jack was the lost one and appeared more adrift than me. He became moody, joyless. Work couldn't console him, as he never liked the post office. I was able to focus on my career, which I loved. It proved to be a therapeutic distraction.

My CBC colleagues were very kind to me after Dad's death. I got plenty of hugs. Even our resident curmudgeon, Doug Brophy, made a point of finding me. He approached, teary-eyed, and embraced me. It was a warm, sincere embrace. It meant a lot. Radio producers helped to make my work more interesting by offering some acting assignments. This was unusual because these were current affairs producers, not arts producers. But the idea of using fictional characters to perform satirical sketches on their shows began to appeal to them. So, I started performing various characters for *The Morning Show* and *Radio Noon.* Most of the sketches were written by Fred Armstrong and later by Ray Guy. I also wrote a few.

The first character I performed was Pottle of the Constabulary, written by Fred Armstrong. The fictional Pottle was a constable in what was then called the Newfoundland Constabulary. Although a constable, he operated more as an investigator or crime solver. He had a "trusty police dog," T. Alex, named after the 1978 Newfoundland Minister of Justice, T. Alex Hickman. The dog wore slippers and smoked a pipe.

In one of the early instalments, we used as inspiration an actual news story that fluorspar mining at St. Lawrence, on Newfoundland's Burin Peninsula, was being threatened by fierce competition from Mexico. Fred crafted a sketch that turned illegal immigration from Mexico on its head. In our sketch, St. Lawrence miners were being smuggled into Mexico to work for less than Mexicans. The Mexican authorities also had another concern. Our miners were such good soccer players (St. Lawrence residents are known for their soccer prowess) that it was feared they might infiltrate the Mexican national team and embarrass the Mexican players.

Here's a small portion of the script Fred wrote, picking up where Pottle, played by yours truly, has just finished listening to a request from Mexican police officers for help in ending the problem:

> I agreed to help them.
>
> [Thriller music]
>
> Upon being informed that the stream of illegal immigrants was passing through St. John's I disguised myself with a miner's hard hat and lantern, and kicking a soccer ball, set out to investigate.
>
> In Brazil Square, I came upon a boarding house I thought might provide a clue.
>
> It was called Pancho Villa . . .
>
> Then I heard it.
>
> Voices with Burin Peninsula accents chanting uno, dos, uno, dos.
>
> Pushing past the proprietor, I came upon a group of miners in sombreros, practising the Aztec two-step.
>
> "Don't do it," I sez.

"How can you even tink of going somewhere where fresh vegetables grow all year round, where the sun shines fifty-three weeks a year, where tequila sells for only pesedas a gallon?"

I could see I was movin' them to the depths of their souls.

"Think of missing the satisfaction of supporting the oil industry with your heating bills," I said.

"Think of your native fog, think of snow."

[Theme up and fade]

We're due to leave on a tramp freighter next week.

Following Pottle, I performed another weekly character, The Honourable Member, also written by Fred Armstrong, for Friday's edition of *The Morning Show*. The conceit was simple: satirize the goings-on at the Newfoundland House of Assembly and the machinations of the government of Premier Frank Moores. My character was a newly minted Member of the House of Assembly representing a rural district.

Every week our honourable young fellow would write a letter to his mother back home in which he'd update her on what was happening in the legislature and government. His take on things was often quirky, with occasional innuendo. We began each instalment with the sound of a fountain pen gliding across paper, as The Honourable Member began with "Dear Mom." He then went on to voice what he was writing until the letter and our weekly instalment ended.

No doubt there were politicians, especially those we skewered, who didn't care for the attention, but the radio audience loved the character. Here's what theatre, TV, and radio critic Sylvia Wigh wrote about The Honourable Member in her *Daily News* column of July 10, 1979:

> "I like to catch the Honourable Member on CBC's early morning show Friday. He is priceless! I especially enjoyed his discussion on the deprogramming of Gerry Ottenheimer and the various committees on which he serves in the House.
>
> "CBC can come up with some very witty moments and they do have some very talented people among their staff. Usually they are the local boys, but they are kept well in the background. However, we know they are there, and we enjoy them."

In the spring of 1978, something else happened that changed the trajectory of my CBC career. I became a fill-in weatherman on *Here and Now*, CBC's suppertime TV news and current affairs program. While acting and creating characters for the CBC was challenging, general announcing—essentially reading out loud—was often boring. And frankly, that's what most CBC announcers did. Unless, like Doug Brophy, you hosted your own interview show. News announcers (anchors, if you like) on radio and television read news, which was written for them. Sometimes they'd ad lib a little. Yes, and sometimes they did interviews, but even then, many of the questions were written for them by producers and story editors. I longed for an assignment that would free me from those constraints.

Patricia White, also a CBC announcer, was the *Here and Now* weatherperson. Whenever Pat was off, she was replaced by one of the senior announcers, sometimes by Geoff Seymour, sometimes by John O'Mara or Bob Cole. Filling in for Pat became a goal for me. Presenting the weather on *Here and Now* was perfect because there was no script. You learned what the weather was going to be and told the audience about it in your own words, as colourfully as you wanted. It would free me from having to read something that had been handed me by a producer.

At the time, *Here and Now* was run by two producers who each controlled approximately fifty percent of the show. One, Bob Ross, oversaw the news portion read by Bob Cole, and the other, Bill Gough, handled everything else—as well as all freelancers who worked for *Here and Now*. (The newsroom was divided down the middle, with permanent CBC News staff on one side and freelancers on the other.) When my name was put forward by the scheduling office as a weather fill-in, Bill refused to allow me to appear on the show without seeing an audition. I auditioned and got the assignment.

I loved filling in for Pat. In the '70s the *Here and Now* weather board was a brown-on-marine-blue map of Newfoundland and Labrador covered in plexiglass. Each afternoon, a briefing package arrived from the St. John's Weather Office containing everything I needed to know in order to present a comprehensive, up-to-date weather report to our viewers. Presenting the CBC weather took me back to those weekday evenings in my childhood when I'd watch Don Jamieson on CJON TV telling the weather with a stick of chalk and a blackboard.

While each weather report had to be learned well enough to repeat the details on-air, there was one area where this was difficult: temperatures. It would have been hard to commit so many numbers to memory. A method had been devised to solve the problem using a blue grease pencil. Each afternoon, whoever was doing the weather would prep the board by discreetly writing in the temperatures with the blue grease pencil on the blue areas of the map. Colour cameras didn't pick up the blue-on-blue cheat notes. The tiny blue numerals were placed approximately where each temperature would eventually

Standing in front of my first weather board in 1979.

be writ bold by the weatherperson during the live broadcast. We weatherpersons used a thick, white theatrical makeup stick (much like lipstick) to make our high pressure, low pressure and sweeping wind symbols. After each show, either a stagehand or I would clean the board using a soft cloth.

On one of my first live weather broadcasts, I was the target of a practical joke by one of the studio crew. You may think it a cruel joke, but TV and radio people can be sophomoric. What passes for humour in the studio may fall flat elsewhere. At the time, I didn't think it was funny, but I laugh about it now. I'd just been introduced for the weather and launched into my live weather report with gusto. Before going on-air, I'd carefully printed all the temperatures in blue on the board. Unfortunately, someone decided it might be funny to wipe out the temperatures in blue, minutes before the show. When

I turned back to the board to begin jotting the temperatures across the province, I felt the hard pang of fright, and for an instant, I froze. As I stared at the board, I couldn't believe what I was NOT seeing. Not a single temperature in blue. Not a single frigging digit!

I have no explanation for what happened next, or how I remembered them, but I began to hear myself speaking number after number as I trowelled them onto the board using the thick white makeup stick. "16 degrees in Labrador City, 18 in Goose Bay, 12 degrees in L'Anse au Clair." Perhaps the weather gods took pity on me that night. After the show, none of the crew said a word. They just stared down at the floor. Then, with their hands in their pockets, they scuffed out of the studio, kicking camera cables out of the way as they went. It was the new guy's turn to gloat. Their little joke had backfired. Although that trick wasn't repeated, I made sure I never went on the air again without checking my markings. I had learned my lesson.

As my private life became less contented, my CBC career continued its upswing. Things happened early for me. I was top of the list for TV opportunities. Toward the end of 1978, I was asked if I could meet with the director of CBC TV for Newfoundland, Dave Sinnott. Dave came up through the ranks and was a practical decision-maker. He didn't waste time.

Dave all but rubbed his hands together. Clearly, he had something good to tell me. Patricia White, a colleague announcer, was moving to Toronto. CBC management wanted me to replace her as weather reporter on *Here and Now*, the flagship evening news program. I was excited. It came as a package deal. They also wanted me to become the anchor of a new thirty-minute regional late-night news program. It would air following a much-anticipated reinvention of the national network icon, *The National*, which was moving from 11:30 p.m. to 10:30 p.m. I asked if the two assignments were permanently linked. Dave said yes.

I thought there was no way they'd keep me on evenings forever and didn't want to miss the opportunity to take over from Pat White. I accepted Dave's offer, sure that eventually I'd be able to get out of the four-to-midnight shift and move to the *Here and Now* noon-to-eight shift worked by Pat and Bob Cole. It did happen, but not until I'd logged twelve years of evenings. When the CBC finally moved the national news two years later, the new offering was hailed as a ground-breaking package of first-rate journalism. It was called *The National* and *The Journal*, co-hosted by Knowlton Nash, Barbara Frum, and Mary Lou Finlay.

My late news show, which immediately followed *The Journal,* was thirty minutes and was given the name *Newsfinal.* It featured news with video reports, sometimes live interviews, a regional weather report from the weather board, and various sportscasters delivering nightly sports summaries. Before I left *Newsfinal* in 1992 for the noon-to-eight shift, the show I'd anchored for twelve years was averaging about 50,000 viewers nightly across Newfoundland and Labrador. Not bad, considering that for most of the 1980s we were competing against shows like *Dynasty*, *The Equalizer*, and *Miami Vice.*

By the end of 1979, Jack and I had become uneasy roomies. More and more we avoided each other's company. He was clubbing a lot and doing gigs as a piano player at Schroeder's Piano Bar and in the Holiday Inn dining room. My new evening shift meant my social life was limited. Our friends sensed a rift had developed between us, but I told nobody about Jack's infidelity. It was none of their business, and many of our gay friends would probably have said, "What's the big deal?" I began to wonder if there were any gay men out there who favoured monogamy. Thankfully, such a man would soon come into my life—on Saturday, January 5, 1980. His name was Larry.

10

A SMILE THAT INSTANTLY CONVEYED WARMTH

Given my permanent weeknight assignment, Saturday night was my best chance to meet people. I felt comfortable in gay and gay-friendly bars, but I noticed that while old friends were still welcoming, it was becoming difficult to make new friends. One night—ironically, at a bar called Friends (a gay bar above an iconic St. John's watering hole called the El Tico)—I bought a beer and sat at a table occupied by three men. One was an acquaintance. I turned to the stranger next to me and said "Hi, I'm Karl. What's your name?" He stared at me blankly and said, "Why? What do you want to know that for?" I was taken aback. He was treating me like I was the police. "Nothing. I'm just trying to be friendly." He mumbled something that sounded dismissive. I decided to move to another part of the bar.

I thought a great deal about the incident and similar ones that followed. It was bewildering. I talked to friends, and eventually I came to see why I was being marginalized. Most gays in the '70s, even ones who occasionally visited gay-friendly bars on a Saturday night, were still very closeted. Their families and friends didn't know they were gay, nor did acquaintances or co-workers. There was risk in being too open. You could be fired, kicked out of your home, or assaulted.

Even though many gays knew that I worked for CBC, I hadn't been a high-profile TV personality at first, not the kind who attracted a lot of attention from the Newfoundland and Labrador public. Being on *Here and Now*, a program that had a nightly audience of nearly a quarter-million viewers, put me in the limelight. It changed everything. Word that the new weatherman on *Here and Now* was gay was major gossip. The news sped along the provincial grapevine so fast that within months I was receiving hate mail at work from anonymous viewers living in urban and remote areas that I'd never visited. Some letters even contained tracts from the Bible supposedly condemning homosexuality.

I now think the gay community of the '70s and early '80s thought I'd become radioactive by becoming a TV personality with a gay label. Nobody who was closeted outside the darker areas of gay-friendly bars wanted to be seen speaking with Karl Wells. They feared they might be seen and labelled "gay" by association. I understood. And I felt sorry for them. It's extremely difficult for people who are frightened of losing the guardrails they've built around themselves and their lives. Especially those folks who grew up in homes with homophobic parents or were forced to listen to pastors, ministers, or priests talking about the grave sin of homosexuality.

I received troubling phone calls at work. One sniggering man, his voice dripping with hate, called to goad me: "Hey Karl! I hear you're great in bed!" Others called the general CBC TV newsroom number, invoked my name, and spewed their homophobic garbage. Reporters and producers who answered treated me like I was to blame. "Karl, someone just called about you and they were saying some pretty strange stuff." They'd never tell me what was said—"It was weird, that's all." It was obvious to me that it was something homophobic.

My unnerved straight male colleagues' reactions convinced me never to mention my private life at work. Not that anybody asked.

Except one smirking co-worker, a videotape operator, who did once ask me if it was true that I'd married a man in Florida. It was a few decades before gay marriage was legalized. I told him to fuck off. At the CBC, to quote American gay activist David Mixner, I became "a stranger among friends." I continued to nod and smile as they showed me photos of their wives and families, and shared their joys when a son or daughter won a scholarship or got good grades.

Nothing deterred me from living my life, a gay man who was good at his job and making a success of it, despite the homophobes, whoever and wherever they were. Years later, I was told by gay men who were teenagers at the time that they remembered hearing homophobes in their own families making bigoted comments about me every time I appeared on television. Some of those homophobic viewers may have been CBC employees, even managers. But I was confident that as long as I kept doing a good job, and was liked by most viewers, I'd have a degree of job security. Being a permanent employee with solid union representation and a strong collective agreement also helped.

If I wanted to go to a bar, I went, despite one bar manager telling me I didn't belong in his establishment. It was a bar called the Waterfront, toward the east end of Water Street. The bar was hosting a drag show in early May, one of the first in St. John's. The performer was local, and I was enjoying her show. During the chatter and laughter, the manager approached me and said, "You shouldn't be here."

"What?"

"You shouldn't be here."

"Why?" I asked.

"A man in your position shouldn't be here."

I was confused. Was he a self-loathing gay who believed I was too important to mix with the gays he catered to in his establishment?

More likely he, too, felt I was the kryptonite that many gays of that era had to avoid. I drew too much unwanted attention to the bar and its patrons. It was a time when flying under the radar was seen as necessary for survival.

During the Christmas season of 1979, I was scheduled to work through the holidays. As the CBC scheduler, Howard Moore, once put it to me when I questioned always having to work the holidays, "Karl, you're not a family man . . . and, you know, the other boys want to be with their families at Christmas. And that's understandable." I resented the term "family man." It implied I was a lesser mortal. I wanted to let Howard know that gay people had families, too, but I knew that without seniority, it was useless to complain in those days. It was a very different CBC then. So, I worked the holidays.

On Saturday, January 5, 1980, I went to Friends. The bar was hopping. Sipping my usual Black Horse beer, I stood by the side of the dance floor enjoying the dancers, the disco lighting, and the music. The speakers were pumping out Christmas disco by the Salsoul Orchestra: "Deck the Halls," "Jingle Bells," "Joy to the World." I was rocking a brown suede windbreaker with standing collar, white button-down shirt, blue jeans, and loafers.

At the other end of the room, bordering the dance floor, stood a cigarette vending machine. There was a beer bottle on top of the machine, and the hand holding it belonged to a handsome guy standing in the glow of a soft, warm light. He looked about my age, early twenties, with expressive eyes, a short, well-trimmed beard, light-brown hair, and full, sensuous lips. I could tell he was well-built by the fit of his clothing. He wore a short, grey windbreaker with a turned-up collar. Underneath the jacket I saw a grey turtleneck. His jeans were slightly flared at the bottom, and his polished black leather boots had slightly higher than average heels.

Like me, he was on his own. He looked straight, but was staring at me. I assumed he was looking at me because he'd recognized me from TV. I didn't think for a second he was cruising me. Then I got worried because of the hate mail and hateful calls I'd received at work. What if he followed me outside and beat the crap out of me? Just as I was thinking I should leave my friend Clarence Legge tapped me on the shoulder.

Clarence, smiling broadly and holding a beer, always greeted me like a long-lost friend, even if I'd only seen him the week before. I asked if he knew the guy leaning against the cigarette machine, and if he was gay. He confirmed that he was gay, and then nearly fell over laughing when I said, "Thank God. I thought he might be a gay basher."

Clarence was a hairstylist and so practised in the art of innocuous repartee that it carried over and became the way he interacted with everybody. That's why I always found it difficult to know who Clarence was underneath the façade. Of course, gay men of my generation and earlier generations had to be careful to keep swathes of their lives secret. Self-preservation is a powerful motivator. No matter, Clarence was a generous human being with a good heart, which is why he was my friend. He offered to introduce me to my admirer at the cigarette machine.

Having done as promised, Clarence made himself scarce. The handsome stranger was named Larry Kelly. Larry. My near-sightedness hadn't done him justice. Larry was even more handsome close up. He had a smile that instantly conveyed warmth. It made you feel good. We were both a little tongue-tied and awkwardly attempted to make conversation. At first all I could do was pull a cigarette from the pack of filtered Matinees in my pocket and ask Larry for a light.

We managed to share some basic information about each other. He knew who I was and what I did for a living. It turned out he worked across the street from CBC TV at the Health Sciences Centre. He was a medical technician. As the evening progressed, it became clear that we'd made a connection. We liked each other, and we were strongly attracted.

Jack was spending the weekend with his family in Victoria. I invited Larry back to the apartment. As we were leaving, I passed Clarence, who leaned into my ear and began to sing the matchmaker song from *Fiddler on the Roof.* I laughed and waved bye-bye. Before heading out, I needed the men's room. As I was doing a quick mirror check, I felt a tug on my jacket from behind. It was Larry. He pulled me toward him and kissed me on the lips. Not a peck, but a passionate, romantic kiss. Then, together, we left the bar.

As the sun rose and flooded my bedroom with the warm, pale light of early morning, I slowly began to wake. I felt those tender lips delicately kissing my forehead, my nose, my cheeks and lips. One gentle kiss after another. I smiled and wondered: is this love? Everything that had happened the night before played back in my head. Our awkward first conversation, our first kiss, sitting on the apartment sofa sharing our stories, and finally, entering the bedroom hand in hand and making love. I opened my eyes and there, coming slowly into focus was Larry's face, wearing that now familiar, beautiful smile. I wanted what I was feeling at this moment to be a recurring part of my life.

Larry and I promised to stay in touch. I knew we would. It was clear we both had strong feelings for each other. Over the next several weeks, there were successful coffee dates and lunches. Everything pointed toward a permanent partnership developing between us, especially after Larry told me he believed the only true relationship was a monogamous relationship. I was hopeful, and happier than I'd been in a long time. Then Larry dropped a bomb.

He called and wanted to meet to tell me something. I became concerned. His tone was different, troubled. We met at the apartment.

I was desperate to know why he seemed distressed. "What's going on?" I asked. "I'm married," he said. I was so shocked I went into a daze. When my head cleared, he told me he was married to a woman four years his senior. She was also from Glenwood, Larry's hometown. He lived with his wife and her mother. They'd been married almost five years and had no children. He told me his wife, Mary, had known he was gay for some time and was resigned to the inevitability of separation and divorce. I asked him why he got married. Larry said he always felt guilty having sexual feelings for men. He wanted to be like his married uncles and have a wife and children. Mary desperately wanted to marry. Larry, being an immature eighteen-year-old, believed that marrying Mary would finally resolve his feelings toward men and his guilt. The marriage worked for a few years, until he finally accepted that he was gay. I told Larry I needed time to think.

I was angry with Larry and with myself. Getting involved with a married man was something I'd vowed never to do. Now I was being tested. My thinking on the topic of gay men marrying women was unequivocal. I saw it as deception. It was simply wrong to marry, knowing you were gay or questioning whether you were gay. Perhaps I wasn't giving enough credence to the argument that societal pressures to conform, such as ones Larry may have been subjected to growing up in a staunch Catholic family (he'd served as an altar boy), were powerful. Nevertheless, with a large measure of doubt about the decision, I ended things with Larry.

I ignored his calls for a few weeks, but I couldn't stop thinking about him. During worknights I'd stand in the CBC TV newsroom window and look across at the Health Sciences Centre. I'd wonder if Larry was over there, also working. Eventually I answered one of his calls and we decided to meet for coffee. It was after work one night, near midnight. I went across to the hospital when he was on-shift and on a break. We met in the dimly lit, mostly deserted cafeteria, surrounded by large, stark David Blackwood etchings.

A few weeks later, Jack moved out of the apartment and Larry moved in, with his suitcase of clothes and little more. We'd reconciled. My thinking had been black and white. I'd failed to realize that while some gays married and took advantage of women to conceal

Larry about to dine in our first apartment. I made a cheese soufflé.

their homosexuality, others married believing they could build a relationship and family with a woman they loved, or thought they loved. And being human, hell, sometimes we're just confused. Some lesbians had married men for similar reasons.

Sexual orientation is complicated. While I believe in the institution of marriage, I don't believe it's for everyone. Nor do I believe that individuals should be pressured to marry. Both parties must believe in marriage and want it very much. You must also be prepared to continuously work hard to keep it strong. The rewards will make the effort worthwhile.

I agreed to pay Jack what he estimated was his share of all the furniture we'd purchased for the apartment during our relationship. He was anxious to rent a new place with new furniture. I got a loan to pay him. Larry and I were happy that we'd made it through and were on the verge of making a life together. He'd decided to seek a divorce from Mary and to tell his family everything about us. Neither of those decisions was easy, and the reaction to both was swift and bitter. In the case of his family, bitter and cruel.

Mary and her mother were livid. This, even though Larry had told Mary before we met that he was gay, and that he'd had liaisons with men. His mother-in-law told him, "We're gonna take you to the cleaners!" Within weeks I was approached in the second-floor hallway of CBC TV by a man wearing a raglan. I had no idea who he was or why he was making a beeline for me. He stared, saying, "This is for you," handed me an envelope, turned, and quickly left. The man was from the Newfoundland High Sheriff's office.

I'd just been served a court document naming me as a co-respondent in Larry and Mary's divorce. Some months later, John Baker, our *Here and Now* lineup editor, approached me with what looked like a rolled-up sheaf of papers. "Here, take it, you don't want anyone around here to see that," said John as he walked away. It was a copy of the court gazette, routinely received by CBC News back then, which contained, among other items, the record of Larry and Mary's divorce naming me as co-respondent.

While Larry's divorce wasn't as smooth as he thought it might be, neither was it especially difficult. Our greatest and most long-lasting disappointment and hurt came from the reaction of members of his family: Larry's parents Cyril and Joan, and two of his brothers—who expressed a desire to do me physical harm. Their reaction was driven by homophobia, ignorance, and religion. Larry's mother was a devout Roman Catholic, and she'd done her best to make sure her nine children kept the faith. Initially Larry wasn't welcome back home. His father said, "I don't want to see him again." Then his mother made an appointment for Larry to see the bishop of Grand Falls for counselling. She thought the bishop might convince him he was making a terribly sinful mistake.

Joan Kelly didn't know that before Larry and I met he'd already visited two priests for counsel about his homosexual feelings. When Larry first realized he might be gay and that his marriage was in jeopardy, he went to see a priest. He regularly attended mass in those days. The priest showed Larry contempt, not compassion. He lashed out, saying, "You're in for it! It's a very dark road you're going down." Later Larry confided in an older priest who also gave him an icy scolding. Like so very many Roman Catholic gays before him, Larry abandoned the Roman Catholic Church, never to return. He quickly declined his mother's arranged meeting with the bishop. He tried his best to educate his parents, to make them understand that being gay wasn't a sin or unnatural or wrong, but that was an uphill, mostly pointless struggle.

Larry's father later accepted our relationship, but sadly, it took his mother years. Larry was eventually welcomed back into his family home, but not with me. His mother needed something or someone to hold accountable for what had happened to her son, and she blamed me for making Larry gay. Joan Kelly claimed she couldn't watch *Here and Now* anymore, because the sight of me upset her too much. It took ten long and painful years before I was allowed to visit his parents' house.

One evening after dinner, as Larry and I were sitting watching TV in the den of our first real home on Larkhall Street in St. John's, I suddenly became overwhelmed with emotion at the news he was going to make his annual Christmastime trip to Glenwood, to spend a night with his parents. I couldn't go, because even after a decade I was still not welcome by his mother. The heartache of not being able to go home with my spouse yet again was too much. I broke like a dam and sobbed. Larry was shaken. He'd never seen me cry before. He put his arm around me, holding tight as I tried to explain. He decided he'd call his mother and tell her that he wouldn't be going home anymore unless I was welcome to come with him. He bluntly told her, "Either you accept Karl or you don't see me. I'm done." We made the next trip home together. In the following decades Joan and Cyril got to know me and I got to know them. They soon learned I wasn't the demon they'd imagined, and I realized they weren't the heartless people I'd resented for years. Before his parents died, Larry and I shared many happy moments with them. We made them laugh and they made us laugh. I'm thankful that eventually they came to respect and appreciate the loving bond Larry and I share.

Not long after we became a couple, Larry decided he wanted to improve his qualifications and work at a more professional level in health care. He studied nursing. Over the years, he earned an RN, a BN, an MSc, and various diplomas. (Decades later, Larry retired after a career as a hospital manager and administrator.) While Larry pursued his RN, I approached my work with renewed energy, happier than I'd ever been in my life. My on-air performance was noticeably brighter, more energized. On a spring shopping trip downtown in 1980, I ran into gay businessman Bill "Bart" Bartlett. (At the time, Bart owned and operated the late-night eatery Yucci's, near the War Memorial. Lots of us gays frequented Yucci's after the bars. Bart later opened the gay bar Madame's.) Bart said, "Karl, my gosh! What's going on with you? I saw you on TV this week and you looked so energized, so happy!" I nodded. My new relationship with Larry had changed my life for the better.

Career developments since Dad's passing continued to improve my work life as well. With my television career, as in radio, I'd been assigned to host shows outside of news, such as CBC TV's annual *Stars of the Festival* with the Kiwanis Music Festival, and was asked to take on some acting gigs. I appeared on the children's show *Skipper and Company*, with Ray Bellew. It was the first *Skipper* episode and the first local TV production to employ special effects from start to finish. Given my interest in TV production and acting, it was perfect for me, and I enjoyed the experience. CBC producer/director Wayne Guzzwell was very proud of the finished product.

In the episode, Skipper accidentally shrinks himself to the size of a thimble after a magic trick goes wrong. Ray, as Skipper, did his part entirely in green screen to appear thimble size. I played a burglar who breaks into his lighthouse. While I stuffed my sack with loot, Skipper hid behind candlesticks and teacups, occasionally shaking his fist at me while he tried to reverse the spell he'd cast on himself. Ray couldn't stop laughing at the way I looked once the costume and makeup people finished with me. He said, "Karl you look like Ray Milland in *The Lost Weekend!*" I'd been given a very dark five o'clock shadow and wore a battered overcoat. I got Ray's *Lost Weekend* reference, thanks to having watched so many 1940s films on Sunday afternoon TV, but I strongly suspected I looked more like Fred Flintstone in a raglan. At any rate I was happy I'd given Ray several good giggles that day. He was one of my favourite colleagues. Ray Bellew had an encyclopedic knowledge of Hollywood movies and showbiz. He lived to entertain people and was enormous fun to be around.

An opportunity also came my way to act on *90 Minutes Live* with Peter Gzowski, a national weeknight talk show that was meant to be CBC's more highbrow answer to Johnny Carson's *The Tonight Show* on NBC. Occasionally the program travelled, sets and all, outside its Toronto base to major cities in provinces west and east. It made one trip to St. John's toward the end of its short life of two seasons. Our station was buzzing with preparation. It was rare for a live national show to originate from St. John's. Local resources were stretched to the limit, sometimes because of concessions that had to be made to accommodate the star. For example, he required a personal dressing room. We had separate dressing and makeup rooms for men and women, which were perfectly fine, but Gzowski wanted his own dedicated space.

Appearing on 90 Minutes Live *with Peter Gzowski.*

There was neither time nor inclination to build a new dressing room, so it was decided that the women's staff powder room would be converted into Peter Gzowski's private dressing room, complete with his name and star on the door. It wasn't opulent, but it was larger and better appointed than the men's facilities. The only other women's restroom in the building was the public one on the main floor. Unfortunately, nobody thought to inform women staff members that their main restroom was on loan to Peter Gzowski for his exclusive use—for a full week. Imagine Gzowski's surprise when he was joined in his private sanctuary by a woman startled to find a man in her powder room. He hightailed it out of there. Delicate diplomatic negotiations ensued, and the less appropriate men's restroom was reassigned to the women. Major crisis averted.

Meanwhile a look-alike for Queen Elizabeth II had been booked and was flying over from England to appear on *90 Minutes Live*. Her name was Jeannette Charles, an actress then making a name for herself impersonating the Queen in movies and TV shows such as *Saturday Night Live*. I was asked to play her companion, a viceregal type. The makeup people greyed my hair and eyebrows and gave me a bushy grey moustache. I wore tails and a bunch of fake medals. Her Majesty was indeed majestic in white fur stole, a crown, and jewellery that looked as if it had been borrowed from the Tower of London.

Jeannette was very kind and treated me like a fellow professional. She sensed I was a little nervous, and like a true pro tried to put me at ease by telling me exactly how a viceregal character would walk, gesture, speak and generally behave. My job was to ride with her in a Rolls-Royce borrowed from businessman Andrew Crosbie. A chauffeur would deliver us to the front entrance of the CBC building, where I would alight with Her Majesty (Jeannette) and accompany her up the steps of the CBC to the landing where Peter Gzowski was standing. I'd make a formal introduction, after which Gzowski would walk with

With Queen Elizabeth II impersonator, Jeannette Charles.

Her Majesty into the building and studio. It went perfectly, like a dream, all done live and covered seamlessly by a team of cameramen.

Peter Gzowski was not made for live TV. It wasn't his medium. He looked nervous, tentative, and uncomfortable before live TV cameras. But on radio he was exquisite. There'd never been a CBC network host or interviewer who could match him. I was in awe of Gzowski when I first listened to him on *This Country in the Morning* and later radio shows he hosted on CBC FM and CBC Radio. His aw-shucks, warm radio personality sounded too genuine to be insincere. Sadly, I was wrong. After observing Peter Gzowski for a week, I observed that he wasn't warm and friendly off-air. He was surly, never smiled, and rarely responded when greeted. Sometimes he'd mumble a hi. Basic courtesy was beyond him. After I'd been dressed and made up for his show, I approached him to say hello; he turned and walked away.

I was having more fun getting to know my local CBC co-workers. The *Here and Now* director installed an overhead camera to get a live aerial shot of the studio, showing all the sets and hosts in their various settings. The overhead shots were used as bumpers to transition from one segment of the show to another or to take us to a commercial break. For example, a nightly shot was an overhead showing me walking across the studio floor after I'd done the weather. It took in the weather board, the anchor desk with Glenn Tilley, and me walking across the studio away from the weather set. Then the program cut to a slow zoom-in shot of Glenn Tilley at the desk taken by the floor camera that had just been shooting my weather report.

One night, before the advent of wireless microphones, I finished the weather and was a few seconds late beginning my walk across the studio for the overhead shot. I made a dash but was stopped in my tracks by my microphone cable. Someone had replaced my regular long cable with a very short one. It was plugged into an audio port in the studio wall. I was about to get caught in the middle of the floor camera shot picking up Glenn. Our floor director screamed, "Get out of the shot!" Knowing I was stuck in Glenn's shot, I panicked and threw myself onto the studio floor. My action put so much pressure on the stretched mic cable that it came flying out of the wall socket like a severed bungee cord. It twirled in the air and dropped, nearly clipping me in the head. The live overhead and floor shots revealed the whole farrago. I looked like someone ducking sudden gunfire as I face-planted myself onto the shiny black studio floor.

You may be wondering how Glenn Tilley reacted. He didn't. Not even a whisper of a smile. I was amazed by how Glenn would never break up when something ridiculous happened while he was on-air. He focused relentlessly on his own performance, nothing else. I was a giggler and always the first person on the show to crack. Never Glenn.

A highlight for me in those early CBC TV years was the arrival of WGB, the Wonderful Grand Band. Producer Jack Kellum had taken in one or two of the band's shows at the Strand Lounge in the Avalon Mall, and loved them, especially the comedy of actors Tommy Sexton and Greg Malone. Jack quickly pulled together an idea for a TV series eventually called *Wonderful Grand Band*. He had a reputation for getting what he wanted, and the series was given the green light. The production, the band, and actors created an exciting, energy-filled atmosphere in the building. While I was involved very peripherally by lending my voice to weekly promos for the series, I have fond memories of getting to know Tommy Sexton.

On Here and Now *with Glenn Tilley, 1978.*

Tommy and I frequently shared the men's makeup/dressing room while I was putting on my makeup for *Here and Now* and he was taking his off. The fact that we were both gay influenced our friendship. Tommy was one of the sweetest people I've ever known and possessed the brightest eyes and brightest smile. He loved to gossip and enjoyed hearing whatever bits were on the go. Sometimes our conversations were serious. We held the same dim view of gays who married women specifically to conceal their sexuality to get work promotions and further their careers. In one of our chats, Tommy made it clear that he didn't think much of certain gay actors he knew who'd deliberately married American women to obtain a green card. (This allowed them to live and work in the United States.)

Wonderful Grand Band, the TV show, unfortunately had a brief life—just three seasons when it was quietly cancelled. Only the CBC would kill an original Canadian show with record-breaking ratings. It was costly to make, but the significant commercial revenue should have helped offset *WGB's* high production budget. The reason for its cancellation was never given, although I had my suspicions. Occasionally the show featured sketches targeting religion and clerics, and these episodes drew complaints from church leaders. Petty complaints from CBC staff may have contributed as well. One day a props person was sent to Mary Jane's, a health food store, to purchase lettuce cigarettes for the *WGB* actors, because they wouldn't smoke tobacco cigarettes in a sketch. It was a busy traffic day, and unfortunately the props person was involved in a minor car accident. I saw him in the lobby when he returned and can still see his flushed face and hear him swearing about the actors wanting those "God damn lettuce cigarettes!"

One of the band members was a practitioner of tai chi. On nice days he'd spend his breaks practising it on the front lawn of CBC TV. A certain top level CBC manager who'd witnessed one of these sessions was convinced the musician was on drugs—presumably because he felt only someone on drugs would behave that way in public. Then there were the staff homophobes who had their hackles raised by the sight of Tommy and Greg in drag. It was quite usual to see the guys in the halls or canteen in costume, either as female or male characters. I heard one cameraman, clearly angry, say under his breath, "This is all bullshit!" as he followed Tommy and Greg (in drag) into the studio. Or perhaps CBC management didn't want provincial political leaders witnessing men in dresses when they came to CBC to be interviewed for *Here and Now*.

Bigotry of this sort was so acceptable in Newfoundland and Labrador at the time that certain provincial cabinet ministers had no qualms about making homophobic comments on TV and radio. I was shocked and angered one day in the 1980s when I heard a provincial cabinet minister say in an interview, "We can't give homosexuals special rights, because the next thing you know, we'll have men walking down Water Street in dresses." Liberal and PC politicians made homophobic comments with impunity.

CBC TV in Halifax was the biggest beneficiary of the cancellation of our Newfoundland and Labrador hit TV show by the CBC in St. John's. Halifax eventually signed contracts with several of the principals, and others, to develop and make a show there. It was called *CODCO* and aired on the national network. To this day Halifax is producing *This Hour Has 22 Minutes*, a national TV show with roots that trace directly back to St. John's and *Wonderful Grand Band*.

By 1981, Larry and I had settled into a comfortable domestic life. We were living in the rented top floor of a house in Kilbride. We still enjoyed going to clubs and socializing, although the joy was lessened by incidents such as one that occurred on George Street. It was a sunny spring afternoon, and we were casually walking. There was a group of guys drinking beer on the veranda attached to the

George Street entrance of the Rob Roy, a popular bar. I happened to glance their way and they were staring straight at us. Then one in the middle shouted menacingly, "There's that queer that works at CBC!" His voice was filled with contempt. We kept on walking and decided to go back home. The incident was upsetting, although I was more upset for Larry. It was the first time he'd been confronted by blatant hatred and homophobia in public. I couldn't help wondering if he'd realized what he was getting into by becoming my partner.

After that ugly incident I kept thinking about what might have happened if we'd been walking on George Street at night instead of in bright afternoon sunlight. Might those guys, emboldened by drink and pack mentality, have thrown their beer bottles at us, or chased and attacked us? We decided to put going to clubs and bars in the rearview mirror. We didn't know it then, but there was a tsunami of homophobia headed directly toward gay men around the globe.

Later that summer of 1981, after one evening meal, I picked up a magazine on the coffee table. As I leafed through it, the word "homosexuals" caught my eye. It was in the headline of a story about a rare form of cancer affecting gay men in New York and California. It was called Kaposi's sarcoma. The disease was appearing as violet spots on the legs of those affected. Worse still, eight of the forty-one victims had died less than twenty-four months after diagnosis. Doctors had no idea why the outbreak involved so many gay men.

I was gripped by foreboding. Somehow, I knew this wasn't going to stop at New York and California. I was also convinced that whatever this was, it was most certainly a disease that affected human beings, not just the gay ones. There had to be a logical reason why, in these cases, gay men were falling victim to what some would later despicably refer to as the Gay Plague. While darker and darker clouds were building all around our gay community, we braced ourselves for what was about to be unleashed.

11

YOU KNOW THAT DISEASE . . .

A strong winter storm that had been developing near Newfoundland for several days brought about devastating events on Sunday, February 14, and in the early hours of February 15, 1982. I woke up that Monday morning, switched on CBC Radio and heard my colleague Doug Laite read the news about the oil rig *Ocean Ranger* being in trouble on the Grand Banks, off Newfoundland's southeast coast. The rig had been reported listing in an area of the banks where the storm had been especially fierce. It was stunning news.

A ship caught in a wild North Atlantic storm is at risk, but a semi-submersible oil rig in the North Atlantic is also vulnerable. The *Ocean Ranger* was crewed by eighty-four people. I tried to recall the weather report I'd given the previous Friday, February 12. Strong storms in February weren't uncommon, and the predicted storm (at least on Friday) wasn't extraordinarily different. Of course, weather can change in forty-eight hours, and I presented inland, not marine weather on *Here and Now*. Those forecasts are different.

I knew it would be busy and pressurized in our TV newsroom that day, so I decided to get to work early. I had no idea how surreal it would be. Our newsroom was then situated in the rear of the CBC TV building, on the second floor. If you entered the building through the staff entrance off Westerland Road, you only had to take a few steps and turn left and you were inside one of the largest and busiest newsrooms in Newfoundland.

Normally I'd walk into the newsroom on a Monday and things would be relaxed and upbeat. A friendly face might catch my eye and ask, "Hello young fella, how was your weekend?" Not that day. I could have entered the room wearing a NASA spacesuit and nobody would have noticed. The room was fuller than usual, and the atmosphere was charged. I saw faces I didn't recognize. More unfamiliar faces would turn up over the next twenty-four hours. Many in the room were on the phone while frantically taking notes or typing. Groups of two, three, or four were huddled around the room, discussing, planning. Every desk was occupied. Some were using the tops of filing cabinets as writing desks.

It turned out the unfamiliar faces belonged to visiting network reporters with the CBC French and English services, and several loud, waste-no-time American journalists. The Americans and their crews worked for CBS and NBC. They were with us because the CBC had resource-sharing agreements with both networks. The NBC reporter was so loud you could hear him from the other side of the building. The indifference the American journalists showed toward each other was obviously feigned. They were fierce competitors. They'd roll over anybody or anything to get a story and get it first.

I headed for the St. John's Weather Office for my regular daily weather briefing. It was a gloomy drive on a gloomy day. When I walked into the airport office, weather specialist Walter Pearce, my briefer that day, was on the phone with a citizen of St. John's. I stood against a counter and waited. Then I heard Walter raise his voice to the caller. "Sir! You just accused me of being responsible for every marine disaster for the last thirty years!" I didn't need to ask what it was about. Lots of indiscriminate and misplaced lashing out took place over the following weeks and months.

In 1982, CBC field cameraman John O'Brien was enjoying life. He'd been with CBC TV for over a decade and was a well-respected professional in 16 mm photography. John had the weathered face and attitude of a farmer and would not look out of place plowing a field. His grey hair made him appear older than his fifty-six years. I liked and admired John very much. He was a gentleman and an uncompromising professional. Sometimes we'd chat while he was waiting in the newsroom to discuss an assignment with a producer or reporter.

But on one occasion he was more animated and enthusiastic than I'd ever seen him. I sat near the CBC's Newfoundland and Labrador national TV reporter, Barbara Yaffe. Barbara had a corner of the room to herself, with wall space—prime real estate. She had done some stories on the province's burgeoning oil industry, and on one of her coveted walls she'd hung a large picture of the *Ocean Ranger* oil rig. On the afternoon of John's display of unusual enthusiasm, he'd been pointing to the *Ocean Ranger* picture and giving me detail after detail about its construction. "Karl, ya see that deck? That deck's the size of two football fields. She's unsinkable," he'd say with the conviction of a religious convert. I'd nod politely, but oil rig statistics didn't really fire me up.

On February 15, 1982, I noticed John keeping to himself in the newsroom. He'd been there since I arrived earlier that day. He appeared to be deep in thought. He'd stand near groups who were conferencing, head slightly tilted, hand on chin, listening and processing the information. John didn't miss a single word. During the day, frustration was slowly developing in the room because Mobil Oil was providing so little information. Mobil was responsible for the *Ocean Ranger's* activities, but its representatives were reluctant to answer basic questions about the disaster. While reporters dealt with their frustrations by venting, I saw that John, who still hadn't left the room, was dealing with something else. His face was pale, a picture of distress. I asked producer Kevin Norman why John looked so worried. "His son Ken is on the *Ranger*." I'd had no idea.

John rightly thought that when word came, any word, the newsroom would be the first to hear it. That's why he wouldn't go home. It was heartbreaking to see a father slowly coming to grips with the fact that he might never see, hold, or speak to his son again. Sadly, our worst fears were realized. John's son Ken was lost. John stayed strong until the end.

There were no survivors of the *Ocean Ranger* sinking. Of the eighty-four souls lost, only twenty bodies were recovered. Kenneth O'Brien was one of them, which at least afforded his family some closure. Ken was twenty-two years old. John, my colleague, was never the same after that dark day. He died twelve years later at sixty-eight. Anyone old enough to remember the *Ocean Ranger* will never forget that tragic time in our history.

On the night of Thursday, September 30, 1982, I was working with reporter Maureen Anonsen in the St. John's CBC TV newsroom. We were preparing news and weather for that night's *Newsfinal*. Maureen was trying to track down more details on a brutal downtown murder. The crime had been committed the previous night inside the Alley Pub, an after-hours tavern on Water Street with a mostly gay and gay-friendly clientele. (Larry and I had visited the Alley Pub a few times. One visit was memorable because a very intoxicated leading light of the St. John's theatre community, for no apparent reason, tried to goad Larry into a fight by hurling insults at him. Larry eventually shut him up by insulting his acting. He was a good actor really, but the poor guy was so devastated by Larry's comeback that he shut like a clam.) Although neither I nor Maureen was aware of the victim's name or the circumstances of the murder, it later turned out that we both knew the deceased personally.

Frank Howse was a generous, cheerful man. He was thin, balding, and handsome, with unblemished skin and eyes that twinkled. His clothes were often tight fitting and colourful. I once saw him wearing bright red plaid pants, a look I admired but could never carry off. Frank could, while wearing a signature smile that engaged every inch of his face, from his receding hairline down to his chin. I'd known Frank since I was a kid being taken by my parents to the Candlelight restaurant on Harvey Road. Frank was a waiter there, at times the only waiter. Years later I'd see him serving in the dining room of the Battery Hotel, delivering a tray of freshly made cocktails to a table, flaming pepper steak, or carving Chateaubriand for a couple of lovebirds. Sometimes he also tended bar at various downtown establishments, including the Alley Pub.

Maureen had been on the phone with the constabulary for some time. She was sitting at the editorial desk at the back of the room. I heard her hang up the phone and looked in her direction. She appeared shaken.

"What is it?" I asked.

"Frank Howse is dead."

"Oh my God. What happened?"

"He was alone in the bar with this guy, after it closed, and apparently the guy attacked Frank and beat him to death with a beer bottle."

Maureen went on to reveal more of her conversation with the constabulary officer. She had been pressing him to find out the name of the perpetrator.

"Do you know what the cop said to me when I asked for the name of the guy who killed Frank?"

I could tell she was about to reveal something she thought reprehensible. "What?" I asked.

"He said, 'Why don't ya give the guy a break? The fella made a pass at him.'"

Both Maureen and I were angered by what the cop had said, but not really surprised. The Royal Newfoundland Constabulary, at the time, was not unique in turning a blind eye to the homophobia and bigotry within its ranks. So did institutions such as the CBC. The facts were clear: Frank was brutally attacked and beaten in the head with blunt force until he was unconscious and left for dead. There's no way of knowing for sure what transpired immediately before the attack, but there is evidence that the murder of Frank Howse was a hate crime.

We later learned that Frank Howse was murdered by an offshore oil worker named John Robert Edwards. Another Alley Pub patron had heard him that night muttering under his breath about "queers and faggots."

That night's lead story on *Newsfinal* was about the Alley Pub murder. As I announced details of what had transpired, the director ran film footage taken outside the pub. It showed a body bag being removed from the premises and carried through a narrow alley to a waiting ambulance. As I was speaking, I looked at the images on the sunken desk monitor next to me. It was hard, reading the words Maureen had written, aware that our friend Frank's blood-soaked body was inside that black bag. Knowing that that bright, compassionate, loving human being would no longer be spreading his own brand of joy in our corner of the world.

An uneasy calm pervaded the St. John's gay community following first reports of the mysterious illness in New York and San Francisco. Some of our friends chose to bury their heads and ignore the reports, while others took the view that since it wasn't happening in Newfoundland, there was no reason to be alarmed. Larry and I thought otherwise. We reasoned that it would likely soon arrive on our shores and not leave without taking lives with it. If it was spreading from gay man to gay man, and since a number of Newfoundland gays vacationed in Montreal, Toronto, New York, and San Francisco, it was reasonable to assume that some might become ill. They could, unknowingly, give the sickness to others in Newfoundland and Labrador.

The US Centers for Disease Control and Prevention (CDC) soon had a name for the malady: Gay-Related Immune Deficiency, or GRID. Sadly, this epidemic fed into the growing homophobia that began in the late 1970s, first in America, then in Canada and other western countries. American singer and born-again Christian Anita Bryant had successfully campaigned to repeal a Florida ordinance banning discrimination against gays and lesbians, while a year later, in 1978, a California ballot initiative unsuccessfully looked to ban gay and lesbian teachers.

Some Newfoundlanders echoed the homophobic rhetoric taking hold in the US. I remember driving my second-hand Ford Galaxy along Pennywell Road in St. John's during this time. It was midday and the car radio was tuned to a commercial AM station. A St. John's–based news commentator came on with an editorial endorsing the banning of homosexuals from teaching in schools. I remember him saying, "I wouldn't want my children to be taught by a homosexual." This was a prominent local voice saying he wouldn't want anyone of my sexual orientation teaching his children. I drove on, now feeling worthless and unfit to do the job for which I'd just received a bachelor's of education degree, to teach high school English.

It wasn't long before the cause of GRID was discovered and a new acronym was coined: AIDS, for Acquired Immune Deficiency Syndrome. A virus—HIV, or Human Immunodeficiency Virus—caused AIDS and was transmitted from human to human by the exchange of bodily fluids. Then we heard of an incubation period possibly lasting years, meaning some of the dying had been infected back in the 1970s.

Suddenly Larry and I felt we had the sword of Damocles hanging over us. We'd thought that because we'd only had sex with each other since beginning our relationship, we'd be okay. Now we felt there was a good chance HIV was inside us, biding its time. We had wills drawn up and for years bore the mental strain of the possibility of an early death.

Soon we began to receive word of gays in Toronto becoming ill, followed in the mid-1980s by news of the first cases of AIDS in Newfoundland. I was shocked to learn about Paul, an early victim—an acquaintance from one of the first gay house parties I attended in 1977. Paul always assumed he'd contracted AIDS and, even before being diagnosed, had adopted a fatalistic attitude. He didn't live long. An inexorable list of ill friends and acquaintances began, with a name added every few months. Often the death was not attributed to AIDS, but we knew the cause. Maxim Mazumdar was one, a theatre director and actor acquaintance who'd partied in my apartment in the late 1970s. I was a huge fan of Maxim's because of his exceptional talent and kindness.

In the early years of the AIDS epidemic, most people developed an irrational fear of folks with AIDS, or anybody who looked like they might have it. Of course, in those days most of society already feared gay men. I found the increasing fear of me in the CBC workplace almost too painful to bear. The most egregious example was an ugly broadside by then *Here and Now* sportscaster Carl Lake. It happened one afternoon while I was alone in CBC TV's Studio One. I was working at the large weather map, preparing it for my evening broadcast. Referring to notes I was holding in my left hand, every so often I'd make a small cheat note or symbol on the board, a memory aid for that night's forecast. I hadn't heard the control room door behind the news set open. Nor did I hear Carl Lake's slow, deliberate footsteps as he approached.

When he was about four yards away, I sensed a presence, looked up, and saw him. Lake was wearing his CBC-issued sportscaster jacket and a malevolent expression. With neither of us saying anything, he came to within two feet of my face and looked directly at me with cold, dead eyes. Finally, he spoke.

"You know that disease that those guys in New York got, with those purple spots all over their legs? You're gonna get that, and you're gonna die."

His words were delivered with heavy emphasis on the word "die," as he pointed his finger accusingly in my face. As I stood paralyzed with shock and fear, he calmly turned and walked out of the studio. That night I had to appear on *Here and Now* with Lake and Glenn Tilley, and act as if nothing had happened. I didn't report him because I believed he had voiced what many of my co-workers, including some CBC management, were thinking. My working relationship with Lake was frosty until the day he left CBC in the late 1980s.

Generally, it became common for CBC co-workers to treat me like I had skull and crossbones on my forehead. Many would pass me in the hallway hugging the wall, face cast downward. A few even appeared to hold their breath as they passed. One reporter, "Tom," was the worst. Tom was so fearful of getting physically close to me, he'd take detours to avoid me. People stopped offering me a chip, if they had a bag of chips—unless the bag was almost empty. Then they'd say, "Keep the bag. You have the rest."

I was ordering a coffee in the CBC canteen one day and the proprietor said, "Hello darling, how are you feeling now?"

"I'm good, good."

"Oh, I'm glad, dear. I heard you were in Montreal for treatment."

"Treatment? Treatment for what?"

"Oh, nothing. I just heard you were sick that's all."

Clearly the rumour mill had me down as a person with AIDS, desperately seeking treatment from specialists in Montreal. In fact, I had been in Montreal for a few days hoping to decompress from the heavy atmosphere in St. John's and at work. It helped, although whenever I spent time with my friend Jerry Bartlett, then studying law at McGill, black humour and serious topics were frequently on the agenda. At that time Jerry was using dark humour more and more as his way of coping with the horror happening around us.

Once we were in Le Mystique, a gay bar on Stanley Street, a favourite of Jerry's. As we stood drinking our beers at a high-top pub table, I noticed Jerry staring contemplatively at a rail-thin young man several yards away. Jerry said quietly with a sigh, "God, I wish I had a touch of AIDS. I'd love to lose some weight." Then, to my surprise, Jerry brought up the topic of death. I asked him if he was afraid of dying. He told me he wasn't but that he didn't want to die in pain. "I can't bear pain, Karl. I really can't bear pain." Not long after I was back home in St. John's, Jerry announced he'd be moving to Toronto after his graduation. I looked forward to seeing him there.

John Murphy, famous owner of the Arcade budget retail store on Water Street, became mayor of St. John's in 1981. His election as mayor, and my ability to mimic Murphy's voice, brought another radio acting opportunity my way a few years into his term of office. I sometimes entertained the *Here and Now* crew by doing my impression of the mayor just before going on-air. I'd repeat and sometimes add to things I'd heard him say in a news report or on an open-line show. For example, in the summer of 1978 he'd told CBC reporter Mary McKim he intended to have "all Arcade employees up on the roof of the Arcade waving Union Jacks" to honour Queen Elizabeth II during her visit to St. John's. I had great fun with that little skit, which was based on an interview with Murphy about a shortage of red, white, and blue Royal Tour bunting in St. John's.

Quite unexpectedly one day, well into the mayor's term of office, I received a call from John Furlong, the new producer of CBC Radio's *The Morning Show*. He asked if it was true I could "talk like John Murphy" and if he could hear me say something in the mayor's voice. I obliged. Then he asked if I'd be interested in doing a weekly impression on *The Morning Show*. I wasn't interested in what he proposed, which was for me to appear on his show and ad lib or write up "something funny" to perform every week. It sounded uncooked to me. We ended the conversation after I told John Furlong I'd only do it if he could find a writer who could deliver a well-tailored, topical script every week. I suggested a few names and we ended the call amicably.

Several days later, Furlong called again and asked if I'd do the John Murphy impression if Ray Guy wrote the scripts. I had tremendous respect for Ray and had admired his writing since the days of his newspaper column covering the Smallwood years. Because I also liked and respected John Murphy, I reserved the right to omit anything in a script I found to be off-colour or in bad taste.

Shortly after I agreed to perform Murphy on *The Morning Show*, I received a call from Ray Guy. Ray asked me to do the impression for him. He chuckled and we chatted about how the scripts should be crafted. I reminded him about Max Ferguson's satirical sketches from the 1960s. I saw the Murphy pieces along the same lines, with plenty of sound effects. I told Ray how I created a caricature of someone's voice much like a cartoonist does someone's face. The cartoonist emphasizes certain facial features that stand out. If a person has a large nose, the cartoonist makes it bigger, and so on.

For me, as an impressionist, it's certain vocal tics or habits and whether a person has a unique pronunciation of certain words. John Murphy had the habit of starting many sentences with, "Well, you know," and he always pronounced the word "tremendous" as "tremenjus," and the word "after" as "arfter." I told Ray I would send him a list of the phrases, words, and vocal habits he should emphasize in the scripts. We discussed a title for the series and Ray suggested *His Honour*. I recommended we go with *His Worship*, because in

With His Worship John Murphy and his second wife, Sheilagh Guy Murphy.

Canada, mayors are addressed as "Your Worship." That's how *His Worship* was born.

His Worship was an instant hit, and became the most popular weekly feature on *The Morning Show*. Sometimes the pieces were based on things happening at City Hall and sometimes they were hilarious sketches originating solely from the imagination of Ray Guy. Several, for example, were set on St. Pete's Beach, Florida, where Murphy had a condo that he occasionally visited in wintertime. Huge positive reaction came when we had the mayor strolling along St. Pete's Beach wearing nothing but bathing trunks and his chain of office ("so hot to the touch!"). That image alone was priceless.

Ray had created a scenario in which His Worship, while walking along the sand, was constantly bumping into powerful and prominent people from St. John's, prostrate on their colourful towels, soaking up the rays of St. Pete's sun. As he bid good day to each of them, he'd deliver witty, sometimes catty asides. Ray had Premier Frank Moores's current wife and both exes on the same stretch of beach. As His Worship greeted them, he'd identify the Mmes Moores with, "Oh hello, Mrs. Moores!" or "There's the other Mrs. Moores," or "Here's another Mrs. Moores." Brilliant writing and very easy for listeners to know what we were up to. I had a ball performing Ray's lines and was grateful he'd agreed to allow me to tweak scripts as I saw fit. It was a delightful, satisfying partnership for both of us.

Among the listener compliments that came our way was a handwritten letter on expensive, cream-coloured, personalized stationery with "Smithville Crescent" at the top. It was dated April 15, 1983, and sent me personally by Mayor Murphy's wife, Marjorie Murphy.

> Dear Karl,
>
> Just a note to tell you we really enjoyed the CBC program *His Worship*—You sounded so much like John that we had many calls asking if it was or not! In our opinion, (especially mine!) it was very witty—unfortunately we will be out of town and will miss the next two—is there any way we could hear them later? Good luck.
>
> Sincerely,
> Marjorie Murphy

I was pleasantly surprised by Mrs. Murphy's reaction to *His Worship*. Politicians and their families usually grin and bear being satirized. They never signal enthusiasm. A few months later I read a second letter from Marjorie Murphy, in the same hand, on the same stationery, addressed to the regional director of CBC Newfoundland and Labrador, John Power. It would call into question everything she had said in her personal letter to me.

His Worship had been going strong and in production for just under twelve months when *The Morning Show* producer, John Furlong, asked if I could come to his office. I did. Furlong was sitting behind his desk. "What's this about, John?" I asked. He was silent, but he slowly, deliberately opened the top desk drawer to his right and took out a cream-coloured sheet of paper. He laid the paper in front of me, remaining silent. It was as if he were rehearsing a scene from an espionage movie. I looked at the sheet and immediately recognized the handwriting and letterhead. It was a letter from Marjorie Murphy to our regional director, John Power, whom she addressed as "John." I picked it up and read it.

The letter was in stark contrast to the one Marjorie Murphy had sent me. Essentially it came across as a letter from one friend to another, imploring John Power to cancel *His Worship* immediately. One line that stood out was, "It may be fun for Ray Guy and Karl Wells but it's not fun for me." Her main complaint was that I sounded so much like Mayor Murphy that "people actually think it's John!" She wrote that friends were calling her to ask if John was all right. Her objection was, in my view, without merit. We hadn't done anything controversial. There had not been a single other complaint.

I looked at Furlong with a so-what expression. He continued doing his impression of the Sphinx, shrugging his shoulders and not saying a word. I walked out. Furlong cancelled *His Worship* immediately. All it took was John Power passing on Marjorie Murphy's letter. The subject of the satire, the mayor himself, had never complained. It was his wife. Years later I learned from John Murphy that he had loved *His Worship*, had "got a great kick out of it." The CBC axed it based on one letter of complaint.

Ray Guy might not have known about Marjorie Murphy's involvement in *His Worship's* cancellation, given John Furlong's covert way of handling her letter. That may account for him laying the blame at the feet of John Power and the former mayor in a column he penned for the *Evening Telegram* on Sunday, March 5, 1995, titled "Preparing to Take Umbrage."

After some vintage Guy paragraphs about being harassed by the "aggrieved folk" who read his column, he wrote:

> Since then, I've had attacks on my livelihood and a public call for a contract on my life . . . both from religious champions among us.
>
> Mayor John J. Murphy is always after my scalp. Mostly on grounds of blasphemy. Either against the Creator or against himself, he can't seem to differentiate.
>
> For instance, I used to have a spot on CBC Radio *His Worship* with Karl Wells doing a great imitation of Johnny the Walker. But one day it was cut off square with no notice, no explanation.
>
> It was only after John Power retired as regional director of the CBC that he admitted that, yes, it got the chop because it annoyed His Worship.
>
> Thus, your Public Broadcaster.

His Worship had been a bright spot in my life. Whatever brightness existed in the world for Larry, me, and the gay community of the 1980s, was dimming. Bad news was about to be followed by worse. My friend Clarence Legge, who had introduced me to Larry, was beginning to look unwell.

12

I CAN'T LIVE MY LIFE IN FEAR

One afternoon we went to a party at Jerry Kelland's Duckworth Street apartment. We'd gotten to know Jerry through a mutual friend, Allan Davidson, who taught figure skating throughout Newfoundland and Labrador. Jerry Kelland, a sophisticated, erudite man and a great listener, was also an excellent chef. He once cooked a delicious dinner for Larry and me on a tiny two-burner stove. It was the first time I'd seen someone grate fresh nutmeg into a saucepan.

By 1985, the number of gay house parties was dwindling. They'd become much quieter, as if we were just going through the motions, pretending to have a good time. Little wonder. We were starting to see friends fade before our eyes. As we entered Jerry's apartment and turned to enter his small kitchen, I glanced in the living room and saw a face that looked familiar. It was Clarence Legge, staring into space, seated on a dull, shabby sofa. Everything about that afternoon was pale and drab. The atmosphere of the times had sucked all the colour out of the place.

I hadn't recognized Clarence immediately because he'd lost weight. His face was blemished by an angry spot on his forehead and a larger one on his left cheek. We'd last seen Clarence in Toronto where, after a night on the town, we spent another hour with him as he searched for a panzerotti takeaway. Pizza in a turnover was the new rage then. Along with Clarence, many of our other friends had moved to Toronto in the early or mid-'80s. Even Jerry Bartlett had just moved there, having graduated from McGill law school. That afternoon at Jerry Kelland's, Clarence said he was "just home for a quick visit." We made a date for him to come to our place for lunch later that week. It was summertime.

Clarence came over the following weekend. We sat at the kitchen table in the big picture window at the front of our Larkhall Street house. The cloudy north sky cast a dim light on the table and us. Clarence wore shorts and a thin, loose-fitting beige sweater. I was surprised he'd chosen shorts, because they exposed some purple scablike lesions on his legs. He now had a spot on the bridge of his nose. We tried our best to keep the conversation light as Clarence picked at the stir-fry I'd made. Neither of us asked him any questions about his health. He looked like a person being stalked by the Grim Reaper. Our hearts were breaking as he struggled to explain his appearance, but none of his reasons rang true. He knew it. Clarence had full-blown AIDS. It was the last time we saw our lovely matchmaker alive.

"Yes, Clarence went fast," agreed Jack Clarke, my ex, from behind the dark wood bar at Schroeder's, where he was working as a bartender and piano player. I was surprised to see Jack tending bar and even more shocked when he told me he'd quit his job at Canada Post. I asked him why and he told me he was fed up working a boring job and wanted to pursue music. I didn't buy it. Jack was too much of a penny-pincher to give up a job with security and a pension. We dropped the topic. Thereafter, the rare time we visited Schroeder's and Jack was working the bar, he'd update us on what news we may have missed about mutual friends in St. John's or on the mainland. Sadly, there was one update Jack deliberately chose not to provide.

Jack had AIDS and didn't tell me, his former partner. He kept this information from me until the day he died. It was only when he was approaching death that I was told, but not by Jack. My ex-sister-in-law, Marg, who had maintained a friendship with Jack after we'd broken up, told me. She knew but didn't want to be the person who gave me the news. Marg had been encouraging Jack to tell me because I deserved and needed to know. Jack would only say, "Oh Marg, he must know," or "he must know by now." Of course, I didn't. When Marg finally told me Jack was dying of AIDS, I went numb. After the information finally sank in, I felt sorrowful and angry. If I'd contracted AIDS, I might have given it to Larry. If I hadn't been monogamous, I could have given it to others.

Before he died, according to Marg, Jack repented his "sins" before God by way of the Pentecostal Church. When I heard this and realized he'd also repented for being gay, I got angry again. I decided, because of my frame of mind, that my speaking to Jack wouldn't have been good for him. I wasn't sure whether his decision to repent was something he wanted for himself or did under family and church pressure. Maybe it was a decision made in the fog of AIDS-related dementia. Whatever the reason, I hope it gave dear Jack some peace.

Although Larry and I had cut back considerably on our weekend visits to downtown clubs, occasionally we'd spend a night at one of the handful of gay bars. We liked to listen to the music, and Larry loved to dance. During the worsening AIDS epidemic, we went to a popular Duckworth Street second-storey gay spot. Usually, we stood at the large bar to have our beers and sometimes we'd bump into someone we knew. One night I used the club's restroom, and while I was washing my hands, in the dim light I noticed a pile of handbills in the garbage can. There must have been forty or fifty printed sheets. I fished one out of the trash and read it. My heart sank. They were handouts from GAIN (Gay Association in Newfoundland) warning gay men about AIDS and strongly advising the use of condoms. Someone had thrown them in the garbage.

I walked back to the bar shaking my head, thinking there must be some logical reason for what I'd seen. It didn't make sense that anyone would get rid of notices that could potentially save lives. Later that night someone I knew stopped to chat and I asked if they had any idea why the leaflets were tossed in the garbage.

"Oh yeah, I know. It happens all the time. The owner doesn't want them in the place because he thinks it's bad for business. Too much of a downer."

It flew in the face of reason that anyone with a conscience could hold such an attitude. If the spread of AIDS wasn't curbed—and at the time HIV infection was a death sentence—the owner or owners of the club could be seen as refusing to assist in preventing the spread of a disease that might result in the deaths of their customers. No customers, no business. It made no sense. Perhaps the decision to get rid of the pamphlets was simply a result of panic and fear. There was a lot of both going around in the 1980s.

Larry and I didn't discuss our previous boyfriends much, but it was unavoidable when they showed up at our front door. Keith Noseworthy, for example, was Larry's beau before me. He was ex-Navy, from Pouch Cove, in his mid-twenties. They met when Keith was working in retail in St. John's, after serving in the Navy for years. I later discovered that he and I had attended Prince of Wales Collegiate at the same time. In our 1970 yearbook Keith wrote that his ambition was "to become a doctor." Mine was "Broadcasting." Keith had moved to Toronto after his St. John's retail work ended. Larry considered moving there with him but ultimately decided it wouldn't have worked out.

It was fall when Keith showed up at our door on Larkhall Street. He breezed into the house like an autumn gale, the kind that sends leaves swirling high into the air. Keith was up—too up—all the time. He wore a short brown leather jacket and white chinos. His dark brown hair was full, longish, and expertly cut. Beneath his slightly stubby nose was an irresistible grin. On the surface, Keith was a glib charmer. Underneath, he was a decent, caring guy.

He irritated me like hell the first few times we met. I suspected he was either trying to win Larry back or make me jealous. (It wasn't difficult to make me jealous.) It was never enough for Keith to greet Larry with a hug and peck on the cheek. He would grab Larry and kiss him on the lips, while holding him in a tight body-on-body press. He'd look Larry in the eyes and say, "Wow! How are you, handsome?" He overwhelmed us, and when he'd leave, we'd let out a long sigh of relief.

Eventually we adjusted to a happy friendship with Keith and even visited him and his roommate when they lived in Toronto's Cabbagetown neighbourhood. Keith found it difficult to find and establish a satisfying career for himself after the Navy. (I don't believe he was ever serious about becoming a physician.) The happiest we ever saw him was when he worked at a beautiful upscale Yorkville restaurant called Sassafraz. Being a server suited his ebullient personality. Many of his co-workers were gay and, of course, he earned big tips.

Keith visited us when AIDS was starting to gain a foothold in Toronto's gay community. I tried to have a serious conversation with him about AIDS, but he would have none of it. He didn't want to hear about precautions or condoms or anything else. "No. I can't. I won't live my life that way. I can't live my life in fear. Whatever happens, happens," he stated flatly. I got the impression it wasn't the first time he'd made that speech. Keith's was not an isolated attitude. I'd received a similar response from gay friends and acquaintances in St. John's.

A few years later, Larry got a call from Keith. He was in town and wanted to have lunch. On the phone he didn't sound quite like the old

Keith, not as upbeat. They arranged to meet at Papa's Place restaurant in Churchill Square. When Larry arrived, Keith was already there. By this time, we'd seen so many people with AIDS that when Larry saw Keith, he didn't need to hear the diagnosis. He was emaciated and a few of his teeth were missing. His hair was dull and thinner; his light shirt and dark pants, both faded from wear, didn't fit properly anymore.

Keith made no mention of his illness, not even to explain why he needed to go to the men's room so often during lunch. It was a quiet meal with conversation of shared yet still vivid memories of happy, carefree times. He and Larry both realized it might be the last time they would see each other. It was. Several years later when we were in Toronto's gay village, we visited Cawthra Square Park and the AIDS memorial. Among the names listed on one of the metal plates was Keith Noseworthy. We both touched his name and remembered the relentlessly upbeat, smiling Keith who had been our friend in the blossoming of our lives.

Having so many friends who were or had been very close to us become ill and die so young was frightening and depressing. The weight of the stress we carried grew daily. HIV testing put our minds at rest a little: we were not infected. But there was no stopping the monthly, then weekly phone calls or casual conversations that brought more bad news, more names. We became accustomed to all news being bad news.

Larry and I both knew, given how close we'd been to so many people with AIDS, that if we had not become partners in 1980 and maintained a monogamous relationship, we would probably have contracted AIDS, like Clarence, Jack, and Keith. Despite our relatives having knowledge of the health crisis affecting our friends and community, I found it disappointing that none of them ever asked us how we were coping. It wasn't surprising, I suppose, given the ingrained reluctance of most of the population to discuss 2SLGBTQI+ topics.

The *Cambridge Dictionary* describes survivor's guilt as "difficult and painful feelings caused by the fact that you are still alive after a situation in which other people died." These days, some professionals consider survivor's guilt to be a form of PTSD. I had survivor's guilt. I thought I should be dead. I asked myself questions: why have I been spared? I'm gay, my friends were gay, so why am I not wasting away and covered with lesions? Why am I still alive? I still ask those questions.

If you're very fortunate, an extraordinary person may enter your life at some point. A person with whom you connect on multiple levels. You may share a similar sense of humour, political views, artistic sensibility, et cetera. And that person will become a friend like no other. They will lift you up, enable you to see beyond the narrow confines of your life, encourage you to be better. My husband Larry is such a friend. I thank God daily that Clarence introduced us that January night. Such friends aren't always people with whom you become romantically involved, but the ability these friends have in common is to profoundly influence you in a positive way. If such a friend comes into your life, cherish them, nurture their friendship, and never take it for granted, because there is no guarantee that they will be in your life for years, or even months.

Jerry Bartlett was also one of my extraordinary friends. The day we learned that Jerry was dying of AIDS felt like a thousand pieces of the world Larry and I shared had suddenly crumbled to dust. He had kept his illness quiet, stubbornly deciding to fight it on his own and maintain a normal life. He wanted to remain in Toronto and in the apartment he loved. Of course, at the time, there was little chance an AIDS sufferer would be able to maintain a normal life.

When I'd receive word that yet another friend was gravely ill, my mind would always take me back to certain moments in the times we shared. Jerry loved to choose feminine names for his close gay friends. A mutual friend from St. John's, living in Dorval during

Jerry's Montreal years, was given the name Millie. We walked into our friend's house one day and Jerry saw a photo of our friend and his St. John's family. He quipped, "Oh look, Millie and the Millettes!"

I was honoured when Jerry decided I was worthy of a feminine name. He started calling me Karlotta, and sometimes Karlotte. He was famous for pulling stunts out of the blue. On several occasions, I stayed with him and his good friend Neil (who also died of AIDS) when they shared a rented Victorian house in Rosemont, Montreal. The last time I stayed there, before Jerry graduated from McGill, he approached me on the final day of my visit with a large brown envelope. I could tell by the slight smirk and twinkle in his eye that he was up to something. He handed me the envelope. "What's this?" I asked, suspiciously. "Oh nothing, Karlotte, just some articles I thought you might find *amusant*."

The envelope did contain articles, plenty of them. I thumbed through one after another. All had headlines like "Man Brutally Murdered in Rosemont Home." I read one of the articles and soon realized that the murder of a few decades previous had taken place in the house Jerry and Neil were renting. Not only that, but I had stayed, several times, in the very room where the victim had been bludgeoned to death. It had been a truly gruesome murder. I was momentarily stunned—and, well, creeped out. Then Jerry and I silently stared at each other for about three seconds and burst into wild laughter. "You bastard!" I shouted. "Well, Karlotte, you'd never have stayed here if you knew, and I couldn't have that." I have no idea how Jerry learned of the grisly historical crime; his neighbours may have mentioned something. Given Jerry's nature, it was quite conceivable that he'd promptly visited a library to retrieve all the gory details.

Jerry devoured information. He was an avid reader and cherished great writers, especially if they were gay. Once, in Key West, Florida, he reasoned that playwright Tennessee Williams might attend a small

Enjoying an evening at Allan Davidson's with Jerry Bartlett (right), 1983.

production of one of his own plays. Williams was living in Key West at the time. Jerry purchased a copy of the play and attended the performance. Sure enough, the playwright was there. Jerry marched up to Tennessee Williams, introduced himself and handed him a pen. "Mr. Williams, would you do me the honour of autographing my copy of your play?" He did, and wrote "Tennessee Williams" in his plain, readable hand.

If Jerry couldn't get an author's signature in person, he did something I found remarkable but that was totally in character for Jerry. Let's assume he wanted his copies of Christopher Isherwood's books signed. Jerry would find a credible mailing address for the author or his agent and mail the books to him, with postage-paid self-addressed return packaging enclosed. His unorthodox method usually worked, and he never lost a book.

When we lived on Larkhall Street, there was an apartment building directly across the road. The apartments had big sliding glass balcony doors. Our kitchen was at the front of our house and had a huge picture window facing the apartments. Sometimes while we sat at our kitchen table it was possible to see the apartment dwellers walking about inside their units. Larry was always up before me, and one morning while eating his breakfast, he noticed that a tenant across the street was standing stark naked in his window drinking a cup of coffee or tea. These nudist displays became a daily occurrence. Sometimes the man was joined by a stark-naked woman—his spouse, we assumed. Jerry came to our house one day, and as we were sitting at our kitchen table having coffee, I said:

"Jerry, see that apartment across the street on the second floor, second from the left?"

"What about it?" answered Jerry.

"Lately, every morning there's a man standing in the window totally naked."

Jerry paused for a few seconds to consider matters, then spoke.

"Is he good looking?"

"Not especially."

"Call the police!" he said with mock outrage.

Larry worked with Jerry's sister, Bernadine, a nurse. Jerry told Bernie and members of his family that he had AIDS. They tried several times to convince him to leave Toronto and return to Newfoundland, where they could look after him. Members of his family even went to Toronto to convince him to come home. Inevitably, he gave in and flew home, where his family cared for him. Jerry was a difficult patient at times. He didn't want to see or talk to anybody. Even close family members were only permitted to spend a few minutes in his bedroom, then he'd kick them out. He was pissed off that he was dying. Who could blame him? A young man with a new career in the law and so much more to do, to see, and to experience.

From the time I heard that Jerry was dying, I frequently thought about the conversation we'd had in Montreal, when he told me he didn't want to die in pain. I kept praying that he wouldn't suffer, that he'd have the kind of exit he wanted. I hope he achieved that at least, and I hope he died having some sense of the positive influence he'd had on people, including me.

A prolonged death from a terminal illness can be largely, but rarely entirely, pain-free. Pain medication wears off, sometimes before the next dose can be administered, or before someone is available to administer it. The in-between times can be unpleasant. Thankfully, today people with terminal illnesses, if cognizant, can choose when they want to die by requesting a medically assisted death. A friend of ours chose that option in 2021. Like Clarence, Jack, Keith, and Jerry, Bruce Hiscock contracted HIV in the 1980s.

I met Bruce through Larry. Bruce, originally from Grand Falls, was a licensed practical nurse. In 1980, he and Larry worked on the same unit at the Health Sciences Centre. Eventually, we three became friends. Bruce was unpretentious and kind. He was quiet at first, but when he got to know you, he'd "talk the head off ya," as he'd say. At costume parties, Bruce's full-on talk came with full-on drag—water-balloon boobs and all. A handsome man became a handsome drag queen.

Bruce had moved to Toronto in 1983, like many gay Newfoundlanders then. He chose to live in the city's gay village, an area where you were unlikely to be harassed for being yourself. It was a place where we felt safe. Unfortunately, unbeknownst to most, HIV was living and multiplying in Toronto then. Bruce was most likely infected by it during his first months in the city. Then he was diagnosed with AIDS.

Bruce was one of the lucky few diagnosed back then who remained alive into his early senior years. But his health was compromised, directly and indirectly, by HIV. In his last years, Bruce needed a wheelchair to get around safely. He remained positive through good and bad, but in 2020 the joy that had always sustained him slowly abandoned our friend. He was diagnosed with stage four cancer and had no desire to fight it. He wanted to die. No amount of gentle persuasion could sway him. He'd had enough. We respected and supported his decision.

He quickly sought professional help in planning his medically assisted death. But Bruce chose not to wait until the facility that agreed to assist him could arrange a date and staff for his exit. In late September 2021, he texted me to say he was feeling tired and generally unwell. I tried to cheer him up and told him how much we admired and respected him. His last text to me was, "Your words mean a lot Karl and thank you for your kindness."

Bruce's medically assisted death was tentatively scheduled for the last week in October. He surprised everybody by taking his own life on October 10, 2021. We pray he had a peaceful death. Larry and I miss our friend but feel blessed that we were able to enjoy his company decades longer than anticipated. Some people with HIV/AIDS endured for a handful of years, while others lasted mere months. Tommy Sexton, for example, kept going in the public eye with spirit and tenacity for as long as he could, but it wasn't nearly long enough.

13

I WANT THE OLD KARL BACK

I spoke with Tommy Sexton for the last time in the summer of 1991. Tommy and his friend and acting partner Greg Malone were in St. John's filming material for an upcoming CBC comedy special called *The National Doubt*. The province had been experiencing record low temperatures, often in the single digits. It was so dreadful that *Maclean's* magazine published a full-page article about it: "A Freezing Summer" (July 29, 1991). I managed to warrant mention:

> Still, many Newfoundlanders remained optimistic, particularly with the arrival of warmer weather last week. Karl Wells, who prepares weather reports for the regular evening news program *Here and Now* on CBC-CBNT in St. John's, two weeks ago promised sunny skies across the province. When the weather turned even colder, Wells wore a paper bag over his head the next evening. Said the forecaster: "I guess if there's nothing you can do about it, you can treat it with a bit of humour." For many Newfoundlanders, that is becoming extremely difficult.

Tommy saw me shortly after I wore the brown paper bag on *Here and Now*. "Oh my God," he said. "Karl, I can't believe you did that!"

He was laughing and flashing that dazzling smile of his. Our chats were a bright spot in an otherwise dull, depressing summer. I was glad I'd given him a laugh and thankful that that was my last personal memory of Tommy. He'd contracted HIV, and 29 months later he would die from AIDS, along with so many of the other beautiful, creative people I'd met and known and loved.

Well into the early 1990s, gay people continued to endure worry and stress caused by the darkest period in our history. A submicroscopic killer continued to wipe out the lives of many thousands of us, across all age groups. A cure seemed far off, if not impossible. Many people, including Larry and me, felt like everything was collapsing around us. What helped keep us going, apart from commiserating with our gay friends, was our bond of love, and our careers. Larry was working toward a degree while holding down a full-time nursing job. I focused on becoming a better TV host, newscaster, and weather reporter.

Throughout my career, it's always been a point of pride to give producers and directors exactly what they expected from me, or at least to do the very best I could to provide it. Hugh Doherty was the second boss I worked for until the mid-1980s, and the first area executive producer for Newfoundland and Labrador. A Montrealer by birth, Hugh had worked in print media across the country. He joined the CBC in Toronto and worked there for several years before getting into CBC regional broadcasting.

Hugh ran CBC news bureaus and television supper-hour shows throughout the province. He came to my desk one afternoon, and with his usual, "Got a second?" escorted me into his corner office overlooking the Canada Games track. Dressed in a clip-on bow tie, ill-fitting white short-sleeved shirt, and baggy brown pants, Hugh looked like a character from a *Blondie* comic, especially with a yellow pencil stuck behind his right ear.

"Have a seat," he said, moving some papers on his desk. He leaned back in his chair and scratched the back of his head. "Yeah, I wanted to talk to you about your on-air performance."

"My performance?"

"Yeah, nothing to do with the information you're giving. That's fine. I'd like to see more of your personality."

"Can you be a little more specific?"

"Have some fun with it. It's the weather, for God's sake. It's the only spot in the show where we can afford to lighten up a bit."

"Okay; I'll do my best."

I smiled as I left Hugh's office and walked back to my desk. The performance I'd been giving on-air was exactly what the CBC expected from all its announcers: bland, well-enunciated homogeneity—a yoke I could now happily cast off. My boss got what he wanted, including my bag-over-the-head weather report.

Over the years I learned that all executive producers like to re-work a show to suit their vision, from studio sets to storytelling, often without giving enough consideration to what the audience might find compelling—unless the ratings are bad, which ours never were in those days. When Hugh Doherty left the position, he was replaced by Ron Crocker. Ed Coady, upon taking the reins as executive producer after Crocker, called me to his office and said, "Just give us the weather straight. Just the weather, that's all." Bob Wakeham, who succeeded Coady, came to my desk one day and asked, "Where's the old Karl? I remember when you were having fun doing the weather. I want the old Karl back."

There was a sure way of knowing when Hugh Doherty was displeased by an edition of *Here and Now*. He used to collect empty cardboard boxes that once held teletype rolls, copy paper, pens, et cetera. They were kept in a closet near the top of the back stairs that led from our studio up to the newsroom. If he didn't like something he saw on the show, a misplaced graphic on a news story, bad sound, a clumsy interview, or any number of what he deemed fails, he would stand at the top of the stairs and wait for all of us to return up those stairs to the newsroom. Then, depending on who he saw ascending, he'd take one of his empty boxes and kick it down the stairs at the offender. If he was really upset with you, he might launch three or four boxes your way. It was all in fun and gave us a good laugh, but the underlying message was clear.

After Hugh's instruction to have fun with the weather broadcast, I assumed I'd eventually become a target for his game of cardboard boxes—for having too much fun. Christmas and holidays provided opportunities to be a little more relaxed. By the late '80s I was donning costumes and presenting the weather at Halloween and Christmas as famous characters from fiction, such as Dracula and Ebenezer Scrooge. Through it all, I managed to avoid the box barrage. Sometimes I'd mildly criticize the crew by poking fun at things that went wrong, or I'd do an impression of a colleague such as Doug Brophy or our

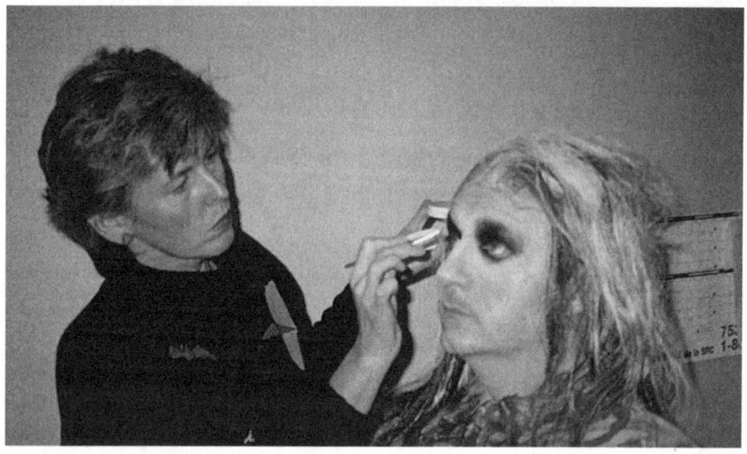

Being given a zombie makeover by CBC *makeup artist Janet Hearn for a Halloween* Here and Now.

ubiquitous freelance rural news reporter, Larry Hudson, who spoke with a very distinctive accent.

Larry Hudson was a reporter and camera person who covered central Newfoundland, the Burin Peninsula, and the island's southwest coast. He was born in England but grew up in Australia and had, as a result, a unique accent. A story about Larry's dedication to the job is one of my favourites. It was wintertime, with lots of snow on Newfoundland's south coast. Larry had his own small, handheld 16 mm film camera at the time. The story he was reporting required footage of the snow-covered roads, narrow road cuts, and towering snow banks.

Always up for trying something different, Larry had the idea to do a long moving road shot from a car—not from inside the car but from the hood. Father "Ed," the local parish priest, volunteered his car for the shoot. Delighted, the two of them drove off to a quiet side road to shoot the creative secondary footage, or B-roll. Larry carefully positioned himself on the hood of Father Ed's wide sedan, using the sloping windshield as a back rest. Larry held his camera firmly and steadily and instructed Father Ed to drive straight ahead, slowly, while Larry turned his camera on the scene ahead: sky, trees, snow, and metre after metre of road that disappeared quickly beneath the car.

Things were going well until Larry saw that the car was veering precariously to the right. Father's view of the road was becoming more and more obstructed by falling snow, the blinding white landscape and the body on his bonnet. Larry began shouting "Go left, Father!" but the priest's window was up and he couldn't hear a thing. "Go left, Father!" shouted Larry, becoming more concerned as a high snowbank was looming like a titanic iceberg in the near distance. "Father! Go LEFT!!!" Larry only managed to get out one more "Father!" Then CRUNCH! The car hit the snowbank; Larry first slid, then flew off the bonnet like an arrow catapulted into the great pile of snow, still tightly gripping his precious camera. He emerged from the snowbank looking a bit like the abominable snowman as Father Ed frantically spoke holy words and apologies. Larry's pride was a little dented, but he was fine. The story aired minus Larry's foray into creative cinematography.

Most of my colleagues had funny or bizarre things happen to them that got talked about over an after-work beer, or at parties. A few didn't need to rely on work stories to make us laugh. Johnny St. George was one of those rare individuals. When I began with the CBC, Johnny was a film editor, but as CBC TV phased out of film, several of our film editors retired or transitioned to electronic news editing. Johnny became a production assistant (PA), someone who worked either in the control room or in the studio, relaying messages from the director and cueing on-air talent. Johnny and I were a volatile combination in the studio, because we had a similar irreverent sense of humour. I once did my impression for Johnny of CBC producer Paul O'Neill, whom we both knew. Johnny split his sides laughing. After that, at least once a week he'd say, "Karl! Do it, do Paul!"

Johnny had a bag of novelty items and props. On any given night, I might be greeted by Johnny (who was bald) with tresses of auburn hair, or a seriously nearsighted Johnny in horn-rimmed glasses with lenses as thick as Coke-bottle bottoms, or Johnny wearing dentures the size of donkey teeth. The glasses broke me up more effectively than anything. In addition to being thick, they had maniacal bloodshot eyes painted on them. On short-statured Johnny, with his bald head and fringe of greying hair, the glasses made him look like a mad scientist out of a 1950s B movie.

Johnny was a storyteller, and one of his stories was especially memorable. It concerned the time he decided to do some maintenance work on the roof of his house to save money. On the sunny summer day in question, Johnny took a ladder long enough to get him onto

With my comedically gifted CBC *colleague, Johnny St. George —the two gigglers.*

the roof, propped it against his house, stabilized it, and confidently climbed. He didn't look down until he was standing on the roof with a clear view of his neighbours' rooftops, treetops, the street below, even Signal Hill far, far in the background. Then it struck him how high up he was. He felt his legs getting rubbery. As fast as he could, he sat down on the roof. That was the beginning and end of Johnny's budding career as a roofer. Over the course of the day, as his neighbours walked past and saw Johnny sitting on the roof, they'd wave and say, "Hi Johnny! Nice day!" He'd smile, wave back and say, "Just taking a work break! Ha ha." This went on for a couple of hours, as Johnny sat frozen in place, unable to move for fear of falling. Finally, Mrs. St. George returned home and arranged for Johnny to be rescued. He never climbed a ladder again, nor did he ever laugh louder than when he told his roof story.

During the '70s and through the '80s, on- and off-air surprises, practical jokes, and bloopers at the CBC happened with some regularity. At the time CBC employed over 300 people in Newfoundland and Labrador and produced hundreds of radio and TV programs. Unforeseen events were inevitable.

One morning I was assigned to read the sign-on TV news. I arrived at work early, picked up my newscast, read it over, and headed to makeup. Since it was too early to go to the studio, I stopped for a coffee at the canteen. While I was there, Gordon Wilson, the technician responsible for getting the sign-on news to air, came in. We smiled and nodded good morning. At the time I was engaged in a conversation with CBC communications officer Roy Baetzel. I lost track of the time and totally forgot about the five-minute TV newscast. The scheduled news window had come and gone. Racing to the master control room, not wanting to believe I had missed not only a cue but an entire broadcast, I arrived just in time to see Gordon putting up the station ID slide, CBNT Channel 8—CBC Newfoundland and Labrador, and rejoining the national network for the first children's show of the day.

"Gordon?" I said, "You knew I was a few steps away in the canteen, why didn't you call for me?"

"Not my job, sir," answered Gordon.

"Well, what did you put on the air for the last five minutes?"

"According to my log [schedule] here," said he, "when that clock strikes 9 a.m. I push this button right here and take the feed from camera two. That's what I did sir, and we aired a lovely live shot of an empty chair for exactly four minutes and fifty seconds." I wanted to throttle him. But it was totally my fault. I was to blame, and I've never had any problem taking responsibility for my mistakes. I went straight upstairs to confess and take my punishment. Dave Sinnott was station manager or director of television then, and he was very sympathetic. He told me to try not to let it happen again and not to worry about it.

A fellow announcer, Art Andrews, once pulled a practical joke on me when I was a CBC summer relief rookie. I was live on-air in the downtown CBC Radio building reading a newscast when Art came rushing into the small studio, conveying a sense of urgency. He thrust what I assumed was a breaking news story in front of me. It turned out to be baseball line scores.

Line scores are essentially a two-line chart containing each baseball team's total runs, hits and errors, with the visiting team on the top line—a bunch of numerals and letters. Only a seasoned announcer and devoted baseball fan could have delivered such raw information smoothly. I didn't have a clue what I was looking at. Yet, inconceivably, after staring at the sheet with glazed eyes, I could hear myself speaking—total gibberish. I regained my composure when I saw my budding career about to evaporate. Through the studio window I saw Art Andrews and technician Dave Bastow doubled over in tears laughing. They got me good. It was a painful lesson, but a lesson nonetheless: never read something cold on-air.

Sometimes fate stung colleagues who were senior to me in years and experience. Once, when Bob Cole anchored the *Here and Now* news in 1976, he almost missed the show's opening. *Here and Now* started at 6:30 p.m. and Bob usually sat in for the show's news rehearsal at approximately 5 p.m. This night, instead of waiting in Studio Two until airtime, Bob decided to relax on a couch in the makeup room.

Unfortunately, he fell asleep. When the show was about to air, a production assistant came running out of the studio, frantically shouting, "Bob! Bob Cole! Two minutes! Bob Cole!"

I was in the hallway outside the studio and heard Bob shout two clear expletives. In what seemed a split second I saw him running to the studio while struggling to put on his jacket. He barely made it. I watched the show's opening on the TV at reception. The right side of Bob's face was wrinkled from being slept on, and a few hairs were sticking up from his head. I secretly thanked Bob, because after that I never felt as bad about having missed the sign-on news.

Bren Walsh was the unchallenged senior reporter in our newsroom—the dean of news reporters. When Bren was regularly reporting from the House of Assembly, a Liberal politician, "Reg Dickson," had spoken on the floor of the legislature about homosexuals working for the CBC. The next day, Bren was walking through the lobby of Confederation Building. He looked up and saw the politician in question at the railing of the lobby's mezzanine level. He waved, and shouted for all to hear, "Hey Reggie! I'm not sleepin' with you no more! You tells!"

Ken Lang was a CBC announcer who specialized in classical music programs in the early '70s. Sometimes he filled in on sign-on and sign-off TV newscasts. In the community of Long Harbour there was an ERCO phosphorus production plant that employed several hundred workers. On one Christmas Eve, trying to be clever, Lang signed off his newscast with, "Merry Christmas everyone and to you folks in Long Harbour, Merry Christmas and a Phosphorus New Year!"

My friend and fellow announcer Richard Beaton was doing a live newscast once and read a story about the inaugural run of a shiny new Marine Atlantic ferry. Richard was mortified by what came out of his mouth when he got his tongue twisted on the words, "flags flying." He read, "A new Marine Atlantic ferry made its first voyage to North

Sydney today. *The Clara and Joseph Smallwood* left Port aux Basques this morning with all fags flying."

Richard made my favourite blooper when he signed off the late TV news on Easter weekend with, "Goodnight everyone and have a happy Weester Eeekend."

In the early 1990s I was offered extra work at CBC that presented interesting challenges. One offer included the opportunity to work with my former *His Worship* collaborator, Ray Guy. Our new executive producer, Bob Wakeham, was keen to introduce a weekly satirical commentary on *Here and Now*. He wanted Ray to write the script, but he wanted me to perform the material as a fictional character. I asked Bob what type of character he had in mind.

"Oh, you know, some outport salt type."

"I don't know, Bob. To be honest, I'm not sure I can do a good enough outport accent."

"Oh, for Chrissakes, don't be so foolish," said Bob dismissively, not sounding like he was ever going to take no for an answer.

Perhaps I was being foolish. Maybe I was unsure about what I was getting into and was self-sabotaging. I had a gut feeling that something big was on the horizon for me. Was this it, or was something else coming my way?

14

IT HAD TO BE ABOUT COMMUNITY

Bob Wakeham arranged a meeting in his office in our new newsroom at the front of the CBC TV building, where he would sometimes gaze thoughtfully out his narrow floor-to-ceiling window and take in the view of Prince Philip Drive. He had a beard with patches of grey, and longish brown hair. His cheeks were broad, his eyes hooded. Ray Guy had straight black hair, parted on the side, thick eyebrows, piercing eyes, a prominent nose and jutting chin.

It was a meeting to nail down what type of character I would play. Should he be my age or older? A fisherman, a clergyman, a teacher? We quickly settled on a shopkeeper. Ray Guy's father, George Hynes Guy, had operated a grocery/general store in Arnold's Cove for years. Ray liked the idea. Hundreds of these family-operated stores were flourishing throughout the province in 1990. These stores sold lotto tickets, and so would our fictional store. They rented VHS movies, and so would we. Building a store set and sourcing props wouldn't be difficult.

Bob was also eager to name our character, but we were all drawing blanks. When Bob suggested naming the character "Raymond" after Ray Guy, Ray became visibly uncomfortable and said, "My name is not Raymond." His parents had given him a simple three-letter name, Ray, as in "ray of sunshine." I suggested we give the character a name preceded by an initial, using as an example the actor F. Murray Abraham.

I felt it would make the character's name more memorable. Everyone was fine with the idea. Later I suggested the name P. Michael, but a surname eluded me. Bob and Ray agreed that P. Michael was a good name. Someone suggested the surname Hynes. It may well have been Ray, because his father's second name was Hynes. And that's how we devised the name and title P. Michael Hynes.

Paul Heale, our *Here and Now* control room director—thoroughly professional and with a sharp sense of humour—came in, and we briefed him. It would be Paul's responsibility to have a set constructed and dressed, furnish theme music and title design, and oversee the shooting and packaging of each *P. Michael Hynes* instalment. The final set consisted of a counter in front of well-stocked, narrow store shelves accented here and there with a Lotto 649 sign or commercial poster. We put canned food, junk food, VHS movies, and sundries on the shelves.

Neither Bob nor I wanted my face recognized. P. Michael needed his own face, his own look, just as he would have his own words to speak. The easiest fix was to have me wear a full wig and full beard. The bits of my face still exposed could be aged with thick fake eyebrows and makeup. Norma Mercer designed the makeup. My standard costume was a plaid shirt with necktie and cardigan.

The words spoken by P. Michael were Ray Guy's responsibility. How I spoke those words was my job. The conceit to have each instalment begin with the sound of the shop door opening and P. Michael addressing the camera as if he were greeting a newly arrived customer was mine. It worked well, and the imaginary customer, Mrs. Purchase—wife of our imaginary town's mayor—became as real as P. Michael. But Mrs. Purchase, unlike P. Michael, never appeared or spoke.

I found it impossible to act on television using a teleprompter. I had to memorize every word or else I couldn't be convincing.

On set with CBC *producer-director, Paul Heale, preparing to film another P. Michael Hynes installment.*

Receiving Ray's scripts only a day or two before we shot meant several hours of fast memorizing and rehearsing. We filmed in the afternoon, as soon as I arrived for my shift. Studio time was at a premium. There was no time for screw-ups. I'd go to makeup, get into my wig, have my beard and eyebrows glued on and my makeup applied, rush to the studio, do the performance, rush to makeup to get my makeup removed, get dressed for my regular job, and head to the newsroom to prepare my *Here and Now* weather report for that night's show.

Despite the stress, I loved playing P. Michael because he was so outrageous. And there were no limits with Ray Guy's writing. He pushed the envelope as far as he wanted. It was up to editors to rein him in, and if they weren't on their toes it could lead to grief. Fortunately, *P. Michael Hynes* managed to remain within the parameters of fair comment, though there were times when editors made cuts. Invariably I was told it was because of time constraints and, although I sometimes had my doubts, I was happy to accept that reason.

Ray Guy wrote a character that was edgy, unpredictable, opinionated, a Newfoundland nationalist, gossipy, anti-Quebec, anti-Ottawa, sometimes nasty, and politically incorrect. P. Michael Hynes was not a satirical character to love but rather one you often loved to hate . . . much like columnist Ray Guy himself. Ray relished being able to say things through P. Michael that he might think twice about saying himself on TV. I sensed early on that while many viewers appreciated the monologue, many found him too defiant. Bob Wakeham, to his credit, leaned toward not cutting or changing Ray's material.

We were shooting *P. Michael Hynes* at a very politically contentious time for Canada. Premier Clyde Wells had rescinded Newfoundland and Labrador's approval of the Meech Lake Accord, the historic agreement which would finally bring about the province of Quebec's inclusion in the Constitution of Canada. Pundits predicted the end of Canada if Quebec continued to be excluded from the Constitution. Ray was having none of it. His strong anti-Meech stance came through in the scripts he wrote for *P. Michael Hynes*.

We forged ahead and produced one weekly segment after another for a year. But since the audience wasn't embracing the character, Bob Wakeham killed *P. Michael Hynes*. The next season, he gave Ray Guy his own weekly spot, complete with leather armchair and set, where Ray happily presented his opinions on current events. I was disappointed with the demise of P. Michael, his pet cat Meech, and Mrs. Purchase, but proud of the work I'd done to bring P. Michael Hynes to life. I was also proud to have collaborated with the great Ray Guy, winner of the Leacock Medal for Humour, and to have had the privilege of performing over a hundred pages of Ray's original material on both radio and television during my CBC career.

Before long, Bob Wakeham would give me a platform from which I could make my mark on live TV broadcasting in Newfoundland and Labrador. It was mine to use in a half-hearted way or to make the most of through imagination and creativity. Bob told me that he was in a management meeting and casually voiced a thought: "Wouldn't it be great if we could have Karl outside every night, from a different location, doing the weather?" He didn't think it would be possible because CBC St. John's didn't have a TV remote broadcasting truck, and likely wouldn't budget for one.

To Bob's surprise and delight, Lloyd Noel, our technical manager, said, "Bob, that might be possible, actually." The station had an old microwave transmitter in storage, and with the acquisition of a few other bits and pieces, one of our news vans could be converted into a microwave van, capable of broadcasting from anywhere in line of sight of either of our CBC receiving towers. The van would be dubbed the CBC Live Eye, but was also called the Weather Van or Karl's Van.

Bob told me the van would be ready to test in a few weeks and that I should think about how I planned to do the weather report remotely, without my green screen and electronic maps, which by then I was using instead of physically marking temperatures and weather symbols in white stick on a real map. It was an exciting development with all kinds of possibilities. Instinctively I knew that this could have a huge impact on our show. It could inject energy, sparkle, and excitement into *Here and Now*. But it had to be about more than a weather forecast. It had to be about community.

There may have been a few naysayers, but most of my CBC colleagues embraced the idea of making my contribution to *Here and Now* about the weather as well as noteworthy things happening in our communities. I regret that I was often deprived of enough time to do a thorough job of reporting both. Because my portion was live and near the end of *Here and Now*, I had to give up precious minutes when other reporters' items ran long; otherwise, the show couldn't end on time. I had to decide whether to cut time from the weather or from my community guest or guests. Weather took priority, especially when there was a storm brewing.

Having overcome the original obstacle of broadcasting live from around the Avalon Peninsula, we would soon employ methods—including satellite and fibre optic technology—to broadcast live from anywhere in the province. One of our first forays to the Burin Peninsula in the freezing spring of 1997 was for a broadcast from Grand Bank, and led to my meeting a gentleman of eighty-eight years called Freeman Johnson. Freeman was a retired fisherman who had worked on the Grand Banks off Newfoundland. During his youth, Freeman had travelled regularly to Lunenburg, Nova Scotia, where he'd sign on with a schooner. He'd toil hour after hour in a rocking dory on the Grand Banks, using a handline to catch cod and haddock.

Freeman was a fit, lean man. He wore strong, metal-framed glasses. His hair was grey, his eyebrows dark and thick. Altogether, Freeman's appearance conveyed the impression that you were in the presence of someone with wisdom. He looked comfortable in his heavy plaid shirt and wool cardigan the day we met for a chat about his life and model boat hobby. We sat in the kitchen where he'd cook his daily meals. He served us tea and pieces of fruit cake. On the wall behind him was a framed Nova Scotia tourism poster featuring the Bluenose, the famous Nova Scotia racing schooner. Remote producer Kevin Harvey was there rolling his camera as Freeman described his life as a dory fisherman. When he spoke to me about his hobby of handcrafting wooden dories (the same type he'd spent countless hours in), he spoke with the authority of someone who knew everything there was to know about dories and schooners and how they're built.

He described the materials he used: the woods, the glue, the paint (dory buff and green for trim). Freeman's dories were beautifully rendered replicas, works of art. Before we said our goodbyes, the elderly man surprised me. We'd been using a 17-inch dory he'd just made as an example of Freeman's work. It was a handsome finished piece. As we were packing our equipment to leave, Freeman took the dory in his weathered hands and held it out to me.

"Mr. Wells, this is for you. I finished it so you could have it," Freeman said.

I felt very honoured by the gesture but knew I couldn't accept such a valuable gift. It would be unethical, and I was, in fact, not permitted to accept gifts of such value.

"Oh Freeman, I'd love to have it, but I'm sorry. I can't accept such a valuable gift," I said.

Eighty-eight-year-old Freeman Johnson proudly shows me his handcrafted dory.

I wasn't prepared for his reaction. He looked at me as though I'd done him a grave injury or stolen his most prized possession, and perhaps I had: his pride. Utterly crestfallen, his eyes welling up, Freeman began to weep. I felt like the biggest jerk that ever lived.

Begging him not to cry, I offered to buy the boat for whatever he charged the public. (At the time he was asking $100 for a dory.) Freeman said he wouldn't take any money for it from me. Then I suggested something he could agree with—I would accept the dory provided he allowed me to give him $100, which he could then donate to his favourite charity. He said he would give the money to the local Anglican church.

Freeman Johnson was a kind man. He experienced an important part of our history, and it was my privilege to hear him talk about his life as a Grand Banks dory fisherman.

Another Burin Peninsula elder still very much engaged in her community was waiting for us as we travelled southeast to the other side of the peninsula. Like Freeman, she had an interesting story to tell. A cherub-cheeked, diminutive woman in a smart black suit met me in the St. Lawrence Miners' Museum. Her name was Ena Farrell Edwards.

In our interview, Ena told me that early on the morning of February 18, 1942, she awoke to learn that two ships had gone aground nearby, one at Lawn Point and another at Chambers Cove, and that a rescue effort by the men and women of St. Lawrence was underway. Ena bundled up against the freezing weather, grabbed her rudimentary camera, and hurried to the rescue site.

The ships were the USS *Pollux* and the naval destroyer USS *Truxton*. They'd left Iceland headed for naval station Argentia in Newfoundland. Ena, perhaps instinctively, realized she was witnessing important wartime military history and began documenting as much of the scene as she could with her camera. She shot well-composed photos

Ena Farrell Edwards told me about the Truxton-Pollux *tragedy as if it had just happened.*

of a team of rescuers pulling the lifeline that brought injured sailors up the steep cliffs from the mayhem and death on the rocky beach below. Other photos showed the wreckage.

Ena told me the touching story of *Truxton* sailor Lanier Phillips. He was one of the 186 sailors who survived the disaster, which, in both shipwrecks combined, killed 203 men. Dark, heavy oil from the wrecked vessels covered the dead and living sailors. Survivors, including eighteen-year-old Lanier, were immediately laid out on tables at the St. Lawrence Mine, to have the viscous fuel washed from their skin. Ena said the woman washing Lanier was heard to say, "This fellow really got covered, 'cause the oil's gone right into his pores. I can't do anything with it. I've scrubbed and scrubbed."

Phillips, an African American, managed to say, "That's because he's Black." According to Ena, in 1942 most people in St. Lawrence had never met a Black person. Later I learned that Lanier Phillips, a boy raised in Lithonia, Georgia, had, until then, only known white people to be cruel racists. He would never forget the compassion and kindness shown him in St. Lawrence. Several years after my meeting with Ena, Lanier's story, including his experience with the people of St. Lawrence, was told in a TV documentary.

Ena Farrell Edwards told me her *Truxton-Pollux* story—an event that had happened over fifty years before—as if it had just happened. She was animated, articulate, and energetic, a born storyteller. I left the Burin Peninsula feeling richer for having met Ena and Freeman, and thankful that they allowed me to share their stories on *Here and Now*.

While bringing personal stories like Ena's and Freeman's to light was, by far, the most satisfying aspect of the job, occasionally an assignment came along that could not be matched for the excitement it generated in me, the crew, and our viewers—as when we flew 315 kilometres from St. John's to the Grand Banks on a Super Puma helicopter owned by Cougar Helicopters and stayed overnight. It was the most memorable remote broadcast trip of my career.

We made a two-day visit to the *Hibernia* platform, the fourth biggest offshore oil platform in the world. I had always wanted to make the trip, being fascinated by this artificial island called a drilling platform, towed out to the Grand Banks and cemented onto the Continental Shelf. Dave Murphy, my community segment producer in 1998, was the driving force behind the project. Dave made contact with the *Hibernia* people and negotiated the two-day trip I would make along with cameraman Tony Snow and technician Derek Howell.

CBC news bosses were happy to have us make the trip. It would mark the first time a live TV broadcast originated from *Hibernia*. (We'd make use of the platform's own telephone video technology.) Later, once we were packed and ready to fly, I learned of another reason they were so keen. It was the only time a CBC camera had been allowed on the *Hibernia* platform. News producers saw it as a rare chance to gather footage of as many key production areas of the platform as possible. Such footage could then be used in any future CBC news stories about *Hibernia*. I'd forgotten the plan until I noticed cameraman Tony dutifully (if somewhat covertly) shooting video of things that I knew would never be needed for my reports.

Before leaving the Cougar terminal in St. John's, we'd been dressed in survival suits and shown a safety video on how to escape the chopper if it ditched in the ocean. We were not permitted to carry alcohol, lighters, or any device that might spark. Our flight from St. John's to the platform hundreds of kilometres away was claustrophobic, because once we were airborne and over the Atlantic, our helicopter was shrouded in thick cloud and fog. Every window looked like it was covered in cotton wool, including the pilot's. I asked Captain Rick Burt how it was possible to fly in such conditions. He told me that we were being flown by automatic pilot all the way to the platform. (Years later, Captain Burt would become the general manager of Cougar Helicopters in Newfoundland and Labrador. He was Cougar's GM when Flight 491 went down on Thursday, March 12, 2009. Seventeen people died. One survived.) I was usually the nervous one when it came to heights and flying in small planes and helicopters, but this time I was perfectly calm.

But after flying in a noisy, confining helicopter for over an hour, I was eager to land. Captain Burt had warned us that unless there was excellent visibility immediately above and around the platform, we'd have to turn around and fly back to St. John's. That's why we'd been told to make sure we peed before leaving the airport. Looking out my window, I wasn't hopeful, but as I stared at the cotton wool, it suddenly receded from the centre and there in the distance was a big flame tinged with black burning bright yellow and orange from the flare boom at the top of the mammoth *Hibernia* platform. (The boom burns off excess gas produced in the oil recovery process.)

The sight of the artificial structure—33 metres taller from its base than the Calgary Tower—was stunning. I felt a flood of excitement. In an otherwise deserted setting, this functional construction of steel and concrete looked completely incongruous, yet in a way majestic. Captain Burt and co-pilot Captain Don Roche manoeuvred the Super Puma directly over the opening in the fog above *Hibernia* and gently brought the helicopter down, down, down for the softest of landings on the helipad.

Tony, Derek, and I were welcomed inside the housing module on the platform. Upon arrival we were required to turn over our prescription medications (if any) to the platform's nurse, who would dispense them to us as required. Fire is a major concern on oil rigs and

Flying to the Hibernia *drilling platform with expert pilot Captain Rick Burt.*

platforms, and we were shown a special room for smoking. To light a cigarette in the smoking room, you had to use a device like a car lighter that pulled out from the wall on a cord. When you're on what is essentially a tiny dot of an island in the middle of the vast Atlantic Ocean, none of the safety precautions seem unreasonable.

Because oil rig or platform workers spend several weeks isolated, working twelve-hour shifts before they get to fly home for a break, the platform's amenities help them pass the time. There were places to watch TV and movies, a fully equipped gym, and recreation areas with pool tables. *Hibernia* also employed experienced chefs who ensured workers received the best meals made from premium ingredients. Chef Gerard Aucoin was in overall charge of the kitchens (pastry and main) in 1998 and described an evening meal that included roast hip of beef, shrimp and scallop tetrazzini, pork ribs, fondant potatoes, pease pudding, apricot and date loaf, strawberry shortcake and other pastries, as well as low-sugar, low-salt, and low-fat options. A freezer in the dining area contained multiple flavours of ice cream available at any time.

By far the most interesting area of the platform we showed our *Here and Now* viewers was the drill floor. I was fascinated by the role modern technology plays in the offshore oil recovery process. In the middle of the pristine room, positioned downward through an opening in the floor, was the drill apparatus, the motion-creating mechanism. Off to the side in an enclosed booth, sitting before a control panel, video screens, computer screens and keyboards, was a balding middle-aged man. The scene was reminiscent of the wizard in *The Wizard of Oz* behind his curtain, turning knobs. Of course, *Hibernia* drill operator Jack Bell wasn't a con artist like the wizard. He was a highly skilled technician who was drilling the longest well in Canada at a depth of approximately 150 metres, or 492 feet. The antiseptic atmosphere of the drill floor and control room surrounding Jack Bell was the opposite of the smelly, messy, oily operation I'd imagined.

I left the Hibernia platform with lasting memories of a place I thought resembled what a base on the moon or some barren, uninhabited planet would be like. Look out any window and you see nothing but a grey and sometimes angry ocean, the distant horizon and limitless sky. Underfoot you feel, without question, that you're standing on land, not floating on water. With you are people—trained, highly skilled people—working toward a goal, on a mission that will one day end, and all will fly home.

My *Here and Now* remotes created many memorable experiences, and several featured animals. All were unpredictable, but viewers remember one of them to this day, and it involved a St. John's seagull.

I was doing a live broadcast from the small boat basin, close to the Narrows near the mouth of the harbour. I'd just returned from a trip to the coast of Labrador, where I'd addressed the graduating class of Our Lady of Labrador School in West St. Modeste. I was wearing a traditional Labrador hooded coat of cotton duck called a cossack, which I'd brought back with me. It was a bright evening, and I was about to give the weather forecast, having just described my cossack and the trip to Labrador. I could hear gulls calling to one another as they circled just above my head. Suddenly I felt and heard a plop on my left shoulder. I felt the watery spray from the guano on the side of my neck. One of the gulls had shat on me—a direct hit. I was indignant. "A seagull just got me! It happened live, folks, right there on my new Labrador cossack! I don't believe it, a seagull!"

The next day, executive producer Bob Wakeham was bent over with laughter when he saw me. "Karl! Ha! Karl, swear to God, if that gull was in the union, I would have happily paid it for shittin' on you last night!" More laughter. Apparently, Bob's nose for talent included the avian world.

It wasn't the last time I'd be shat on by an animal. During one live broadcast from Roaches Line, I held a sweet little lamb as it nuzzled me. After a minute I could feel something like warm lava running down my front. Yes, even the innocent lamb pooped on me on live TV. It was a small price to pay for an engaging broadcast, but I was beginning to wish the next animal to upstage me would do it with something less stinky.

A long procession of animals did steal the show: a pickpocket horse, a microphone-hogging golden retriever, a neck-hugging python, a kicking cow, and another cow with a penchant for using its nose to misbehave. That one was a cow at an Avalon Peninsula livestock exhibition. I was standing in front of it for a live weather preview when, just as I went to air, it started goosing me with its nose. Up, down, up, down, up, down I went. Elsie had lots of fun with me during that broadcast.

Then came the turkeys.

One autumn day, my live-eye cameraman Tom Voisey and I set up to do a pre-Christmas broadcast inside a big barn on the outskirts of St. John's. It housed hundreds of free-range turkeys of various sizes. We were occupying their living space, and they were pecking at our feet and legs, and at literally anything they came in contact with. It's what turkeys do. I was to give the weather forecast, then interview the turkey farmer while surrounded by the hundreds of excited turkeys all going at me and the farmer. It was a scene made for unpredictable and potentially interesting live TV. In my Telex IFB earphone, I could hear the control room telling me to stand by. Then, "Fifteen . . . ten . . . five . . . " Tom switched on his camera lighting. "You're on." I was temporarily stunned by what I saw unfolding before me—something the audience couldn't see because the camera was pointed at me, not at Tom. As soon as he'd turned on his TV lights, every turkey in the barn abandoned me and moved toward him.

On-air with an unruly canine guest determined to eat my microphone.

More importantly, they'd all trotted out of the live camera shot and abandoned our *Here and Now* audience. A turkey army was now mounting a full-scale assault on my cameraman. I watched with a tinge of jealousy as poor Tom tried his best to fend them off, but they were unrelenting. I wanted to shout, "No, you fools! It's me you need to attack! I'm the one on TV! Here! For God's sake, peck me!" It was like a scene from Alfred Hitchcock's *The Birds*. Turkeys can't fly, but an aspiring airborne unit going after Tom's upper body was achieving almost enough lift to reach his chest. Poor Tom was inside a cyclone of flapping wings, pecking beaks, and swirling white feathers, all while I appeared in a turkey-less sea of tranquility. We never worked with turkeys again.

Once I was in the middle of a meadow to talk about horses. When we finally went live, we were struggling to remain standing in gale-force winds and sideways sheets of rain. The four or five horses we'd gathered ran away to take shelter under a copse of trees. Horses are noble, intelligent animals. They knew better than to expose themselves to horrendous weather for the sake of a few minutes of television with a couple of thoroughly saturated humans. Who could blame them?

Watching me outside, unsheltered from the weather every night, our audience began to empathize, and viewers did something quite unexpected. They began sending me homemade items of clothing. First it was a pair of grey-and-white patterned mitts, knitted by the sender. Then came dozens of hand-knitted wool caps, scarves long and short, and more mitts, even a few pairs of hunting or trigger-finger mitts, with a thumb and index finger. In my case, they were perfect for handling a microphone and note card. Once I even got a painstakingly knitted blue sweater.

Many of these gifts arrived with sweet notes, including the wish that I try to keep myself warm and dry in bad weather. Our audience's sincere expressions of kindness toward me made a lasting impression. They were evidence of warm affection, of the fact that regardless of my fears and my uncertainty about my performance, viewers were saying they valued me, that I was welcome in their living rooms. I will always be grateful for that, and will never forget.

There was lots of fun in doing a decade of daily live remote broadcasts, but as time passed, I faced challenges and demons that, unfortunately, would bring me closer and closer to a mental health crisis.

15

I WAS NUMB, SPENT, DEVOID OF BASIC EMOTIONS

"They told me you were comin' here t'night. I know you're a queer, an' I got no time for queers. These fellas say you're alright . . . that's it. I said what I wanna say."

He used the word "queer" as profanity. Poison, poured in my ear by a thin, sinister-looking man who confronted me at the Benevolent Irish Society meeting rooms on Queen's Road. I'd been invited there to do a live broadcast for St. Patrick's Day. The unbenevolent man wasn't a BIS leader and I received a warm welcome from others. But the bigoted greeting lodged in my heart like a splinter.

After I began doing remote broadcasts, I was always on guard because I knew I was vulnerable to in-person anti-gay abuse. It was challenging to endure because I couldn't say much. I needed to maintain my composure, act like nothing was out of the ordinary, and get on with doing my job. While feeling abused and worthless, I still needed to appear upbeat and full of energy for a TV audience of over 150,000.

I also had drive-by abusers. They showed up several times after I did my live weather preview early in the show from an easily identifiable outdoor location. If I was at Quidi Vidi Lake in St. John's, for example, they'd have watched the show and recognized the location, then they'd get in their car and head to the lake. As they were driving by us, they'd put down the window and scream, "KARL WELLS is a FAGGOT!" It was painful. If my guests heard, they'd look uncomfortable. This made me feel (wrongly) that it was my fault. My cameraman's attitude was to pretend he'd heard nothing. I'd drive home afterward feeling depressed and angry but determined not to let the abuse bother me. It wasn't easy. I was fortunate to have Larry, as always, giving me his unconditional love and support. It hurt him to see me dispirited and in pain.

We were also dealing with something else. The negative pressures of my job exacerbated my OCD, which was becoming unbearable. I'd been suffering from obsessive-compulsive disorder for over twenty-five years. It had begun in 1967.

The illness arrived suddenly, in my last year of junior high school. My family had recently moved into a new bungalow, within walking distance of Bowring Park. Mom and Dad were very proud of their purchase, a big change from living over a store. Our new bathroom's shower wall divided the shower from the toilet. At the corner of the wall where the shower tiles met the vinyl wall covering, I realized how easy it would be to work my thumbnail under the vinyl and pull it away from the wall. I suddenly feared I would do it, and then go on to cause worse damage by pulling sheet after sheet of vinyl off the walls. I was panicked by the thought that I'd really do it. This irrational, obsessive thought made me so anxious that I had to leave the bathroom.

Every time I went into the bathroom after that, I had the same thought, the same fear. I calmed down a little when I succeeded in avoiding looking at the area of the wall that triggered my OCD, but the fear and obsessive thoughts never went away. I knew I'd never act on those thoughts, but that didn't matter. I still feared I might, and the fear was overwhelming. My OCD might have been brought on by moving to our new home, but the manifestation of OCD at some point in my life was inevitable, because (as I was told later by my doctor) my brain doesn't produce enough of a chemical messenger called serotonin.

Later I developed more fears and began performing rituals, like arranging objects to line up perfectly. Over time my OCD intensified and manifested itself in many pernicious ways. Worst of all were the terrible unwanted thoughts that would repeatedly pop into my head. OCD became a daily part of my life and caused stress, pain, and tears for almost three decades.

My OCD was always rooted in the general fear that I might do something harmful to others or something self-destructive or career-ending. As years passed, the intrusive thoughts became scary. I'd see a kitchen knife and think I was going to stab someone with it. The sharper and more pointed the knife, the more frightening it became. I'd have to quickly put it in a drawer or get out of the kitchen to find relief. Eventually any object that could be used to physically hurt someone created the same overwhelming fear: a hammer, a screw-driver, a wrench, a shovel.

The obsessive thought of doing harm to someone with a weapon escalated to the fear that I might deliberately run someone over with a car. When I'd drive to work, if I passed someone riding a bicycle, by the time I got to the CBC parking lot I would have convinced myself (even though I knew otherwise) that I might have struck the cyclist and that they might be lying bleeding and dying in the gutter. Then I'd turn the car around and drive back to the spot where I'd originally passed the cyclist. If I didn't see anyone or any evidence of an accident, I'd feel relieved, although I might repeat the behaviour and drive back a second time just to make sure.

It was as if my brain were constantly malfunctioning. One day I was in line at my bank and became convinced that at any second

I might start shouting obscenities: the vilest, most obscene curse words. I knew I wouldn't, but OCD is the fear of fear. (In other words, the panic you feel when you fear you're on the verge of doing something unthinkably bad.) It was a struggle to make it to the teller without fleeing the bank in panic. Fighting off all these urges was incredibly tiring, but for me it was a choice between withdrawing from life altogether or carrying on, pushing through the mental anguish to maintain some semblance of a normal life.

Severe OCD is a lifelong struggle, but it can be managed in most cases. I waited too long to seek professional help, and my illness worsened. A plague of intrusive thoughts began to interfere with my work. I'd go to a CBC meeting and be overcome with panic, fearing I might say something intensely offensive, or even grope someone (despite knowing I wouldn't). One night during a live studio broadcast, while explaining what track a low-pressure system would likely take, I suddenly feared I was going to look straight into the camera and shout, "You're all a bunch of cunts!" I stumbled, quickly regained my composure, and wrapped up the weather report as fast as I could.

Night after night, live broadcast after live broadcast, I struggled with trying to remember weather information, while at the same time fearing I'd slip and call the viewers something grossly obscene. The fear wasn't as great when I taped something, because I reasoned that if I said something horrible it would only be seen by the crew and could be reshot. But on live TV there could be no reshoot, no taking it back. I sometimes wonder how I managed to do my job effectively. Perhaps the adrenaline rush of being on live TV helped give me a slight edge—enough, at least, to enable me to give a professional performance.

Larry and I made the decision to keep my struggle with OCD secret. The reason it took me decades to seek help was that I'd become a CBC TV broadcaster, a public face. I needed, and was determined, to live an open life as a gay man. That alone would raise questions about my character. When I began my career, many people believed homosexuality was pathological, a disease. Some ignorant people still do. I decided that, rather than seek professional help with my OCD and risk being spotted going into a psychiatrist's office—with the inevitable fallout gossip about Karl Wells having treatment for whatever the toxic grapevine might conjure up—we'd try to cope with my illness on our own. Larry's love and support got me through the darkest days. He possesses empathy in abundance, and I've been blessed to have benefited from it.

I continued to read about OCD, listen to self-help recordings, practice relaxation and positive thinking techniques. I'd meditate. I'd do anything I thought might help me. But because of the stigma of mental illness, I couldn't risk the CBC finding out. I had no confidence that my bosses would be understanding, and thought they'd react negatively. At the CBC, until the late 1990s, I'd always felt more tolerated than accepted as a gay person. I felt vulnerable. Learning I was dealing with a potentially disabling mental disorder, I feared, would lead to dismissal or reassignment to a job shuffling paper in a corner. My concerns weren't unfounded. I was aware of decisions affecting people's lives that were made by the CBC because of expediency.

OCD can be mild. Some may even laugh it off, make a joke of it. But it can also be extremely severe, so much so that it has caused some sufferers to take their own lives. If you've tried every treatment available, including medication, and nothing works, you just want to escape the torture of it. My OCD was severe. After nearly three decades I reached a point where I couldn't handle it anymore. I felt it was profoundly lessening the quality of our lives—mine and Larry's. The simple joys of life had vanished.

Every self-help aid I could find, I'd tried. Books to help me understand OCD, like *The Boy Who Couldn't Stop Washing*, were informative, but offered little I could do on my own. I took a home study course to learn techniques that claimed to help eliminate anxiety, but any relief I got was short-lived. It was the same with meditation. Meditating for thirty minutes a day was effective for thirty minutes—that was it.

My brain was relentlessly generating destructive obsessive thoughts, one after another, all unwanted and frightening. I might suddenly think about physically hurting Larry, sexually assaulting somebody, swearing or hurling insults in public, at my boss, my colleagues, or on the air. I even purchased a home recording device to view my broadcasts, to make sure I hadn't sworn or done anything obscene on *Here and Now*. Logically, of course, I knew if I had done such a thing, there would have been immediate repercussions. I could never have left the building without confirmation I'd done something horrendous. But that's the kind of unreasonable, cognitive shitshow that OCD creates in your head.

I was past being able to cope. Life no longer felt worth living. It was too hard. I came home depressed and exhausted every day. Most mornings I didn't want to get out of bed but I'd force myself to get up. Obsessive compulsive disorder was winning the battle I'd been having with it for so long. I was numb, spent, devoid of basic emotions. Thankfully, I realized what a dangerous situation I was in, and had enough sense to go to my family doctor before it was too late.

Dr. Lydia Hatcher entered the examining room, which was decorated with anatomy posters, children's drawings and a few framed photos of her family. She began with her usual warm smile and said, "What can I do for you today?" I was seated in a corner by the window. The weather was sunny, which always seemed to make Dr. Hatcher more upbeat. She looked at me quizzically as I shifted in my chair.

I began to tell her about my OCD. She listened intently. I unburdened myself, relating in detail the entire story of my many years struggling through the hell of it. By the time I'd finished, tears were running down both our faces. It was a relief to have finally told someone who could officially diagnose my illness and help me find some relief. As we wiped the tears from our cheeks, the doctor suggested we try medication. I was happy to hear there might be a drug that could help. Given my lack of success with various coping strategies, I thought medication would be my best chance to get my life back. It was.

I started taking one specific drug at a low dosage for six weeks and noticed it was having a calming effect on me. My symptoms hadn't disappeared, but they had lessened. Eventually we decided on a higher dose, three times stronger, that largely reduced my most severe OCD symptom, the intrusive thoughts. I asked the doctor how long I'd need to be on the medication; I naively thought it would cure my OCD, like penicillin cures pneumonia. Dr. Hatcher explained that I should think of myself as needing to take a daily pill for this disorder, similar to how a diabetic needs to take insulin daily. Neither malady disappears. Although I still have symptoms, and sometimes scary intrusive thoughts, thanks to daily medication my overall mental health is good.

Despite my concern that the calibre of my on-air work might have been adversely affected by my OCD, something happened on June 24, 1997, that reassured me. It was the 500th anniversary of the arrival in Newfoundland of Giovanni Caboto, an Italian explorer known to us as John Cabot. A full-sized replica of Cabot's ship, *Matthew*, was being sailed from Bristol, England, and was scheduled to make landfall at Bonavista. Her Majesty Queen Elizabeth II and Prince Philip were to be there for the colourful ceremony welcoming the vessel and her crew. The CBC had organized major national TV coverage with a live broadcast anchored by Peter Mansbridge. The provincial government was producing a major TV show at dockside. Thousands of visitors were expected in and around Bonavista for the event.

A special *Here and Now* broadcast was scheduled to originate live from Bonavista that evening. All the show's principal hosts would be there, reporters, producers, production assistants, camerapersons, and mobile unit technicians. We CBC locals all piled aboard a rented school bus before dawn on the 24th and headed to Bonavista for the historic broadcast. It was a happy, fun-filled trip there and back with singing, storytelling, and joking. At one point driving down the Bonavista Peninsula we heard the loud, distinctive propellor of a helicopter overhead. We turned into a bunch of excited teenagers, shouting, "It's the Queen! It's the Queen! It's the Queen!" When we saw the large military helicopter was about to land at a nearby parking lot, we had our driver stop the bus. What luck, we thought: a *Here and Now*

Interviewing Janice Winsor on the Bonavista wharf. Janice organized the luncheon for Queen Elizabeth II at Bonavista in 1997.

scoop—first video of Her Majesty at Bonavista, Newfoundland. We watched and waited with bated breath as the helicopter door opened. Descending the steps was a group of garden-variety VIPs. It was a false alarm. We piled back into our bus and resumed our journey. Before long we were laughing like grade schoolers again. That bus trip was a great morale builder, one of the few times I saw my colleagues really happy together, upbeat and enthusiastic.

Once we arrived in Bonavista, we were dropped off some distance from our location and had to take our scripts and gear and walk to our dockside set-up. Bonavista had swelled from about 5,000 people to a population of 30,000 that day. We were given permission by security officials to walk down the middle of Church Street to access our temporary piece of CBC real estate near the waterfront. Each side of the street was jammed with rows of thousands of eager spectators behind rope lines. When Debbie Cooper, Doug Letto, and I walked down the middle of the road, we were very much on display, because the street had been completely cleared for the imminent arrival of the royal motorcade.

Not long after we began our walk—Debbie in the middle, flanked by me and Doug on either side—someone shouted, "Karl!" Then someone else, "Karl!" And another, "Karl!" As if a fuse had been lit, a chant began amongst a group, "Karl! Karl! Karl! Karl!" This was followed by wave after wave of "Karl! Karl! Karl! Karl!" Thousands began picking up the chant, and it grew louder and louder, following us all the way to the dock. I waved and smiled self-consciously as we walked along, but it made me uncomfortable that I was the only person being cheered. At one point during the walk, I heard Debbie say under her breath, "This is humbling."

I found out later that several UK reporters who'd flown over from Britain to cover the Royal Tour were asking spectators and local journalists who this chap "Karl" was who drew bigger cheers than

Her Majesty Queen Elizabeth. Well after the excitement of that day, I looked back on people's reaction as an indication of the affection and respect they had for me, a loyal friend who'd been coming into their living rooms every weeknight for almost twenty years. It was a good feeling and a memory I'll always cherish.

I'd never taken our audience for granted, nor any audience, from the first moment I spoke into a microphone at VOWR. There wouldn't be much point in putting words on paper or on a device, or broadcasting or streaming sound and video, if nobody read, listened, or watched. I sensed—and was told by CBC colleagues with access to focus group information—that my weather and community segment appealed strongly to viewers of *Here and Now*. Part of that may have been the anticipation generated by the unpredictability of my segment, since viewers never knew where I'd be, whether I'd be serious or having fun, what I'd be talking about, or who my guests might be.

Apart from the homophobes, I did have detractors both inside and outside the CBC. Some, including a few CBC mandarins, preferred a more staid, scripted approach—in the style of a traditional strait-laced broadcaster. A *Here and Now* reporter stopped by my desk one day after reading the daily compilation of viewer comments taken by our switchboard operator. It noted reaction to my Halloween night weather report, which I'd presented in costume as Count Dracula or some other Halloween character. He looked at me and said in an exasperated tone, "I don't get it. I spend weeks working on a documentary and it gets no reaction. You go on and play the fool on Halloween and we get 60 or 70 positive calls."

I understood his frustration or, perhaps, his envy (we all had bigger than average egos), but it was a ridiculous comparison; I was a little shocked he'd made it. My once-a-year turn as a Halloween character bringing a little levity to a special night and the fact that viewers called to say, "Thanks for that, well done," should never have been compared to a piece of long-form journalism. As I explained to my colleague, if my segment of *Here and Now* was resonating with viewers and increasing our viewership, it was potentially bringing more viewers to his *Here and Now* documentaries and everything else on the show.

Our audience always seemed to get and appreciate what I was doing and noticed more than some of my colleagues that most of my broadcasts were meant to inform and educate. My community segment regularly highlighted topics such as AIDS, homophobia, cancer, water safety, first aid, the arts, education, food banks, grocery budgeting, sports events, theatre, charitable causes, literacy campaigns, and dozens of other worthwhile subjects. Not to mention mine and my crew's widespread travel throughout Newfoundland and Labrador talking to people, highlighting communities and what was happening beyond the overpass.

My biggest fan through all my CBC TV career was my mom. She watched *Here and Now* devotedly from the time I first appeared on the program until I retired from the CBC. She became my personal one-woman publicity agent. Everywhere she went, she told people she was my mother. "Karl Wells is my son," she'd say. Frequently I'd take a taxi and if the driver recognized me, they'd say, "I drove your mom the other day." I'd ask, "You know Mom?" They'd answer with a smile, "No. She told me she was your mom." My mother was very proud of me. I know that the only thing she wanted was to hear people say something nice or positive about me. I like to think she sometimes did.

It seems surreal to me now, but one night at my brother Len's Pleasantville apartment I saved my mother's life. Larry, Mom, and I went to have dinner with my brother and his wife. He'd cooked rabbit stew. We were all enjoying the meal, when in the middle of dinner, Mom got up and went to the bathroom. After some time,

Larry and Mom in her living room. She loved him like her own.

I became concerned because she'd been gone too long. I went to the bathroom and got no answer at the door. I turned the handle. It wasn't locked. Pushing the door open, I saw Mom standing at the sink. I spoke and she turned toward me. Her face was blue, and she looked totally terrified. She began pointing at her open mouth. I knew right away that she was choking.

Despite having always thought I'd fall to pieces in an emergency, I felt a calm come over me. I said, "Mom I'm gonna help you. Now turn around because I need to put my arms around your belly." She did so immediately. I placed my arms around her, making a fist with my left hand. I positioned my fist just above her navel and with my right hand over my left fist I quickly and forcefully pushed inward and upward at the same time on Mom's stomach. As soon as I did, a short, round rabbit bone popped out of my mother's mouth.

"Thank God!" I said as the reality of what just occurred hit me. Mom was very relieved and happy. "You saved your mother's life, my son," she whispered.

We both realized that if I hadn't known what to do, the outcome would have been very different. The manoeuvre I performed is the Heimlich, named after the doctor who invented it. Luckily, I'd seen Dr. Henry Heimlich demonstrate the manoeuvre on TV in the 1980s. His demonstration made such an impression on me that I never forgot it. Mom continued to enjoy her life and all it offered for many more years. She had a circle of friends with whom she sometimes travelled on short sightseeing trips; she attended social events; she cooked and pursued many other activities. Living life was a joy for my mother.

16

THERE'S SOME SPIRIT OVER ME . . .

One of the most evocative trips I made in rural Newfoundland for *Here and Now* was in the early 1990s. I knew very little about St. Brendan's, the island community in Bonavista Bay. When a trip to Bonavista Bay and central Newfoundland was suggested to me, my producer Bill Maher pitched St. Brendan's as a community to highlight. Billy's pitch included the opportunity to film a ferry trip across the bay, sailing between and around clusters of small islands, many of which had been inhabited at one time or another. People had lived in St. Brendan's for 150 years.

We began our St. Brendan's adventure early in the morning, heading for Burnside, where the car ferry *Hamilton Sound* would be loading vehicles. Among them, we hoped, would be our small red, white, and blue van bearing the CBC logo and the words Weather with Wells. The trip to St. Brendan's (on Cottel Island, Bonavista Bay) took about one hour, giving cameraman Kevin Hanlon plenty of time to shoot a seascape of greys and green: ocean, sky, and of course, Bonavista Bay's many islands dressed in mist and stunted vegetation. Familiar deserted islands: Willis, Flat and Great Black Island, Tumbler and Bessy, and many more with simple names. Islands formed millions of years ago that made you think of all the mariners, explorers, fishers, and pirates who'd set eyes upon them and navigated those waters over centuries.

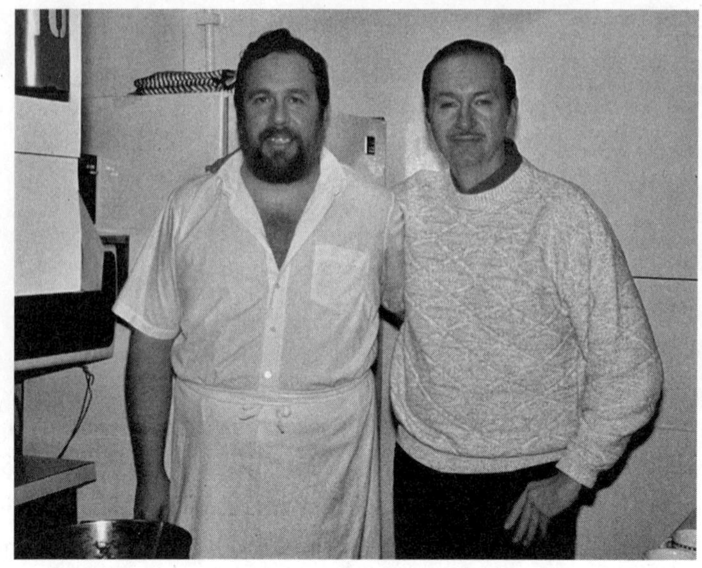

En route to St. Brendan's aboard the Hamilton Sound. I'm in the galley waiting to be fed some of chef's pea soup.

Despite the breezy weather, or perhaps because of it, Captain Charlie Janes had the *Hamilton Sound* on automatic pilot for our trip. "It sure beats havin' to crank that old wheel back and forth," Captain Charlie told me. His ferry was a substitute for the regular St. Brendan's ferry, which was away for a refit. After chatting with the captain, I met the cook assigned to the *Hamilton Sound*—a jolly, bearded guy wearing a white apron that covered his ample front.

In the vessel's small galley kitchen, I watched as he made dumplings, each about the size of a large Timbit. The dumplings would join the pea soup with salt meat that was bubbling gently on the stove. It was the crew's lunch. Later I tasted a dumpling with some of the thick creamy soup. It was delicious. During a coffee break, the cook told me he'd studied marine cooking at college. He enjoyed his job on the boats, but his goal was to get a position as a cook in the offshore oil industry, perhaps on the *Hibernia* platform or on one of the rigs. Offshore employment was the dream of many young Newfoundlanders in 1994: jobs with good pay and a future.

We'd seen so many uninhabited islands during our trip that it was slightly jarring to suddenly see the boats, wharves, lobster pots, and houses of St. Brendan's. We saw men gathering hay in a field, a sight that made St. Brendan's seem like a place where time had stood still. I felt I was getting a taste of the quiet of the Newfoundland outports of my mother and father's generation.

Most of the homes and buildings were in good repair. Many were painted white. The only signs of disrepair were the usual things: an abandoned rowboat, a collapsing shed. One large building housed a retail business that had been serving the small community—then consisting of 350 residents (down from a high of 800)—since 1951. It was Croke's General Store. The sign above the door read John Croke Ltd. I smiled when I saw the store's counter with its backdrop of shelves containing various goods, with items pinned to the narrow edges of the wooden framework. It looked so much like the outport shop that CBC design had created for my P. Michael Hynes *Here and Now* character several years earlier.

Ruby White, a pleasant, neatly dressed woman of nineteen or twenty, was on duty at Croke's that day. I was interested in how she saw her future unfolding. Her answer took me aback. I was expecting to hear her say that she planned to go to college or university, begin a career, and settle in a larger provincial centre or on the mainland. Instead, she told me that she saw her future in St. Brendan's and that she had no plans to leave her hometown.

Ruby explained that she loved growing up in such a close-knit community with large families, and that she didn't feel she was isolated or missing out on anything. She was resolved to stay in St. Brendan's, and, I assumed, get married and raise a family. I admired Ruby's resolve, but I did wonder if her optimism about the future of St. Brendan's might be misplaced. At the time there was no cod fishery because of the moratorium, and St. Brendan's fishermen were fishing part-time for lumpfish and lobster. As we sailed back to Burnside aboard the *Hamilton Sound* with Captain Janes and crew, I thought if everyone on Cottel Island was of Ruby White's mind, then it certainly wouldn't be wise to bet against a future for St. Brendan's. As of this writing, the ferry still runs between Burnside and St. Brendan's.

Labrador is lovingly called the Big Land. I didn't appreciate how well chosen the term was until I flew over Labrador in a small Provincial Airlines plane in the early 1990s. Flying over Newfoundland from St. John's had its scenic joys, but my first sight of Labrador from approximately 30,000 feet was a gift. Limitless unsullied land, sky, and water; ponds, rivers, streams reflecting blue sky. I saw snow, too. Everything was pristine, breathtaking, and yes, BIG. And wondrous. When I looked out the window, I knew immediately why people say, "Labrador calls you back, again and again." The Big Land reminds you that nature and its forces are powerful and eternal. In Labrador they speak to your spirit and say, "We've got this. Forget your worries. Rest easy."

Prior to the millennium, I made many trips to Labrador. My travels took me to all regions: the north and Nain, the southern coast and Red Bay, West St. Modeste, L'Anse au Loup and L'Anse au Clair, central Labrador and Happy Valley-Goose Bay, Sheshatshiu, Northwest River and Mud Lake, and western Labrador, Wabush, and Labrador City. In all these communities, I was impressed by the calm, steady demeanour of Labradorians.

In Sheshatshiu I was privileged to sit in the large kitchen of a home and meet two distinguished Innu Elders, 95-year-old Michel Pastene and Shimun Michel Sr. Shimun wore a grey pullover and white collared shirt. The older man, Michel, had a lined face, greyer hair and a moustache. He wore a traditional hooded parka, tailored from waterproofed fabric. They were among the few Innu who played the sacred ceremonial drum. Only Elders play the instrument. The drum itself, called a *teueikan*, was wooden framed, about two feet in diameter, narrow, and covered tightly with caribou hide.

Using a long piece of string, Shimun attached the drum to two poles suspended from the ceiling. It hung like a pendulum just above his knees when he sat in front of it. He took a long-handled beater, shaped with a small hammer at the top, and beat the drum rhythmically. Then he began a singing chant in Innu-aimun. Later Shimun deferred to Michel, who played the drum in similar fashion. I felt very honoured to be permitted to witness this ceremony. It was a spiritual and emotional experience.

Learning about the Innu drumming tradition from Labrador Elder and icon Shimun Michel Sr. at Sheshatshiu.

Speaking in Innu-aimun, with the aid of a young woman interpreter, Shimun told me about the significance of the drum ceremony.

"There's some spirit over me, who is taking care of me," he began. "Before hunting for caribou, we play the drum, so we know where to send our children for the caribou . . . When I hit the drum, you always get a caribou. You see it in your dreams when you hit the drum. Sometimes you see in the vision tracks or a sign, a light, a light that gives you directions to the caribou."

Before leaving, I asked if it was important to continue this tradition. Shimun replied quickly: "Yes, it's very important that it goes on, because it went on for generations. My great-grandfather played the drum, and my people lived here for thousands of years. I would like it to go on."

Both Shimun and Michel continued to make lasting contributions until they passed. In fact, Shimun lived until 2018 and left us at the remarkable age of 103.

Mud Lake is a village of fewer than 100 people, inaccessible except by boat and located across the river from Happy Valley-Goose Bay. Most of the people who lived there in the '90s worked in Happy Valley-Goose Bay. They commuted back and forth by boat unless the river was frozen over, then they travelled by snow machine. My cameraman and central Labrador producer, Tony Dawson, accompanied me on a trip to Mud Lake with Sam Broomfield. It was a beautiful morning, and Sam and his outboard-powered boat were waiting for us on a small stretch of beach, not far from the CBC station.

Sam was a long-time resident who'd made the trip hundreds of times. He handled his boat with such assurance that you could easily imagine him successfully steering it blindfolded, right to his cozy waterside home. We crossed a wide part of the Churchill River, entered an even calmer narrow channel and leisurely cruised southwest. In the far distance, I could see hills. Sam told me I was looking at

Sharing a laugh with Marion and Sam Broomfield on our sunny day in Mud Lake, Labrador.

the Mealy Mountains. As we neared Mud Lake, we saw debris in the shallow part of the river near shore: large, rusted metal objects, obviously some sort of heavy machinery. I was surprised to learn they were remnants of a tugboat once owned by the Grand River Pulp & Lumber Company. It had operated a lumber mill in Mud Lake more than a century earlier.

Houses, mostly small ones, came into view. Sam pointed out that the houses on our left were on what he referred to as the mainland part of Mud Lake, but to our right was the island part of Mud Lake. I saw a narrow footbridge stretching across the channel to the island. It was needed so the children of Mud Lake could walk to the school on the island, where there wasn't much else. We were invited to visit Mud Lake School, a little wooden schoolhouse that consisted of two rooms. The young teacher was responsible for nine students and taught every grade from kindergarten to grade nine. The students sang a song for me and recited a poem about CBC. I blushed when I heard the line, "B is for the best weather reporter in the world."

After our school visit, we were invited to Sam's for a bowl of his wife Marion Broomfield's excellent caribou soup. Marion was a quiet, kind woman who told me she was born in Mud Lake and had lived in this tiny piece of central Labrador her entire life. I asked Marion why she chose to stay. She thought for a moment and said, "Well it's peaceful. You're on your own. It's just a nice place to be." I suspect most of Mud Lake would have agreed with her.

A trip to Labrador in the fall would be followed by a variety of remote broadcast trips in winter. The Corner Brook Winter Carnival was always a popular choice, and the Newfoundland and Labrador Winter Games. Once we did a broadcast from the games in Clarenville, and I decided to have a go at figure skating as part of an interview with one of the athletes. The fun for *Here and Now* viewers was watching me attempt (and usually fail at doing) things for which I had little aptitude.

Quite often I was hilariously incompetent, be it at line dancing, directing traffic on Duckworth Street, wall climbing, arm wrestling, or, as it turned out, figure skating. My attempt to do a figure eight at the Clarenville Arena failed miserably. I fell and ended up on my butt. Like a trooper, I laughed off my folly and carried on with the broadcast. I didn't say anything at the time, but I knew I'd hurt myself. A skating surface is hard. Turns out I'd fractured a rib. I had to put up with several weeks of wincing pain, but I thought it was worth it if we'd managed to spice up our information with a little entertainment.

For the most part, I avoided doing myself mischief on TV, though I had plenty of near misses. Nearly injuring my skull on a door frame while driving a car in a demolition derby in the Goulds comes to mind. Then there was the time I had to prematurely end a TV broadcast near Confederation Building in St. John's. It was midwinter, a clear, cold, dark evening. Plenty of snow had fallen that week and, thanks to settling and subtle temperature changes, it had acquired just the right texture for snowballs.

Stirling Snow, my appropriately named cameraman, had picked a location for our weather report just west of the front of Confederation Building, in a sort of sheltered valley. The land behind where I was standing gently rose to meet the lip of a parking lot behind the building. Light from pole lamps in the area and from our TV lights, reflected by snow, created an almost magical effect. It was a simple set-up: two standing lights, my hand-held microphone tethered to a mixer on Stirling's camera, which, in turn was tethered to a fibre optic box connected by a cable to our nearby remote van.

We were a two-person team, the only personnel necessary for a straightforward live stand-up. Everything was going fine until we got

Perhaps one of my most reckless and ill-advised on-air capers was driving in a demolition derby.

to the final few minutes of my report. Stirling, who normally would be relaxed and motionless as he peered into his viewfinder, began to look agitated. He'd stop looking at his shot, step away from the camera and look directly at me. Or so I thought. This went on for some time, but when he began looking at me with an angry expression, which gradually got angrier and angrier, I became scared. It was when Stirling stepped away from the camera and started shaking his fist at me that I thought he was having some sort of episode—a lapse in sanity. He looked furious, as if he wanted to come for me. I decided I needed to pull the plug on the broadcast, so with a full minute remaining, I quickly wrapped up the weather and handed the show back to the studio.

Before I had a chance to ask him what was wrong, Stirling fled, running like a whippet, past me and up the hill behind us toward the parking lot. I didn't have a clue what was going on. When I looked down at the ground just behind where I'd been standing, I immediately knew what had happened. An unidentified duo behind me on the hill had been steadily lobbing snowballs at me throughout our broadcast. They must have pinpointed where I was from my first weather hit on that night's show and concealed themselves in the dark lot behind us. I could see the spent ammunition from their barrage—too many snowballs and pieces of ice to count.

The snowballs had come so close that Stirling thought I could be hit in the head and seriously hurt. Three or four minutes after his chase, he returned red-faced and out of breath. The culprits had jumped into a pickup truck and sped away. Stirling tried his best to get the truck's licence number, but it was impossible. After that incident I knew that Stirling Snow would always have my back, especially if someone was trying to use it for target practice.

Perhaps Stirling's concern resonated with me because, at the time, I was preoccupied with health and safety. In 1997, Larry and I were both worried about my mom, Elizabeth. She was forgetting things to a point where we wondered if it was normal aging or something more. Mom began to ask the same questions again, not long after we'd answered them. When I pointed this out, she'd laugh and say, "Your mother's losin' it, my dear. You'd better keep an eye on me." She was eighty, and the comment made me wonder if she believed her cognitive health was in decline. I decided to speak with her doctor, who later gave Mom something called a mini mental exam. It involved remembering words, drawing the face of a clock and other tasks. Mom passed the test. Months later, Larry suggested I make an appointment with a colleague of his, Dr. Howard Strong, who specialized in geriatric psychiatry.

Dr. Strong was a warm, caring man. Mom liked him. After seeing her, he took me aside and told me that while he couldn't make a definitive diagnosis, he did think it was possible my mother might be heading for Alzheimer's disease. All we could do at that point was keep an eye on her for the next year or so. If any change in Mom's cognitive ability developed, I could ask Dr. Strong to test her again. Mom didn't improve. Over the next few years, her forgetfulness increased. She also became slightly paranoid and would, for example, complain to me that certain men in a room had been staring at her in a lustful way. She gave up bowling, an activity she loved. It was a decision I later suspected may have been linked to her paranoia.

Mom was also telling me dubious stories about things that had happened in her daily life—at the supermarket or the bank, for example. The stories never rang true. She'd also forgotten that certain friends and relatives had died. Then Mom began to forget our birthdays, which was the final alarm bell. When Dr. Strong tested Mom again, the diagnosis, although expected, was difficult to hear. My mother had Alzheimer's. Fortunately, she was able to carry on for a few more years living on her own in a small apartment. Larry and I lived just around the corner and would often look in on her. Dr. Strong prescribed Aricept, an Alzheimer's drug that significantly improved Mom's cognition. When she reached the stage where she required long-term care, she was admitted to St. Luke's Home. The move revived her in many ways.

Being a social butterfly, Mom thrived on interacting with other residents. She also loved participating in the recreational activities—the singalongs (she remembered the words to every song she'd ever sung), the card playing (while she was mentally able), and even the seniors fashion shows. Inevitably, because of the Alzheimer's disease, there was a final deep slide. She became wobbly and needed a walker; then she lost the use of her legs and needed a wheelchair. She no longer recognized me; she lost her ability to speak and to feed herself.

With Mom at St. Luke's. She still knew who I was. Time spent together was becoming more precious.

I'd sit with her and hold her hand, and sometimes if there was music playing, she'd move our clasped hands in time to the music. Once she feebly raised my hand to her lips and gently kissed it. I wanted to cry. It was a sign that inside somewhere, my mother knew that I was special to her. I felt her love. It was palpable, like an embrace. At the same time, I felt deeply sad that Mom's life was ending this way. Seeing my mother go from dancing and walking independently to using a walker and then a wheelchair, unable to communicate, was painful. I was losing a little of my mother each day.

In her 94th year Mom had what we believed was a series of minor strokes. She only partially recovered from them. St. Luke's staff were still able to dress her and put her in her wheelchair, but her quality of life was worse than ever. She spent most of the last year of her life slumped over in a wheelchair on the sidelines of a lounge outside her room. In Mom's 96th year, I received a call from Diane, the nurse who usually informed me of anything I needed to know about Mom's health and care. She said, "Karl, your mom's not eating." I asked why. "Well, she's refusing to eat."

I went to see Mom. At this stage in her life, she had to be spoon-fed a puréed diet, which hadn't curbed her appetite at all. (Baked beans pulsed in a food processor is one meal I remember feeding her.) I put the spoon to Mom's mouth to coax her to eat. She kept her mouth shut tightly as I spilled a bit of food on her chin. I wiped her mouth and looked into her eyes. They were fixed. She lay in her bed staring at the ceiling, as if something fascinating was up there.

Sometimes people refuse to eat when they're ready to die. Maybe the nurse wanted to tell me this but didn't feel I was ready to hear it. She needn't have waited. I knew as soon as I saw my mom that she was ready to go. Later that day I was asked if I wanted Mom to be fed through a tube. I understood why they asked, but the thought of my dying mother being fed that way horrified me. On behalf of my mother, I declined the offer. There was no doubt her end was close. I wanted Mom to pass with dignity, free of pain and stress. I asked that she be kept as comfortable as possible and given morphine when needed.

I informed my sister and brother about our mother. Like me, they knew this day had been approaching. My sister was in Halifax and wouldn't make it home. I was asked if we'd like Mom moved to a special palliative suite upstairs, one designed for family visits. We agreed and Mom was moved to the quiet end of an upstairs corridor. The suite consisted of two areas. One area had a hospital bed, some chairs, a sofa, and bathroom. An inner area had a kitchenette with fridge, and more seating. The suite was painted in warm pastels. As it turned out, Mom wouldn't spend more than forty-eight hours there. It was a blessing. On her final day, Larry and I went back to see Mom a second time. Brother Len had been earlier in the day. While we were home having dinner, Larry said, "I think we should go back and stay with your mother. There was something about the way she looked. I think she might go tonight." I hadn't noticed any change in Mom, but Larry had medical training and experience, so we returned to St. Luke's immediately.

Mom was lying on the bed as we'd left her, wearing a simple hospital smock, with bed sheets drawn up to just below her neck. She remained wide-eyed, staring upward. Her hair, once a prominent and attractive feature of her appearance, was now a sparse, delicate grey fringe framing her thin but mostly unlined face. Mom was breathing in and out through her mouth, very deliberately. Each time she exhaled, her cheeks filled like balloons as she blew the air out. I held her hand, and thought about the past, the happy past, all our joking and joyous laughter, our trips to Bowring Park, to downtown and lunches at Marty's, the Sweet Shop and Woolworth's. I thought, too, about the nearly three decades she'd spent raising us, the time she'd spent cooking and baking, cleaning, ironing, and sewing. She had given so much of herself to Betty, Len, and me. I told Mom how much I loved her.

We called Len to say he should come and see Mom as soon as possible. Larry and I kept vigil by her side. He spoke to the evening nurse, and she'd not seen much change in Mom. At one point Mom had been wincing and was given some morphine to keep her comfortable. We'd been back in Mom's room less than an hour when Larry turned to me and said, "She's dying now." I looked at him incredulously. I'd seen no change. "She's dying now, talk to her, talk to her," Larry said. Holding my mother's hand and leaning in, I spoke softly into her ear and said, "It's okay Mom, don't be afraid. You're going to be with Dad, and your mom and dad, and all your brothers and sisters. We love you very much, Mom. Don't be afraid. I love you, Mom." Then, for the first time in two years, my mother smiled; she drew her last breath and exhaled quietly. An unexpectedly fast yet very peaceful death. Larry hugged me tightly. We stood and looked at Mom's frail, now lifeless body. Just Mom and the two of us. As I looked, I thought, this was my mother, and I'm so grateful this woman gave birth to me, so grateful she raised me. We felt sorrow but were happy she was finally free, released from the cruellest phase of Alzheimer's. Our dear Mom was in a much better place.

17

YOU DIDN'T HAVE TO TELL HER WHO YOU SLEEP WITH!

The year 2000 did not begin well for me, mainly because it marked the beginning of a period of harassment toward me by a CBC TV senior producer. The result was my leaving the CBC as soon as I was eligible for early retirement.

On May 16, 2000, the CBC's top national management held a closed-circuit nationwide meeting with employees. In my experience, these national in-house meetings consistently yielded bad news. Typically, at the appointed time, those of us who could spare a few minutes would turn to the nearest TV and the appropriate in-house channel and wait for the feed from Toronto to start . . . and there he was, Harold Redekopp, VP for English TV, flanked by assistants and communications and HR staff. A nondescript man with slightly sunken eyes and blondish hair, Redekopp was, like several top managers, a Toronto-centric bean counter. His first significant national pronouncement to employees would hit like a hypersonic missile.

Redekopp announced that all regional supper-hour news programs were to be cancelled and replaced by a single national early-evening newscast. The newsroom went quiet as a tomb as either the news sank in or we asked ourselves if we'd heard him correctly. It felt as if we'd just been told bluntly, coldly, of a death in our immediate family. That night, we were the news. *Here and Now* led with the story of its own imminent demise. Reporters and hosts were interviewed for their thoughts. I remember expressing disbelief that a program with such a large viewership was to be axed. My colleague Brenda Murray, a reporter, was succinct in her reaction: "This ship is going down!" she exclaimed with a wry smile.

Public reaction across the country was negative, especially in Atlantic Canada. The CBC regional director in Alberta, Joe Novak, resigned in protest three days later. Newfoundlanders and Labradorians responded as we expected they would. They were angry that the loyalty shown *Here and Now* for thirty-plus years was being thrown back in their faces. Who could blame them? Within weeks, public and political pressure forced CBC management to partially reverse its decision. Rather than totally abandon the plan for a national suppertime show (which they should have done), they opted to create a hybrid called *Canada Now*. It featured a thirty-minute regional program (*Here and Now* lite) preceding a thirty-minute national program from Vancouver. Our viewers were not impressed, but a "30 minutes is not enough!" campaign failed to change anything. *Canada Now* launched in the fall.

All hands did their best to produce a telescoped yet comprehensive package of provincial news and weather. Autumn television ratings for *Canada Now* (formerly *Here and Now*) were even worse than anticipated. The loss wasn't a trickle—we were bleeding out. The bulk of our audience had abandoned us for the competition's (NTV's) suppertime news. That winter, in mid-February, I was sent to Corner Brook, along with my friend Linda Lambe, a CBC communications officer and unofficial production assistant. Linda was the first person I had come out to at work, in the early 1990s. Soon after, I came out to many co-workers, except those I'd heard make homophobic or bigoted remarks (a dozen or so people, including four bosses).

Corner Brook is a city I love and had visited many times before to broadcast from its famous winter carnival. Our task this time, in addition to my doing the weather from Corner Brook, was to drum up support for the new version of our suppertime show. The agenda included an hour with the Corner Brook newspaper, the *Humber Log*. I'd been asked for an interview for a cover story about *Canada Now* and my career.

The interview took place in the paper's cramped downtown offices. A young reporter, Contessa Small, posed questions from a list. I'd been interviewed many times before, and this one was run-of-the-mill until I was asked, "How does it feel to be a role model for every gay person in Newfoundland?" My being gay had never been brought up in an interview before, but I was flattered by the question. Most of my response was published in the February 28, 2001, edition of the *Humber Log*. The article included a photo of me wearing my *Canada Now* ballcap and red winter coat with flakes of snow falling around me. The piece was titled "More than a weatherman." Contessa didn't include my initial comment, which was, "If anybody considers me to be a good role model then that's fine, I'm honoured." She did include the rest of my answer:

> "I'm a pretty private person. I've always sort of guarded my private life. But it's hard because you're in the public eye and people pay attention to you," said Karl.
>
> As an openly gay man who realizes the power of television as a medium, Karl says his main goal is to present himself as truthfully and honestly as possible.
>
> "I'm not a political person. I don't try to influence people's opinions in any way. I just present myself as myself. I am who

I am. People have seen me on television for 25 years. I think they have a pretty good idea of what I'm like. And I think if you do that, then people will say, 'Hey, he's okay. He's not that different,'" said Karl.

Once CBC management found out about the *Humber Log* interview, to my disappointment, the general response was consternation. The CBC's view (not mine) was that I'd been the victim of an ambush interview, that the newspaper's goal was to "out" me. Management was acting as if the CBC itself had been outed. Consideration was even given to pulling CBC advertising from the *Humber Log*.

If the CBC had been monitoring press coverage of local media and media personalities, they should have noticed that long before the Corner Brook interview, the *Herald* had interviewed me and asked what I'd done that made me most proud. I answered, "maintaining a near 20-year relationship with my spouse, Larry." Since the day I started going to gay bars and meeting other 2SLGBTQI+ folks, I never thought of myself as being closeted. I wasn't a gay activist because my job didn't allow it. Because I chose not to discuss my sexual orientation with homophobes in the workplace, and with CBC leaders (some of whom were homophobic), the CBC assumed that I was in the closet. I didn't feel safe having those discussions. My decision was reinforced by a very stressful meeting I had with John Furlong, then CBC TV's senior news producer for regional news, a man with enough authority to seriously affect my work life and job security. The same John Furlong for whom Ray Guy and I had done *His Worship* when Furlong was producer of CBC Radio's *The Morning Show*.

A few weeks after the Corner Brook trip, around March 5, 2001, John Furlong called me into the newsroom's corner executive office, closing the door behind us. Grim-faced, he sat, arms crossed, his back against a smudged window that overlooked our newsroom. I sat facing him as a few of my curious newsroom colleagues looked on from outside like spectators at a zoo. He stared at me coldly, with piercing eyes, through glasses perched on a long, narrow nose. He got straight to the point, "So what happened at the *Humber Log* interview?" I told him about the gay role model question that was put to me. Before I could continue, he cut in sharply to say that at that point I should have ended the interview and walked out.

I was surprised by the comment coming from a journalist, saying I should have shut down an interview because I was asked a legitimate question. When I told him there was nothing wrong with the question, and that I'd answered by saying I was honoured to be viewed as a role model by anybody, he became angry. The fact that I'd given an ambiguous answer, neither denying nor confirming my sexual orientation was, to John Furlong, tantamount to confirming I was gay. "Jesus Christ!" he shouted. "You didn't have to tell her who you were sleeping with!" At that point I knew I was being harassed and that John Furlong was a homophobe.

When he saw my shocked and worried expression (frankly, I was scared) he made a bizarre pivot. He told me he was an alcoholic and that he knew exactly what it was like for me to have to deal with people gossiping and whispering negative things about me, a gay, behind my back. He said that when he was "on the bottle" he had to deal with the same kind of thing. I felt like I was in a scene from a nightmarish 1950s black and white anti-gay propaganda movie, where my tormentor was equating my being gay with having a serious addiction. By 2001 the world had moved on, but clearly CBC leadership hadn't.

I was speechless. Slowly, I stood up, looked in his direction, nodded, opened the door, and walked out. Back at my desk, I started to feel physically ill. My first thought was to report the encounter to Human Resources. At CBC, Human Resources was then just another branch of management. Our union wasn't much better, with its leadership still being, one way or another, on the corporation's payroll. Since Linda and I had returned from Corner Brook, I sensed that management and communications were generally uncomfortable with my interview in the *Humber Log* and that they wanted it forgotten about as soon as possible. But I didn't complain about John Furlong. Not then.

On September 10, 2001, I went to bed at 9 p.m. It was the beginning of a new and necessary bedtime routine. Weeks earlier, after a campaign of persuasion by producers and colleagues, I'd agreed to take a position as host/weather person for CBC *CountryWide*, a daily cross-Canada morning show on a new cable TV/satellite channel called Country Canada (later renamed CBC Country Canada). While the channel was a joint venture by Corus Entertainment and the CBC, the corporation's main contribution was to produce news programming for the channel, tailored to fit its mandated rural focus. I'd initially refused to join the new program because it meant I'd have to abandon *Here and Now*.

The main argument being made to me for quitting *Here and Now* was that since it had recently been chopped to 30 minutes, its long-term survival was seriously in question. In other words, *CountryWide* had a brighter future and was a better bet. I thought that argument was specious. If a new, low-budget national morning show on a new channel, in a TV landscape that already had two successful morning shows, wasn't rolling the dice, then what was? My determination to stick with the well-established *Here and Now*, a show to which, at that point, I'd devoted twenty-two years, was accommodated. Against my union's advice but with its eventual acquiescence, I received a waiver to work a split shift. I would do both shows. I'd spend roughly four hours with each. This allowed me downtime in the late morning and early afternoon. My *Here and Now* duties would begin at 4 p.m.

After weeks of preparation and rehearsal (while I was still performing my regular duties for *Here and Now*), we were scheduled to launch *CountryWide* live on the morning of September 11, 2001. I was up at 5 a.m. Having been given remote access to my CBC computer, I was able to prepare the weather report for all ten Canadian provinces and the territories at home. I arrived at the station at 7:30 a.m. We went live at 8:30 a.m., which meant viewers in the Eastern time zone would see us at 7 a.m. The show was two hours and a success, according to producers and CBC bosses.

Just after 10:30 a.m. local time I walked into the CBC canteen to grab a coffee. Five or six staff were there. Everybody was staring at the small TV on the wall. It had an image of a skyscraper surrounded by blue sky and what looked like puffs of white smoke coming out of a corner of the building. I was told it looked like a small plane had somehow hit the World Trade Center in New York. The angle of the live shot was deceiving. It made the event appear almost insignificant. Then, at 10:33 a.m. Newfoundland Time, before I'd had a chance to take my eyes off the screen, I saw the second jet, filled with people, fly straight into the South Tower. It disappeared inside the upper part of the building, between floors 77 and 85. Floors filled with people.

The disaster cast a pall. Its emotional impact on me and my colleagues made everything else seem less important. Contacting family became a priority. I called Larry at work. He wasn't aware of what had happened. By the time I reached him, it was clear that the United States was under attack. I remember saying it seemed like the world we knew was coming to an end. We felt dazed. That evening we made dinner together and sat gripped by the news and ghastly images appearing on CNN.

As the next days, weeks, and months unfolded, TV viewers turned to well-established 24-hour news channels for coverage of what occurred on 9/11 and in its aftermath. The Country Canada Channel and a few of the other new digital cable/satellite channels that launched in the fall of 2001 were never able to gain a firm market foothold. *CountryWide* struggled on for a year; the channel itself managed to last until 2008 before it transitioned into a channel called Bold, focused on drama, comedy, and sports.

Not long after my *CountryWide* assignment began, John Furlong—still senior producer for *Here and Now*—continued to badger me. A producer who sat next to me in the newsroom witnessed a couple of these incidents. He asked me to step into the hall with him one day, then motioned me into one of the small viewing booths and closed the door.

"So, why is Furlong always picking on you?" he asked.

"I don't know. I honestly don't know," I said. (Of course, I knew the harassment stemmed from John Furlong's homophobia, but I didn't know this producer well, and I didn't feel comfortable sharing the whole story with him.)

"Well, listen," he continued, "I know Furlong, okay? There's only one way to deal with him. When he comes at you, don't be afraid to go back at him. Go back at him! It's the only way to deal with the guy."

I nodded. "Yeah, thanks."

I appreciated the concern and advice, but I couldn't follow it. I feared that responding in kind to Furlong's baiting might make things much worse for me. John Furlong was in a position of considerable power, influence, and authority. He was able to affect the rest of my CBC work life for good or bad. Demoralized, I carried on, keeping my head down.

One of his frequent taunts was designed to undermine my confidence in my job security. Despite knowing our local supper show's sudden, embarrassingly low ratings were the result of the show being chopped to thirty minutes, producers made futile attempts to find a path to higher ratings. The CBC had upset and alienated its viewers by gutting its highest-rated provincial supper-hour show. Righting the ship required an immediate reversal to a sixty-minute regional news

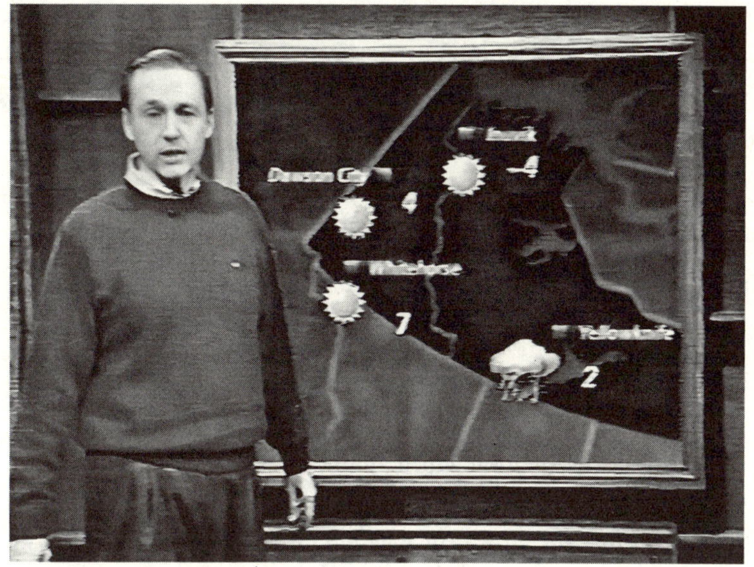

Reporting the nation's weather on CountryWide *for the* CBC *Country Canada Channel.*

program. (Years later a reversal came, too late.) John Furlong sidled up to my desk and whispered to me that newsroom leaders had met for a brainstorming session on how to boost ratings and had unanimously agreed that my weather segment "had to go." Furlong said he wanted to tell me before I "heard it through the grapevine." It was a lie. The executive producer confirmed this, saying the only person suggesting the weather should be dropped was Furlong himself.

Around this time, several of my colleagues in the newsroom and control room told me they'd heard John Furlong making negative comments about me personally. Others, including managers, had told me that Furlong was not a fan of my community segment and was responsible for having it cancelled when *Here and Now* was cut to thirty minutes. CBC regional director Ron Crocker told me, "As long as John Furlong is producing the show, the community segment will never be back." It upset me that this individual had managed to have a worthwhile and well-liked feature axed. Furlong wouldn't even allow me to honour the commitments I'd made to guests and a few local volunteer organizations to do broadcasts with them. A week's reprieve was all I wanted, but the community segment ended the day I was told it was finished. Our competition, NTV *Evening Newshour*, copied the segment from us and kept theirs going successfully for many years.

There was no doubt, given John Furlong's past treatment of me, that his animosity was at the root of his successful effort to have *Here and Now*'s community segments discontinued. The developments reminded me of something I'd put to the back of my mind years earlier. In the mid-1990s my then producer, a very competent guy who went on to work for CBC Newsworld, told me something chilling. It was just before he left for his new job on the mainland. "Karl," he said, "John Furlong is not your friend. Watch your back around the guy." I asked him why, and he appeared uncomfortable. He could only shrug and say, "He just doesn't like you."

In September 2003, the Newfoundland Liquor Corporation's local wines and spirits magazine, *enjoy!*, published an article I wrote about a DIY wine cellar Larry and his brother built. I became concerned when I saw the magazine on John Furlong's desk. Later that afternoon, he picked up the magazine, waved it in the air, and said loudly enough for me and others in the vicinity to hear, "Anybody see the article with Karl's byline in this NLC organ? Somebody must have ghostwritten it for him!"

Subsequently, two *Here and Now* colleagues—both excellent reporters—told me one evening about something they'd witnessed in the story meetings that took place in our conference room twice a day, early in the morning and after lunch. *Here and Now* producers and reporters would attend. The early meeting was to assign stories to individual reporters and tentatively set the show's lineup or agenda for that evening. The follow-up meeting was to check on reporters' progress with stories and lock in that night's show content. The two colleagues standing near my desk seemed exasperated. They told me that John Furlong had been making homophobic comments in story meetings. They were adamant: "He's homophobic!"

On Monday November 3, 2003, CBC News and international outlets reported that the Episcopal church of the United States had consecrated its first openly gay bishop, Reverend Gene Robinson. The consecration had taken place the previous day in New Hampshire. It was a joyful event for me and the 2SLGBTQI+ community worldwide. John Furlong was sitting at his desk reading the story from his computer screen. Finishing, he raised his head and said loudly, "Holy God! There's a story here about the Anglican church in the States consecrating the first GAY BISHOP! That's disgusting! Disgusting!" I deliberately looked around to see my colleagues' reactions. Their heads were down; they were all staring at their keyboards in silence.

I'd had enough. I realized I couldn't live with myself unless I made a complaint against John Furlong. Despite having been exposed to homophobia in various forms most of my life, I'd never made a complaint of harassment against anybody. At fifty years of age, knowing I was close to early retirement after almost thirty years with the CBC, I thought about toughing it out. I certainly didn't take the decision to complain lightly, knowing I was going against a powerful person who had been empowered by the corporation to which I'd be making my allegations. In the end, it was concern for my mental health that held sway. I was feeling miserable all the time. Some days I felt afraid to go to work. Something had to be done. I moved forward with my complaint.

Management's initial reaction, if facial expressions count, was as if I'd just placed a rotten codfish under their noses. I also laid out everything I'd been subjected to for several years to my union representative. He told me that, in his opinion, it was "a *prima facie* case of harassment." A complaint was lodged with CBC Human Resources. The HR manager said she would investigate. I had detailed all incidents of John Furlong's harassment, including the names of people who could confirm he'd made homophobic comments or spoken ill of me, and who had seen him picking on me.

When questioned by HR, John Furlong claimed his private meeting with me in the wake of my interview with the Corner Brook *Humber Log* was purely to lend emotional support, to tell me that as a recovering alcoholic, he understood how I must have felt when people in our newsroom and elsewhere ridiculed me for being gay. This was hogwash. My sexuality was old news to my colleagues and to most people. More important, I was absolutely not bothered by the interview with the paper. I was bothered by the way CBC management had reacted to it. Furlong had called me into a private, closed-door meeting to berate me for answering a reporter's legitimate question involving my sexual orientation. I had left that meeting feeling humiliated and worthless, far from consoled.

As for various comments he made to me in the newsroom and canteen, and general comments that I'd described as harassing or homophobic, he claimed they were just his brand of "black humour."

When HR's enquiries into my complaint were finished, I received a verbal report. (I never received anything in writing.) The HR manager came to see me and told me, as she looked me directly in the eye, "First, I want you to know that we believe YOU. We believe you." She went on to say that none of the people I knew could corroborate what I'd said would go on the record. I wanted to know exactly how they answered. She told me, "They said they couldn't recall or couldn't remember."

"But what about my colleagues who witnessed Furlong's homophobic comments in story meetings?" I asked. The HR manager gave me a stunning answer: "We didn't speak to them." I asked why. "Well, we thought it was best, you know, to keep this inside our own region. Not to go outside." (Both reporters were by then working in other provinces.) She reiterated that the CBC believed me and not John Furlong. She concluded by assuring me that the CBC would see to it that Furlong received "sensitivity training." (To my knowledge he never did.)

I was devastated. The CBC had made a half-hearted attempt to resolve a serious Human Resources complaint, based on several years of harassing behaviour by a senior producer. The fact that they refused to question important witnesses was a dereliction of duty. I was sad but not surprised that my St. John's colleagues chose not to confirm what I knew they'd witnessed. They feared retribution from their immediate boss, John Furlong. But I have no regrets about making my complaint. It was the right thing to do. Thankfully, Furlong soon left *Here and Now* to become host of CBC Radio's *Fisheries Broadcast*, and later *Radio Noon*. I no longer had to deal with him.

18

YOU DON'T LIKE GUNS

"We can get married!" was the collective cheer of the 2SLGBTQI+ community in Newfoundland and Labrador on December 21, 2004. That was the day on which the Supreme Court of Newfoundland and Labrador ordered the provincial government to begin issuing marriage licences to gays. Not long afterwards, the first Newfoundland lesbian and gay couples tied the knot. Marriage commissioners and mayors officiated. It would be years before religious same-sex weddings happened, and then only within a few of the mainline religions. Larry and I were thrilled for our community, but personally, we already considered ourselves married. At that point, we'd been together for twenty-four years. The idea of going through the formal process, at least in 2004, wasn't something we thought much about.

By 2005, *Here and Now* had been fully restored to one hour. The extra time and new bosses gave me an opportunity to do feature pieces and longer interviews. Many of the interviews and feature pieces focused on the province's arts community, such as the profile I did of the famous Newfoundland portrait painter Helen Parsons Shepherd. While I'd never met Helen, I was aware of her work. Many of our former House of Assembly speakers, premiers, governors, and St. John's mayors had been painted by her. Helen's husband, Reginald Shepherd, was my art teacher in high school. Their son,

Scott Shepherd, was a year ahead of me at Prince of Wales and worked with me for years at CBC TV.

Scott was an enigmatic fellow. Nobody at CBC could quite figure him out, and what they had figured was largely off the mark. He had a caring, sensitive side, but Scott was his own worst enemy. He sometimes did and said things that could alienate. He loved guns and owned a collection, along with other lethal weapons. All were legally purchased and properly licensed. Scott had his own personal shooting range and had even learned to make ammunition for some of his guns. He liked working with metal. One day he showed me a belt buckle he'd fashioned. He'd also shown me a bullet he'd made.

Sometimes Scott would bring his weapons into the workplace. He said they weren't loaded, and I believed him. I can't speak for others. More than once I heard a co-worker say, half joking, "One of these days that fella's gonna walk in here and take us all out." At various times Scott showed me (and I assume others at CBC) a Bazooka missile launcher, a hand grenade (a "dummy," Scott said), and what looked like the kind of handgun Clint Eastwood used in the *Dirty Harry* films, a .44 Magnum.

I had a visceral reaction to that one. At the time, Scott was working in an audio control room called "the cage." It had an attached booth where scripts could be recorded, or live reports fed directly to our radio building downtown. Scott had his black leather coat hung on a hook in the cage. My desk was near the cage. One day Scott poked his head out and waved for me to join him. I did.

"I wanna show ya something," he said flashing a Cheshire-cat grin. He reached into one of the hanging coat's pockets and pulled out the Clint Eastwood gun. "Look at this," said Scott. "Isn't that a beauty?"

"Wow," was all my suddenly dry throat could croak out.

"Now that's craftsmanship," he continued, "Here Karl, take it. Just hold it. Get the feel of it."

"No that's okay Scott. I'm good," I said as my mouth got drier.

"No b'y, here, take it for God's sake. Hold it."

Scott placed the gun in my hand. I was shocked by its weight, much heavier than I thought it would be. It had a cold, steely feel. I'd only ever held a toy gun before, and this was no toy. It felt like something lethal. It made me feel woozy. Scott read my face instantly. Clearly annoyed, he snatched the gun out of my hand, saying, "You don't like guns." He put the weapon back inside his coat. He never showed me anything from his collection or mentioned guns to me again. I was thankful.

Unfortunately, like dozens of local CBC employees, Scott lost his job in one of the many rounds of layoffs that occurred during those years. He took it hard. Scott had allowed the CBC to play far too important a part in his life. Being cut adrift from it made him morose and bitter. A few years after his layoff, a reporter in our newsroom called him, thinking he might be able to recall something about a particular story she was working on. His response was to launch into an anti-CBC tirade.

When I contacted Scott's mom, Helen, about my idea to do a feature on her for *Here and Now*, I wasn't sure how she'd respond. The idea of co-operating with the organization that had laid off her son might not be palatable to her. She was living in the bungalow on Oxen Pond Road that she'd shared with her late husband, Reg. Helen was eighty-three and still painting daily. Her process was painstaking, making her output sometimes as low as one canvas a year. She was reluctant to agree to an interview, but I sensed some interest in her voice. With a little coaxing I was confident she'd say yes, and eventually she did. I was sure she'd tell Scott about my call. My hope was that he'd react positively. Even though I felt Scott liked and respected me, by then he despised the CBC.

Before we visited Helen, I'd been able to gather footage of most of her important work, such as *Sunday Morning* and *Spring in Newfoundland.* I knew our feature would be visually rich. All I needed was an interview with interesting answers from Helen and, if we were lucky, some video of Helen at work on a painting. We visited on a mild, grey day with the even light often favoured by photographers and painters. Helen opened the door and cheerfully welcomed us in. She appeared to be on her own. She was talkative and pleasant while we were setting up for the interview. She wore an emerald two-piece suit with white, collarless blouse. At one point she proudly showed me a photo hanging near her kitchen. It was taken at a reception on the lawn of Government House. The photo featured many St. John's notables, including Helen and Reg.

While we were chatting off-camera, I asked Helen if she ever, for pleasure, visited art galleries in St. John's.

"Why would I do that?" she asked with genuine surprise.

"Oh, I was just wondering if you like to keep up with what other local artists are doing." I'll never forget her answer.

"I wouldn't see anyone who's better than me. So why bother?" she asked, with an assuredness I found impressive and astounding.

She allowed no room for the idea that she might derive intellectual stimulation or pleasure from viewing the work of other Newfoundland and Labrador artists. She saw her work as incomparable in its quality to anything else produced here. She simply believed there was nothing she'd see that she could learn from, at least about the kind of portraiture that she produced. Her interest in art galleries was strictly practical: will I learn anything new from the experience?

Just as we were about to begin the interview, Scott Shepherd made a surprise appearance. He was dressed unlike I'd ever seen him dressed before. At work Scott always wore jeans and a casual shirt or T-shirt. This time he was wearing a suit and tie. Had he just come from a wedding or was he trying to make an impression of some kind? I looked at Helen. Her expression changed dramatically. She looked on edge, tentative. I smiled at Scott and as we greeted each other I knew immediately things weren't going to go well. I smelled alcohol on his breath. Maybe he'd had a bracer to give him some confidence. Within a few minutes he was attempting to play the role of TV producer. He left to get something in another room.

Helen turned to me and said, "I shouldn't have told him you were coming." I felt bad for her. Scott's arrival, or more likely his inebriation, had thrown her. Scott returned with a large photo album and sat on the sofa. Above his head was a painting of him as a boy, sitting in bed in pyjamas with his right leg in a cast, elevated on a pillow. The painting was called *Damnation*. Scott began flipping through the album, pointing out photos of various milestones in his parents' careers. He was keen to let me know about the Newfoundland Academy of Art, which Reg and Helen had established in their home in 1949, at 51 Cochrane Street. He did his best to suggest the line of questioning I should use with his mom. When we finally began, with Scott muttering suggestions in the background, I realized we were headed for disaster. Helen wasn't doing well. Off-camera Scott had interjected, "Mom, don't forget about Cochrane Street." Helen shut down. I stopped the interview.

I looked at Scott and approached him. He knew why. I told him it would be best for the interview if he left the room. He was downcast, but left, quietly and respectfully. We finished the interview. If Scott hadn't shown up, it would have been better. After her son's arrival, Helen couldn't muster the enthusiasm she'd shown at the outset. Her best moment was describing meeting Reg at the Ontario College of Art. A mutual friend, knowing they were both Newfoundlanders, had paired them off at a college dance. Helen said it was love at first sight.

After the interview, Helen changed into sweater and slacks, having agreed to allow us to film her at work. Her studio, attached to the back of the house, was bright and immaculately organized. Everything was white: ceiling, walls, cabinets, and fixtures. I noticed a full ashtray next to her easel. As she painted, every so often she'd take a puff on a cigarette. Somehow, I hadn't expected an eighty-three-year-old to be smoking. The mostly finished painting on the easel had an interesting backstory. The painting featured three older, bearded men sitting at a table playing cribbage.

Helen told me that the painting was based on an old photograph given her many years before by the businessman Gerald S. Doyle, collector and publisher of traditional Newfoundland songs. He'd given it to her with the suggestion that it would make a great painting. Helen had recently found the photo between the pages of one of her books, where she'd placed it years before and forgotten about it. As she painted one of the eyes, she told me that in her portraits that was where she spent most of her time. "If you don't get the eyes right, it's not going to work. It's just not. The eyes have to be perfect." When Helen passed, I had the privilege of seeing the finished piece at The Rooms Provincial Art Gallery. The eyes were perfect.

After decades of interviewing, mostly on live TV, I'd gained useful experience in preparing guests for interviews, many of whom had never been on live TV before. They could be divided into categories: nervous and super confident. I was less concerned about recorded interviews because an awkward first take could usually be reshot. Not so with a live interview, which is why I focused beforehand on making the guest feel relaxed and confident. I'd make sure they knew the topics we'd be chatting about, and I'd maintain as calm and relaxed a demeanour as possible before the interview. If I showed any sign of being uptight, the guest might pick up on it and become stressed. The guests who worried me most were the super confident ones. There was one who was particularly memorable.

He was a cop, "Phil." Phil was also a minor hockey coach. We were broadcasting from Twin Rinks in St. John's, where a minor hockey tournament was being held. Phil had been lined up as an expert to talk about the tournament. I was to interview him live on *Here and Now* while a game went on in the background. Phil had a cockiness about him that, for me, was a big red flag. I'd asked him if he'd ever been interviewed on TV before, and without missing a beat he began to boast.

"Oh, I've got no problem talkin'. I've done loads of public speaking. Loads. In front of big crowds. All that stuff."

I decided to pre-interview Phil off-camera, just to get a sense of how he might answer my questions on the air. He breezed through his answers, and then said, "Just give me a shout when you're ready for me!" And off he went, still self-assured, to rejoin other officials.

When we finally began our live interview, I looked at Phil and he seemed fine. After an introduction I asked my first question: "Phil, how many youngsters are taking part in St. John's minor hockey this year?" I looked at him and immediately had a sinking feeling. His face was losing colour like a wine bottle being emptied. His eyes got glassy. He moved his mouth but no words came out, just an unsettling sound like a low wheeze.

I quickly covered: "I believe you were telling me it's over 1,000 kids involved in minor hockey here in St. John's this year." I asked another question, but Phil still couldn't get a word out. He just stood there, zombie-like. Again, I answered my own question. And that's how the entire interview went. I asked, I answered. Phil was done in by an acute case of TV stage fright. When we were off the air, I gave him a consoling pat on the back. "Sorry," he said. "I don't know what happened there." Shoulders drooping, he walked away defeated.

I was told that the next day poor Phil was razzed mercilessly about his performance by his fellow RNC officers. Easy for them.

The unexpected was always expected on my live TV broadcasts, with or without guests. It might be a stand crashing to the floor, a light bulb blowing with a bang, a technical glitch or human error. Sometimes it was a glitch combined with the erring of humans. One incident (actually, multiple incidents) with an art contest broadcast caused a nightmarish occurrence.

At *Here and Now*, we were always searching for ways to increase our viewership, especially during the fall and winter ratings periods. Ever since my earliest weather reports back in the late 1970s, I'd occasionally receive colourful drawings from young viewers: scenes with yellow suns, azure skies, green trees, and dark blue lakes. They'd come from everywhere—anywhere *Here and Now* was seen, even the Lower North Shore of Quebec. I always showed them on TV. Thinking of this, I pitched the idea to do a *Here and Now* weather drawing contest for young kids. We invited submissions for several weeks. Before long, hundreds of entries began to arrive from all over Newfoundland and Labrador. They were wonderful images. A small volunteer group of artists was organized to judge and pick our contest winners. It was all very rewarding, well watched and a great deal of fun. An ultimate live broadcast was planned to show and announce the winning first-, second-, and third-place drawings and to name and congratulate the young artists.

On the day of our contest finale, we decided I should do my live segment from the boardroom at CBC TV, where the judges had been deliberating. To show as many drawings as possible, we pushed the long boardroom table aside and pinned drawings to the walls in front of our camera. There wasn't an inch of space that wasn't covered with artwork. When I went on the air, I could give viewers a walking tour that took in great swathes of drawings at a time. The multicoloured

A contestant's entry for Here and Now*'s weather art contest, where "everyone's a winner."*

backdrop was rich, lively, and perfect for TV. Knowing that thousands of entrants and family members would be watching, I was keen to be inclusive and praise all the youngsters who'd drawn pictures for us. During the live show, with a warm smile and reassuring voice, I said the line, "You are ALL winners."

As soon as I uttered the word "winners," I heard a voice in my right ear say "LOSERS!" It's difficult to describe the complicated tangle of emotions and split-second thinking I experienced at that moment. I knew immediately where the interfering word had come from and who'd said it: "Stacy," our control room production assistant and the person responsible for quietly giving me time cues through my Telex earphone. I realized it was a joke and that nobody was losing their mind or going rogue. In the background I could hear control room tittering and laughter. What bothered me was that it was uncharacteristically unprofessional to play such a stunt on someone live on-camera being watched by thousands of *Here and Now* viewers. What the hell were they thinking? I managed to stay composed and carry on, assuming it was a stupid, one-off wisecrack. It wasn't a one-off. Nor had it been intended for my ear.

Here's what happened. After giving me an initial "You're on" cue, Stacy had accidentally left her talkback microphone on. With her mic still activated I could hear everything being said in the control room while I was on the air. Not knowing I could hear every word, every giggle, every titter, they kept it up, along with occasionally barking, "LOSERS" and "THEY'RE ALL LOSERS!" (Control rooms can sometimes be like junior high.) While I was showing a snowy scene painted by Jenny in Port de Grave, and a sleek sailing ship on a foamy, blue ocean drawn by Kory of Bonne Bay, I began thinking of all the hideous, cruel, painful ways I would torture each individual member of the control room crew once I got off the air.

Finally, I'd had it. I was struggling so much to maintain my concentration during the control room's backtalk, I pulled out my Telex and said, "Pardon me folks, I just want to speak to our control room. I can hear you. Please turn off your talkback switch." I put my Telex back in. Silence. My relief was palpable. I carried on and brought our contest to a happy conclusion. After the show I lost my desire to torture anybody. Stacy showed up, red-faced and looking as sheepish as a human could. Mea culpas and profuse apologies followed. We made up and agreed that one day we'd be laughing about the night of the art contest. We did and still do, about other misadventures, too. Although ever since that broadcast, whenever anyone says, "you're all winners," I still hear Stacy's younger voice saying, "LOSERS!"

19

THEN I SAW THE FUTURE

"I like the planet a lot an' ah, it's one of my favourite planets. 'Cause ah I think, the dog, Pluto, from the show."

"Oh, from the cartoons? Mickey Mouse and Pluto?" I queried.

"Yes," said Nathan with a smile.

Nathan was about five years old. It was August 24, 2006, and the planet Pluto had just been downgraded to a dwarf planet—no longer a member of the big boy planets club. Nathan and his younger, less chatty sister, Meghan, were the only planet watchers at the Geo Centre. I interviewed them for that night's *Here and Now* beneath the beautifully fabricated solar system display in the underground foyer. I also interviewed Paul Dean, the centre's executive director. After Nathan and his Pluto-the-dog reference, I knew everything else in my report would fall on deaf ears. A five-year-old and a cartoon dog are unbeatable.

Pluto wasn't the only entity that had been relegated to lower status that fall. CBC TV's regional and national network ratings continued to slide. In some instances, shockingly so. For example, as Mark Dillon noted in the media trade journal *Playback*, the number of viewers who watched *October 1970*, a costly miniseries partially funded and aired by the CBC, was a "mind-boggling 58,000," which Dillon attributed to "largely ineffectual promotional efforts."

To put this in context, *Here and Now*, in its heyday, was getting close to a quarter-million viewers in a province of only 500,000 people. *October 1970* was a national miniseries aired to a country of almost 33 million people. Yet the best it could manage was an audience of 58,000. Neither lack of promotion nor program content were to blame for *Here and Now*'s by then abysmal five-figure rating. Our numbers problem could be traced directly back to the CBC's stripping down of *Here and Now* and the creation of *Canada Now*.

The re-instatement of the one-hour *Here and Now* had, alas, come too late. Many of us knew it would take years to win our audience back, if ever. The situation had affected our spirits. My co-workers and I were still trying to adjust to the cold fact that ours was no longer the highest-rated news show. Not even close. Unfortunately, this wasn't the only cause of my own worsening morale.

John Furlong, our former senior producer and my tormentor, had moved back into our newsroom as a result of local CBC Radio operations being moved from Duckworth Street to the CBC TV building. The development was causing me mental anguish. Neither of us spoke to or acknowledged the other. Having to pass Furlong in our narrow hallways was literally panic-inducing for me.

The situation caused my mood to descend into a dark place. I was sometimes short with people, even rude. I'll always regret this behaviour and am deeply sorry for it. Although I sometimes failed, I had always worked hard to be professional and treat people kindly.

During my time at the CBC, six presidents of the Crown corporation came and went. I didn't give most of them a second thought. Only two stood out. Anthony "Tony" Manera was a president for whom I had great respect. He'd come, unusually, from within the ranks of the CBC, having been hired in 1985. When Jean Chrétien's Liberal government (the most unfriendly government of all time toward the CBC) cut $44 million from the corporation's annual budget in 1995, Tony Manera immediately resigned as CBC president in protest. Of his decision, he said, "I will not preside over the dismantling of the CBC." The gesture was respected and applauded by staff and CBC supporters across Canada.

Robert Rabinovitch was the sixth and final president of my time. In my opinion, he failed to realize the importance of our news service—local, regional, and national—to Canadians. I've always felt that if anything is dismantled or downsized within the CBC, it should never be at the expense of a robust CBC news service with widespread investigative resources. Otherwise, our democracy is weakened. Media that depends on commercial revenue for its survival is sometimes prone to ignore or soft-pedal important news that might upset sponsors. CBC News is not in that position. I saw no examples of the CBC being afraid to hold the powerful to account.

In 2005, during ongoing negotiations with our union, Rabinovitch locked us out—over 5,000 employees across the country. We were unable to produce and air *Here and Now* for eight weeks: another serious blow to the program we were trying hard to build back up.

In the wake of all this, Robert Rabinovitch embarked on a "listening" tour of CBC stations across the country. Staff leaders would talk, and he'd listen to our thoughts about the current state of the CBC, on building a better CBC, and—although it remained unsaid—how to get more eyeballs on our shows. I suspected the effort was nothing more than a public relations gesture, a president paying lip service to his seriously demoralized staff from Vancouver to St. John's. I attended and gave Robert Rabinovitch my unsolicited analysis of the damage he'd wrought with his supper-hour shows debacle.

I told him I thought the reason CBC prime-time shows were seeing a significant drop in viewership was partly because of what had been done to *Here and Now* and other supper-hour shows. Prime-time shows (from 7 p.m. to 11 p.m.) benefit from the audience delivered to them by lead-in programs like *Here and Now* (6 p.m. to 7 p.m.). If a lead-in has a large audience, many of those viewers may stay tuned to sample the next show on the channel. I pointed out that the CBC had severely damaged its prime-time lead-in show in Newfoundland and Labrador and in so doing had lost revenue and viewers for its prime-time lineup. I added that the CBC (mainly him and a rubber-stamp board) had angered our viewers to the point where they were turning their backs on CBC TV. He didn't respond, except to give me a patronizing smirk. I think my colleagues were shocked by what I said and the frankness with which I said it.

As the room was emptying, and as I was about to stand, a person seated nearby turned toward me, smiling, and spoke. The person was the CBC Human Resources manager—not someone I'd engaged with often since CBC's bungling of my harassment case against John Furlong. She said something I wasn't expecting.

"You must be so excited about next year!"

"Sorry, what?"

"I said you must be excited about next year. You can retire next year."

"To be honest, I haven't given it any thought."

"Oh well, I guess it's something to look forward to anyway."

It was hard to believe I'd been with CBC almost thirty-one years, and indeed more, counting two years of casual employment that included radio and TV announcing duties, and radio acting. In retrospect, I shouldn't have been surprised by the HR manager's comment.

She had given me something to think about. Perhaps it was time for me to at least entertain the idea of a future outside the CBC. Counting the hours, days, weeks, and months to early retirement was a preoccupation of most CBC employees past the age of fifty. The ensuing months would nudge me further and further into the category of the time-left-to-retirement counters.

A CBC *billboard advertisement for our resurrected 60-minute* Here and Now.

Late in 2006, the CBC appeared to abandon the claim that as a public broadcaster it wasn't that concerned about ratings. It had always maintained it was more concerned with providing Canadians solid journalism and programs that celebrated Canadian culture, programs that enlightened and entertained. Tasteless commercials airing on one of the world's leading public broadcasters were a necessary evil, required to supplement shrinking government funding. Yet it was willing to pay several millions to Frank N. Magid Associates, an American consulting firm known in the industry as "show doctors," to revamp all its regional supper-hour shows and CBC Newsworld. It was an American company with very little, if any, experience in the field of public television.

My jaw dropped the day I was told the group of circumspect strangers walking around our newsroom, acting like they were trying to avoid landmines, was the "Magid" team. That name Magid was one I'd known for thirty years. In 1977 I'd read *The Newscasters* by Pulitzer Prize–winning journalist Ron Powers. Magid, and criticism of that company, figured prominently in Powers' book. I knew that Magid's services included researching a show and then recommending how to revamp it—often significantly—to boost ratings and revenue. Magid's approach, which hadn't changed in decades, was to create news shows that gave viewers the news they wanted, not necessarily the news they needed. It wasn't about journalism, and it certainly didn't fit with the CBC's mandate to "inform and enlighten."

The Newscasters includes comments made by the journalist Ralph Renick, president for news at WTVJ TV in Miami, to the Dupont-Columbia University Survey of Broadcast Journalism. Renick, a pioneer American TV journalist, made this unqualified assessment of Magid and its methods after he had "convinced his station to terminate the services of Magid":

> They are really a Trojan horse. They roll it in and suddenly the enemy troops are in your camp. Too often the service is put to political use to permit management to get control of the news when the news director is in conflict with management. . . . These agencies have taken hold of many stations and virtually dictated news policy "in absentia," by the use of their research techniques. Too often stations with consultants end up trying to present news only as the research results suggest the people want. But lost in this concept is that a professional journalist should have the ability and news judgment to determine what is important and significant.

It troubled me that the Canadian public broadcaster would hire such a company, one with expertise, mainly, in reshaping local American news shows with the specific goal of hauling in as much revenue for their owners as possible. A few years later, the CBC would do something even more inconceivable, perhaps in desperation. It outbid Canadian private broadcasters and purchased, for more millions of dollars, Canadian rights to air the American game show *Wheel of Fortune*, starring Pat Sajak and Vanna White. It would take pride of place as the lead-in for all CBC supper-hour shows. I wasn't alone in finding it bizarre and offensive to see Sajak spinning his wheel and Vanna flipping letters on the public TV channel supported by Canadian taxpayers.

Over the next weeks, months, and years, the Magid team kept up a repeating pattern of being among us for days, flying back to the USA, and then returning to our newsroom. Most of us weren't quite sure what they were up to, or what changes might be wrought by Magid at *Here and Now*. We were on tenterhooks. All I knew was that the Magids gave me the creeps. In the end, although I wasn't around to be part of it, the Magid team didn't accomplish much. The great boost in ratings never happened.

There comes a point in the unceasing daily grind when almost all of us feel a crushing kind of weariness that never goes away. I'd always loved my job and was proud to work for the CBC. It brought me joy. But thirty-one years on, the weariness weighed on my shoulders—along with disappointment and defeat. Having the Magids around, as well as the actual and sometimes ghostlike presence of my former workplace tormentor, worsened matters. There was only one thing to do: protect my mental and physical health and get out. I was fortunate. Having put in thirty-one years, I could retire with severance and a monthly pension.

When I told my boss, Janice Stein, that I wanted to retire, she wasn't surprised. At the time she was executive producer for news. She was aware of my unhappiness and promised to take a look at the retirement numbers. I was surprised but also delighted when she asked if I'd help choose my "weather" successor. It turned out not to be a serious offer, because my recommendation was ignored. My gut told me they'd made up their minds even before the auditions.

I felt strongly that it was time for a person of a different gender, someone who reflected the growing diversity of the province, to take this prominent position on *Here and Now*. A young woman, Shilpa Acharya, who from time to time substituted for me on the weather and did a polished, professional job, was the person I recommended. Shilpa demonstrated tremendous potential, but she wasn't selected.

My last *Here and Now* was on Friday July 27, 2007. Signoffs are tough because you're not only saying a public goodbye to the people with whom you've worked, you're saying goodbye to the folks who've depended on you to bring them the weather and the news for decades. I was determined to let our viewers know how much the confidence they'd placed in me meant. Thankfully, I got through my little speech without blubbering. My friends and co-workers threw a party for me, and the CBC hosted a reception where I was presented with a retirement gift: a Labrador carving of an Inuk drummer. It's on our mantle and I cherish it.

After that final show and after I'd wiped off the heavy TV makeup mixed with a few tears, I went up to the newsroom for one last visit. Everyone had left by then. I would spend my final minutes alone in the building I'd first entered at the age of twenty-two. I quietly placed the remaining things on my desk (a coffee cup with a picture of a younger me on it, a cheap plastic pencil holder, a few pictures, and some personal files) into a small cardboard box. A faint twinge of reluctance passed over me as I picked it up. I slowly left, allowing my eyes to take in the newsroom one last time. I thought about the many physical and bureaucratic changes I'd witnessed at 95 University Avenue over my three decades there.

In the very newsroom where I stood, I could visualize the warren of executive and subordinates' offices that used to occupy the space. The general manager (director of TV), assistant to the manager, buildings manager, manager of public relations, commercial sales and acceptance, set design and staging, technical, and production offices: positions that, for the most part, no longer existed. Walking down the hall toward the lobby stairs and elevator (which hadn't existed in 1975), I could faintly hear the past—laughter coming from the duplicating and mail room where the CBC mail carriers gathered. They distributed corporate mail throughout CBC's five locations in St. John's before the invention of personal computers and internet. I saw their bright, young smiling faces, at first a smudge but finally coming into focus, blue canvas mailbags slung over their shoulders. In the background was the whirring of the copier spitting out scripts for another episode of *Skipper & Company.*

I could even smell the distinctive scent of paints and solvents that wafted out from the original graphics department at the end of the hall. I could picture the designers working at their drafting tables—drawing, sketching, and painting by hand the news illustrations that were used on *Here and Now*. Descending the stairs, I remembered how the lobby used to be. I stood and looked briefly at the switchboard operator's window, filled in years ago with concrete. It's where I'd delivered my first CBC job application in 1974. I paused, looked out the glass front entrance and saw Larry sitting in our car, waiting for me. Then I saw the future, our future, and I walked through those CBC doors for the last time, smiling.

20

MY JOY MIRRORED HIS

It all began with four words Larry spoke after a meal one night. We were still seated at the kitchen table having a second glass of wine, not talking much. Sometimes we enjoy holding each other's hand and not speaking for periods of time. Our lips may not be moving, but plenty is being said, a beautiful, non-verbal conversation. Larry eventually broke the silence with those magical words. "Will you marry me?"

I said "Yes." Neither of us could quite believe what had happened, but we both felt the need to yell the news to someone. We got on the phone to our friends Chad and Bill at the other end of town. We ordered them to sit tight because we were on our way over to tell them something.

After a quick cab ride, we were on their doorstep. Then it was more wine and toasting until all four of us were glowing like orbs. The next day I happily assumed the mantle of official wedding planner. It was the dead of winter by the time I started planning, but that summer we had a glorious July wedding—a ceremony complete with harpist, classical organist playing a mighty Casavant pipe organ, two opera singers, and, for our garden reception, Bill Brennan's band playing in our gazebo. Ours was the first gay wedding to take place at Gower Street United Church. Reverend Marion Davis officiated. I asked Reverend Davis about her memories of that July day.

Finally, legally married to the love of my life. A joyful day.

"Joy! It was just so wonderful to see you both, you know, with family and friends around. And to be able after so many years to declare your love for each other. To make that vow, that commitment to remain together in love and devotion for the rest of your lives. You know, Karl, the thought of that day always warms my heart."

What I feel and remember with great clarity is being at the altar with Larry as we said our vows. It was those precious moments. Placing rings on each other's fingers, our embrace, our kiss. And unlike the first time we kissed, almost thirty years before, this time it wasn't impulsive. It was expected and symbolic. A statement, weighted with years of shared love and shared life. As our lips touched, gently, briefly, we acknowledged our survival as a gay couple despite daunting odds. Those present knew. We turned to face our guests, and for a moment, I couldn't take my eyes off Larry. Smiling the most ecstatic smile, he looked happier than I'd ever seen him before. My joy mirrored his. We stood delighted to let everyone share our happiness and pride. We two, deeply in love. We two, who'd made it.

New adventures. Life is good.

ACKNOWLEDGEMENTS

The author thanks the following individuals for any encouragement or assistance given during the writing of the manuscript: Marion Davis, John Drover, Barbara Fong, Pam Frampton, David Goveia, Larry Kelly, Linda Lambe, Sheilagh Guy Murphy, Peter Norman, Don Oravec, Bill Parsons, Mick Stockley, Chad Stride, Bruce Tizzard, Betty Wells, Claire Wilkshire.

Photo: Dave Howells

THE AUTHOR

Karl Wells has been a broadcaster in Newfoundland and Labrador media since he first spoke into a live microphone on VOWR at age 16. His professional career began in 1974 at the CBC, where for 32 years he perfected his skills in hosting, performing, newscasting, and interviewing. He appeared on multiple radio and TV programs including the flagship TV news program, *Here and Now*, during which his dynamic on-location weather and community broadcasts made him a much-loved personality throughout the province. Since leaving the CBC Karl has pursued writing, with a 14-year stint as a weekly telegram restaurant and food columnist, for which he received the Canadian Culinary Federation Sandy Sanderson Award.